English Coordinate Constructions

Drawing on extensive corpus-based research, this book explores the nature and behaviour of coordinate constructions in three case studies, covering order in copulative compounds, binomials (bare phrases) and more complex phrases. Historically, research on order in coordination has concentrated on so-called irreversible binomials, but Lohmann's research places significant focus on reversible ad hoc coordination and also presents a detailed comparison between irreversible and reversible binomials.

This book uses empirical analyses to explore a wide range of factors, from pragmatic to phonetic influences on the ordering process. It also offers readers a processing perspective on the results obtained, and puts forth a processing explanation for the characteristics of irreversible binomials.

The book is ideal for researchers and advanced students working in English linguistics, syntax and psycholinguistics, and due to the multifactorial methodology applied, it will be of particular interest to quantitatively minded corpus linguists.

ARNE LOHMANN is a postdoctoral researcher in the Department of English at the University of Vienna.

STUDIES IN ENGLISH LANGUAGE

General editor
Merja Kytö (Uppsala University)

Editorial Board
Bas Aarts (University College London), John Algeo (University of Georgia), Susan Fitzmaurice (University of Sheffield), Christian Mair (University of Freiburg), Charles F. Meyer (University of Massachusetts)

The aim of this series is to provide a framework for original studies of English, both present-day and past. All books are based securely on empirical research, and represent theoretical and descriptive contributions to our knowledge of national and international varieties of English, both written and spoken. The series covers a broad range of topics and approaches, including syntax, phonology, grammar, vocabulary, discourse, pragmatics, and sociolinguistics, and is aimed at an international readership.

Already published in this series:

English Coordinate Constructions

A Processing Perspective on Constituent Order

ARNE LOHMANN

University of Vienna

CAMBRIDGE
UNIVERSITY PRESS

University Printing House, Cambridge CB2 8BS, United Kingdom

One Liberty Plaza, 20th Floor, New York, NY 10006, USA

477 Williamstown Road, Port Melbourne, VIC 3207, Australia

314-321, 3rd Floor, Plot 3, Splendor Forum, Jasola District Centre, New Delhi - 110025, India

79 Anson Road, #06-04/06, Singapore 079906

Cambridge University Press is part of the University of Cambridge.

It furthers the University's mission by disseminating knowledge in the pursuit of education, learning and research at the highest international levels of excellence.

www.cambridge.org
Information on this title: www.cambridge.org/9781108790871

First published 2014
First paperback edition 2019

A catalogue record for this publication is available from the British Library

Library of Congress Cataloging in Publication data
Lohmann, Arne,
English coordinate constructions : a processing perspective on constituent order / Arne Lohmann.
    pages   cm – (Studies in English Language)
ISBN 978-1-107-04088-5 (hardback)
1. English language – Coordinate constructions – Case studies.   2. English language – Grammar – Case studies.   3. Grammar, Comparative and general – Coordinate constructions – Case studies.   4. Construction grammar – Case studies   I. Title.
PE1385.L64   2014
425–dc23

                                                        2014008647

ISBN 978-1-107-04088-5 Hardback
ISBN 978-1-108-79087-1 Paperback

Contents

Figures

Tables

Acknowledgements

This book grew out of my doctoral dissertation, which I completed at the University of Hamburg while being employed there as a junior researcher. I am immensely grateful to Thomas Berg, my thesis advisor, not only for his academic advice, but also for his words of encouragement when I most needed them.

I thank my colleagues in Hamburg and Vienna for their helpful comments on earlier versions of this study. Florian Dolberg especially needs to be singled out, as he was always willing to interrupt whatever he was doing to discuss what I had on my mind, although I could not always reciprocate the favour. I am grateful to the support of the DFG-funded project on frequency effects in Freiburg (Project 1624/1) for giving me the opportunity to attend a number of inspiring workshops.

Many people have contributed to the successful completion of this book, by sharing their ideas on language with me, as educators, colleagues, collaborators or simply as friends. Ning Hilpert deserves credit for awakening my interest in linguistics and for introducing me to other friendly people sharing that passion. I would like to mention, in alphabetical order: Stefan Gries, Martin Hilpert, Evelien Keizer, Chris Koops, Britta Mondorf, Marion Neubauer, Klaus-Uwe Panther, Günter Radden, Katerina Stathi, Anatol Stefanowitsch, Tayo Takada, Daniel Wiechmann and Arne Zeschel.

Furthermore, I am grateful to Merja Kytö, the editor of this book series, for her feedback and advice. A word of thanks also goes to Helen Barton at Cambridge University Press for assisting me in all practical matters of publishing this book and generally for her positive attitude.

Most importantly I thank Helen, my wife, for all the loving support without which writing this book would have been impossible, and I thank Elsa for making life so much more exciting.

1   Introduction

1.1   Aims of the study

During language production, the users of any given language produce strings of phrases, words, morphemes and, ultimately, phonemes. Mostly unaware of the process, language users master the task of ordering the building blocks of their language on the syntagmatic axis, solving what Lashley (1951: 112) referred to as the 'problem of serial order'. This linearisation process is the primary demand the syntactic system of a language must fulfil. In most constructions, these constituents are hierarchically organized (Bock 1987b: 340–2). Due to this hierarchy, the word order is relatively fixed, at least in analytic languages such as English; thus, a certain meaning can only be conveyed using one particular order. Nevertheless, there are exceptions wherein certain constituents can be ordered in more than one way without a significant change in meaning. Among the more apparent examples of these are *coordinate constructions*.[1] These are, loosely stated, constructions where two elements are conjoined in a non-hierarchical fashion and whose order is in most cases reversible. Let us look at (1a–e) for illustrative purposes, taken from corpus data:

(1)   a. As a <u>singer-dancer</u>, however, she hasn't advanced much beyond the ballet. (COCA corpus, *New York Times*, 18 October 1992)

     b. . . . No there's a scene in Terminator, he's like <u>wood and metal</u> in his new Terminator . . . (BNC, File KE1)

     c. . . . we can take over two of their sponsored events er which is <u>golf and tennis</u> and it would be something like . . . (BNC, File FUG)

     d. . . . the gypsies identify with <u>her nomadic existence and her life as an oppressed servant</u>. (ICE-GB:S2B-027# 116: 1 :A)

     e. . . . <u>rootless populations and beleaguered minorities</u>, feel themselves and indeed are, considerably at risk. (ICE-GB:S2B-050 #79: 1:A)

---

[1] The definition and thus a clarification of what is considered a coordinate construction in this book will be provided further below, in Section 1.2.

In the examples above, speakers coordinated two elements (underlined) in a certain order whose reversal would also have been a possibility. As can be seen, these orderings take place on different linguistic levels. In (1a) the two constituents of a compound are coordinated, (1b) and (1c) are examples of coordinated lexemes, while (1d) and (1e) instantiate the coordination of complex noun phrases, which themselves consist of several words. All examples are constructions in which two conjoined elements occur in a particular order mostly conjoined by a lexical link, a so-called coordinator (except for (1a)). The most general question to be asked in this book is, what are the influences speakers are subject to when serialising elements in such constructions?

In doing so this study distinguishes itself from previous research along a number of dimensions. To begin with the most important point, the present study is different from others in highlighting the aspect of reversibility by putting clearly reversible cases such as (1a–e) at the centre of the investigation. This approach contrasts with most previous research in linguistics, which strongly focused on so-called frozen, irreversible binomials, which are coordinations of two lexemes that occur only in one particular order. Examples are *law and order*, and *house and home*. Due to the focus on these expressions, the more typical case of reversible coordination has been neglected. Even works that recognised this problem, such as Benor and Levy (2006), simply incorporated both groups into their empirical study but did not differentiate between the two categories. An explicit analysis of reversible constructions can however be considered rewarding for the following reasons. First of all, we can assume that the language producer performs an ad hoc decision on how to order the constituents in these instances. These expressions thus enable us to analyse the workings of an online ordering process, investigating what influences speakers' decisions during language use. This question cannot be addressed with irreversible binomials whose order is fixed, as these are stored as holistic units in the mental lexicon.[2] Thus, it remains unclear to what extent identified ordering factors are at work in online ordering tasks, which is an issue to be addressed in this book.

A second reason for the focus on reversible cases is their high frequency, as they greatly outnumber irreversible cases. Hence, the online ordering process I just described is much more representative of the kinds of tasks the linguistic system must perform when processing coordinate constructions and probably also of linearisation as a whole, as compared to the more marginal role of quasi-idiomatic irreversibles.

---

[2]   In current models, irreversible binomials are grouped with other fixed expressions for which storage as holistic units is assumed. The different models and their relevance for irreversible binomials are discussed in greater detail in Chapter 9.

Although this work thus focuses primarily on reversible coordination, it also explicitly compares ad hoc coordination to its irreversible counterpart. Such a comparison is interesting for the study of both groups: First, for reversibles, it can be tested whether the ordering constraints mentioned for irreversibles also hold for online ordering during ad hoc coordination. Secondly, for the group of irreversibles, it will be interesting to see whether these exhibit properties which render them especially suited for developing into frozen, holistically processed, multi-word units. Both of these questions will be pursued in this book.

The mentioned difference between reversibles and irreversibles with regard to processing brings us, moreover, to psycholinguistic research on the phenomenon, in particular to studies on the mechanisms underlying the linearisation of words and phrases during language production. Due to the generally larger scope of these works, which do not focus on individual syntactic phenomena, coordination has been treated only marginally in most studies. Nevertheless, their results are particularly interesting, as they are very controversial. Regarding the central question of this study, viz. which factors influence order during coordination, there is great uncertainty in the relevant literature. Some studies claim that the order of constituents is completely random, or at least that such constructions are not consistently influenced by the same factors at work in other cases of syntactic linearisation (see Branigan et al. 2008). Following these empirical uncertainties, there are widely diverging views on how coordination fits into the bigger picture of linearisation as a whole. Some view it as a construction which is particularly well suited to investigate general properties of the processing system, in particular the influence of accessibility factors on serial order (Bock 1987b: 375). Others, in contrast, argue that we cannot generalise results from coordinate constructions, as these are processed unlike any other construction in putting the usual incremental processing system to a halt (Branigan et al. 2008). These discrepancies show that the question as to how these constructions are processed is far from answered. Another aim of this book is to discuss this question in light of the results obtained and to explore which language production models are best able to explain this process. In doing so, established serial models (e.g. Bock and Levelt 1994) are compared to more interactive models. Thus, this book breaks new ground in discussing the ramifications of order in reversible coordination for language production models.

A further innovation of this study is its multilevel approach: As mentioned above, the ordering process is investigated on several linguistic levels, as coordinative compounds, the coordination of lexemes (binomials) and complex phrases are taken into account. Previous studies, in contrast, restricted themselves to the study of binomials. This book thus breaks new ground in extending the scope beyond the word level, addressing the question as to whether the factors relevant for lexical coordination are also at work at the other two levels. Such an analysis naturally invites a comparative perspective. Regarding possible inter-level differences, Cooper and Ross (1975) suggest a strength hierarchy, with the morphemic level showing the strongest influence of ordering constraints, which gradually weaken towards the syntactic level. Thus the following two questions will be addressed: Do the factors and their cumulative as well as individual influence differ across the respective linguistic levels under consideration? Can a hierarchy of growing strength of constraints from the syntactic to the morphological level be found, as suggested by Cooper and Ross (1975)?

By drawing on usage data from corpora, this work taps methodological resources that have been thus far rarely used in the study of order in coordination. Previous works have been either monofactorial experimental studies (in the field of psycholinguistics), i.e. testing only one variable, or works relying on introspective methods (predominant in the studies on irreversible binomials). Only Benor and Levy (2006) is a notable exception in also using corpus data. Thus, in my opinion, the topic has not received the empirical, corpus-linguistic attention it deserves, although using corpus data comes with specific advantages.

First, regarding data sampling, corpora provide us with a wealth of natural usage data, which are more representative of the language production process than data arrived at through introspection or individual linguistic experience (cf., e.g., Sinclair 1991). Even compared to experimental studies, corpus data has certain advantages: because the data samples arrived at through the use of corpora are generally larger, they may be viewed as more representative than experimental studies with a limited number of subjects.

A second methodological selling point of this study pertains to the method of analysis. Coordinate constructions instantiate a case of grammatical variability, whereby the language user has the choice between two constructions that are formally divergent but largely equivalent regarding semantics. These cases of language variation have previously been found to be difficult to investigate empirically, as researchers began to realise that not just one but a host of different factors influences the choices between alternating constructions. In recent years, however, the empirical study of such alternations has made tremendous progress through the rise of multifactorial research methods, which take into account a multitude of variables simultaneously. While a specific type of such methods has been used to investigate linguistic choices in variationist sociolinguistics since the 1970s (under the name of *Varbrul*, e.g. Cedergren and Sankoff 1974; Sankoff and Labov 1979), multifactorial methods have only recently begun to be applied to alternations in corpus-linguistic research: Gries (2003) and also Bresnan et al. (2007) point out that only through this methodological resource is it possible to determine the influence of a particular variable when acting in concurrence with other factors. For example, with a particular case of coordination, such as *apple and grapefruit*, chances are that *apple* occurs in the first position due to its being shorter than *grapefruit*. However, it could also be due to the fact that *apple* is the more prototypical fruit item. The question thus is whether only one factor or both factors influence the speaker at the same time. Monofactorial research designs in previous studies have invited conclusions of just one factor being responsible for these instances of variation. Yet only a multifactorial approach which takes into account possibly confounding factors can safely answer this question. Furthermore, it allows us to calculate the relative strengths of different influential factors.

In summary, by choosing a multifactorial approach that analyses representative corpus samples, this book aims at a more fine-grained investigation of ordering effects, which has been precluded thus far due to the predominance of introspective methods and monofactorial experimental studies.

1.2   Coordinate constructions in English

1.2.1   Definitions and general properties

In this chapter, definitions and properties of coordinate constructions will be presented, focusing on coordination in English. I will also elaborate on the syntactic analysis of coordination and the question as to which constituents can be coordinated at all. These are the two issues most widely debated in the literature on coordinate constructions.

A common formal definition of coordinate constructions is that all coordinated elements belong to the same syntactic category and together form a constituent of the same category (cf. Haspelmath 2004: 28–9). Quirk et al. (1985: 945), for instance, state that '[we] regard coordination as a type of linkage whereby the resulting conjoint construction is equivalent, structurally speaking, to each of its members'. This structure is illustrated in Figure 1.1 and the example, where the two nouns, *pizza* and *pasta* form a superordinate noun phrase.[3]

We will see later that the aforementioned definition does not capture some constructions which could be viewed as coordinate constructions. Nevertheless, in this book I shall focus on the constructions that adhere to this formal definition.

Generally, three different types of coordination are distinguished: conjunction (conjunctive coordination), disjunction (disjunctive coordination) and adversative coordination. See the examples below:

---

[3] Coordinate constructions contrast with subordinate or dependency constructions because, in the latter, only one constituent (the head) must match the syntactic status of the overall phrase.

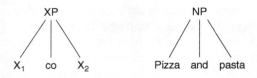

Figure 1.1 Structure of coordinate constructions[4]

(2) a. the tiger and the lion   *conjunctive coordination*
     b. the tiger or the lion   *disjunctive coordination*
     c. He walked fast, but he did not run.   *adversative coordination*

Since the focus of this book is on intra-phrasal phenomena, I will deal only with conjunctive and disjunctive coordination, as adversative coordination is rare outside clausal coordination (Haspelmath 2004).[5]

With regard to the structural elements of a coordinate construction, it usually consists of two (or more) connected constituents (coordinands) which can (but do not have to) be connected by coordinators (e.g. *and*, *or*, *but*) (Haspelmath 2004: 4). When occurring with a coordinator, the constructions are termed *syndetic*, while when occurring in simple juxtaposition without a coordinator they are termed *asyndetic* (Haspelmath 2004: 4; Stassen 2000: 1106). Both variants are possible in English and are instantiated by the following examples.

(3) a. Slowly, stealthily, she crept towards her victim. (example from Haspelmath 2007: 7)
     b. Pizza, pasta and ice cream are my favourite foods.
     c. Pizza and pasta are my favourite foods.

Asyndetic coordination is a minor strategy for English, and with the conjunction of nominal elements, which I focus on in this book, it is not possible with coordinations of only two elements (compare 3b and c) (cf. Stassen 2001: 1105).

Probably the most well-known property of coordinate constructions mentioned in syntactic theory is that they adhere to the Coordinate Structure Constraint (Ross 1967), which states that no conjunct can be extracted from a coordinate construction. Most subordinate constructions, however, allow for such an extraction; the difference can be seen in the following examples by Haspelmath (2007: 5, emphasis in original).

---

[4] Figure 1 implies a non-hierarchical, symmetrical view of coordinate constructions. This is merely for the purpose of exposition; it is not intended to express the author's view on the structural (a-)symmetry of these constructions. This point will be elaborated below.
[5] For examples of adversative coordination with *but*, see Quirk et al. (1985: 952).

(4)   a. dependency (subordination)
       (i)   (basic sentence) You talked to someone before Joan arrived.
      (ii)   (*who* extraction) Who did you talk to _ before Joan arrived?
    b. coordination
       (i)   (basic sentence) You talked to someone **and** then Joan arrived.
      (ii)   (*who* extraction) *Who did you talk to _ **and** then Joan arrived?

While the Coordinate Structure Constraint works with English coordinate constructions, it is not clear whether it can be applied as a linguistic universal (Haspelmath 2004: 26). Thus, Haspelmath (2007: 1) offers a definition of coordinate constructions from a semantic perspective:

The term *coordination* refers to syntactic constructions in which two or more units of the same type are combined into a larger unit and still have the same semantic relations with other surrounding elements.

This can be illustrated with the following example:

(5)   Juan and Pablo went to Argentina.

Both coordinands have the same semantic relations with the rest of the sentence, the VP, in that it is true that both Juan and Pablo went to Argentina.
    A further, semantic definitional criterion of coordinate constructions, which is especially important for the aims of this book, is the reversibility of the conjuncts (Haspelmath 2004: 29–30). It is generally agreed that the two ordering possibilities are truth-conditionally equivalent (Blakemore and Carston 2005b), resulting in the possibility of 'meaning-preserving inversion' (Bock 1987b: 375). It is this property which renders this construction especially interesting; since it is not semantics that constrains the order of elements, the question arises as to which factors influence the order of elements. There are, however, exceptions to the reversibility criterion in English, which pertain to certain contexts featuring the coordinator *and*, where truth-conditions seem to change by a reversal. Consider the example below (from Blakemore and Carston 2005a):

(6)   She handed him the key and he opened the door.

Here the interpretation seems to be not (*A and B*) but (*A and then B*), as a reversal of the two constituents results in a different interpretation. One possible explanation is that the coordinator *and* does not mean solely (*and*) anymore but conveys the meaning of temporal sequence. Another view, in contrast, is that the interpretation of a temporal sequence must be located in the realm of pragmatics and is not the result of the coordinator being polysemous (see, e.g., Quirk et al. 1985; Blakemore and Carston 2005b). According to the latter view, the interpretation of temporal sequence is due to pragmatic inference, as it is the most natural interpretation to assume a chronological ordering. This study follows the latter argumentation and views the aforementioned pragmatic inferencing process as a constraint on ordering whose influence can be empirically investigated. This issue will be discussed in greater detail below (see Chapter 9).

Having dealt with the basic properties of English coordinate constructions, I will now focus on more detailed issues of their analysis. The first issue to be addressed is the syntactic analysis and constituent structure of coordinate constructions, which is a widely debated issue in syntactic theory.

Early syntactic models assumed a flat structure, while in more recent models they are analysed hierarchically, as the coordinator has been argued to exhibit greater structural cohesion with the second conjunct (for an overview, see Ross 1967; Dik 1972: 52–5;[6] Blakemore and Carston 2005a). Hence, most current analyses assume a constituent structure of the form [A[co B]].

One argument Ross (1967: 163) uses to prove this point is that once coordinate clauses are broken up into two clauses, the coordinator is in the second clause.[7] See Ross's (1967: 163) examples for an illustration:

(7)   a. John left and he didn't even say goodbye.
       b. John left. And he didn't even say goodbye.

A further argument by Ross (1967) is a phonological one, as possible intonational pauses typically do not separate the coordinator and the second conjunct, as in the examples below (taken from Ross 1967: 164–5).

(8)   a. (Tom (and Dick) (and Harry)) all love watermelon.
       b. ((Tom and) (Dick and) (Harry)) all love watermelon.
       c. ((Tom) (and) (Dick) (and) (Harry)) all love watermelon.

Hence the bracketing in example (8a) represents a typical intonational pause pattern, while b and c do not. Ross's (1967) examples suggest a hierarchical, right-branching structure, which is the most widespread analysis. It should be noted, however, that it is not universally accepted (see Dik 1972: 25–60, who argues for a symmetrical analysis) and that in many theories, coordinate constructions are treated as a special case due to their controversial status (see Blakemore and Carston 2005a). In addition to these theoretical complications, there 'remains a strong pretheoretic intuition that coordinate structures are in some important sense symmetric' (Blakemore and Carston 2005a: 354). Trying to resolve the conflict between syntactic theory and intuition, Cormack and Smith (2005) assume the simultaneous generation of two asymmetric branching structures, one head-initial and one head-final.

---

[6] An overview of the arguments is given by Dik 1972:45–52, although he himself does not adhere to a hierarchical view.
[7] But see Dik 1972: 54 for a different interpretation.

In summary, the discussion in syntactic theory shows that the theoretical task of modelling phrase structure of coordinate structures is by no means a trivial one. However, since the question of (a-)symmetry does not interfere with the aims of this work – which rely on the observation that the constituents can be produced in either order – the current work will not take a stance on this issue.

A second widely debated issue with coordinate constructions is the question of which constituents can or cannot be coordinated, as it has been observed that the two elements that are coordinated are in some sense equal or alike (see, e.g., Blakemore and Carston 2005a). The question that still seems difficult to answer asks on which level of description the equality must be assumed and what exceptions are allowed. Schachter (1977), in propagating his Coordinate Constituent Constraint (CCC), assumes constraints on three levels: the syntactic, the semantic and, to a lesser degree, also the pragmatic level. All of these constraints are argued to apply jointly, thus no one level explains another. The syntactic constraint states that both constituents have equal syntactic status, thus both belong to the same phrasal category, which is a point I already mentioned above as a first definition of coordinate constructions. This constraint explains why example (9a), a coordination of two adverbial phrases, is grammatical and (9b), where an adjectival phrase and a noun phrase are coordinated, is not (examples taken from Schachter 1977: 87):[8]

(9)　a. John ate quickly and greedily.
　　　b. *John ate quickly and a grilled cheese sandwich.

There are cases, however, that defy the aforementioned syntactic properties, where two phrases that belong to different syntactic categories are coordinated, still constituting a well-formed sentence, see (10) below.

(10)　John ate quickly and with good appetite.

Here an adjectival phrase and a prepositional phrase are coordinated and still result in a well-formed sentence. This is generally not viewed as a violation of the syntactic equality criterion, but a same phrase status is assumed on an underlying level of representation (cf. Schachter 1977). In cases such as (10), the prepositional is assumed to be governed by a higher adjectival phrase node. This solution is of course not without controversy, and different suggestions have been made for how to deal with this coordination of, at least on the surface, different phrasal categories (cf. Bayer 1996).

---

[8] Whether this constraint is a grammatical one or a constraint rooted in processing preferences is still being discussed (cf. Frazier et al. 2000 for an explanation from a processing perspective).

It has also been postulated that both elements must be equal on the semantic level in taking on a parallel function in the construction. Consider (11a) and (11b) for an illustration (11a found from Schachter 1977: 89).

(11)   a. John ate with his mother and with his daughter.
       b. *John ate with his mother and with good appetite.

While undoubtedly both coordinated phrases belong to the same syntactic category, the semantic functions are the same only in (11a) but not in (11b), which is why only the former sentence is grammatical. While in (11a) both phrases denote the company John had – accompaniment phrase according to Schachter (1977) – in (11b) an accompaniment and a manner phrase are coordinated, apparently resulting in a conflict, which makes the sentence ungrammatical.

Another way of dealing with the semantic equality constraint is put forward by Lang (1984, 1991) and also Blühdorn (2008), who argue that the coordinated elements have to be semantically integrated via a *common integrator*. This term refers to a superordinate conceptual category under which both coordinants can be subsumed. For sentence (11a), this common category could be 'company of people John had dinner with'. This common integrator can also be construed ad hoc in discourse, which brings pragmatic concerns into play (see Blühdorn 2008). Consider the following two sentences for illustration ((12a) from Quirk et al. 1985, (12b) my own):

(12)   a. ??The youngsters went off to a dance and the equator is equidistant
            from the two poles.
       b. ?My mum went to the mall and the carpenters fixed the stairs.

Both sentences fulfil the syntactic and the semantic criteria but still sound considerably odd, as a context in which they could be sensibly uttered seems hard to imagine. Nevertheless, appropriate pragmatic contexts can be construed. The second example could be an answer to the question 'What happened today?' And even sentence (12a), although harder to imagine, could be an appropriate answer to the question 'What are two true statements?' in a situation where the interlocutors just watched the youngsters going to a dance. These examples show that the equality of elements in coordination can also be pragmatically licensed; i.e., a common category or integrator can be construed by pragmatic context.

1.2.2   *A typological perspective on coordination in English*

This section will address the properties of English coordination in a typological context. In particular, I will elaborate on the major differentiating properties of coordinating constructions among the languages of the world and how English can be classified with regard to them. I will also mention the frequencies of different coordination strategies to enable an understanding of how widespread is coordination of the type found in Present-Day English. Since the book focuses on the coordination of nominal elements, this focus will also be applied in the present discussion.

Above I explained that English coordination is typically syndetic, with asyndetic coordination in only some contexts. Among the world's languages, most resemble English in that they mostly feature syndetic coordination, with the exception of a small number of languages featuring solely asyndetic coordination (see Stassen 2001: 1106). In a typological context, a further distinction is made between monosyndetic coordination, which involves only a single coordinator, and bi- or polysyndetic coordination, which involves two coordinators which still coordinate only two constituents. An example of the latter type is found in Yoruba (taken from Haspelmath 2007: 10):

(13)   àti èmi àti Kéhìndé
        and I and Kehinde
        'I and Kehinde'

Bisyndetic coordination is not possible in English or in other European languages, but it is found in languages spoken in the Caucasus, Africa, Australia, New Guinea, Southern India and northeastern Asia, according to Stassen (2001: 1107).

A further distinction that is important for the classification of English in a typological context is the difference between comitative and coordinative strategies of coordination. The difference between the two can be illustrated in English (examples from Stassen 2001: 1105–6):

(14)   a. John and Mary left.   *coordinative strategy*
        b. John left with Mary.   *comitative strategy*

While with the coordinative strategy the two constituents are of equal structural rank, this is not the case with the comitative strategy, where the two NPs are not even part of the same constituent/phrase (cf. Stassen 2001: 1106). In a typological context, it is important to note that, unlike English, not all languages have a clear formal differentiation between the two strategies. Some languages employ the comitative strategy across all contexts and are therefore also termed WITH-languages, as opposed to AND-languages such as English which have both possibilities (Stassen 2001: 1109; 2003: 766). There are clear areal parameters involved in the distribution of the two types, with all of Europe being a domain of AND-languages (see Stassen 2000: 40–3). Regarding the frequency of instantiation of the two types, English clusters with the majority, as there are twice as many AND-languages, as there are WITH-languages (Stassen 2001: 1110).

A further issue that defines English coordination in a typological context is the position of the coordinator. Haspelmath (2004: 4) lists the four possible positions of the coordinator in monosyndetic coordination, in descending order of frequency:

(15)   a. [A] [co B]   e.g. English, most other European languages
       b. [A co] [B]   e.g. Lai
       c. [A] [B co]   e.g. Latin
       d. [co A] [B]   unattested

The categories (a) and (b) – the use of a 'medial connective' – are by far the most widely attested options (Stassen 2001: 1107). To distinguish between (a) and (b) is not necessarily straightforward, and a symmetrical analysis of [A] co [B] also remains a possibility, as we saw for English above. Recent research however assumes that all languages which employ a medial connective exhibit some sort of asymmetry in structural cohesion, thus can be categorised as either (a) or (b) (Haspelmath 2004: 4).

Another dimension important for typological classification is the syntactic categories of constituents that can be coordinated by a given coordinator. In English the coordinators *and* and *or* can link a wide range of constituents including a diverse range of categories: noun phrases, verb phrases, adjective phrases, prepositional phrases and also clauses (see Haspelmath 2004: 7–9). Many languages, however, have coordinators which are sensitive to the syntactic category of the constituents they link. The most widespread distinction is between verbal/clausal and nominal constituents, which, according to Haspelmath (2004: 7), can be found in about half of the world's languages. Yet even more fine-grained distinctions with three different coordinators for nominal, verbal and clausal constituents exist (Haspelmath 2004: 8). While category-sensitive coordinators are thus a widespread phenomenon, it is important to note that, like English, the other European languages generally employ universal coordinators for all syntactic constituents.

In a typological context, also meriting distinction are different coordinate constructions dependent on semantic factors. I explained earlier that in English there are three different constructions, namely conjunction, disjunction and adversative coordination. However, languages may exhibit more fine-grained distinctions than these, with such different constructions for animate vs. inanimate constituents or for proper as compared to common nouns (cf. Haspelmath 2004: 9). One especially important distinction in the present context is the use of different constructions for what Wälchli (2005) terms *natural* versus *accidental* coordination, which is evidenced in a number of languages. Natural coordination denotes the coordination of coordinands in 'close relationship' on the semantic dimension (Wälchli 2005: 13). Other researchers describe special forms of coordination which are roughly similar to Wälchli's category of natural coordination as the coordination of entities which 'are closely associated in the real world' (Haspelmath 2004: 10), which 'habitually go together' (Stassen 2003: 768) or form a 'conceptual unit' (Mithun 1988: 332). In contrast, with accidental coordination less predictable combinations of constituents are coordinated: there is thus a 'more distant relationship between the coordinands' (Wälchli 2005: 13). Examples of natural coordination which are frequently mentioned, as they appear in a number of languages, are 'father and mother', 'bow and arrow' or 'husband and wife' (see Wälchli 2005: 45; Stassen 2001: 1106; Haspelmath 2007: 21). Those languages that formally differentiate between the two categories employ a number of different marking patterns for doing so (an overview is given in Wälchli 2005). Most widespread is the use of less explicit forms for natural coordination, as opposed to accidental coordination, with zero-marking, thus the omission of the coordinator being the most frequently found distinction.[9] Since the omission of a medial coordinator results in less distance between the coordinands, the two are more tightly coordinated (Wälchli 2005: 67–89). A language where this difference can be found is Mandarin (Stassen 2001: 1106).

(16)   a. Zjé yué
           sun moon
           sun and moon   (example from Mullie 1947: 232, as cited in Stassen
           2001: 1106)
       b. Lù Wényì gen wo
           Lù Wényì and/with I
           Lù Wényì and I   (example from Li and Thompson 1981: 657, as
           cited in Stassen 2001: 1106)

Example (16a) is zero-marked and can be classified as an instance of natural coordination, while (16b) features the coordinator and would classify as accidental coordination. Summarising, natural coordination means a more predictable semantic relation which frequently co-occurs with a tighter formal relation between the constituents. This category can therefore be viewed as being more lexicalised than accidental coordination and is also referred to as *coordinative compounds*, or *co-compounds* (see Wälchli 2005).

While there is no such formal distinction between natural and accidental coordination in English, it is important to note that the English translations of the aforementioned examples of natural coordination are often classified as irreversible binomials. This irreversibility may thus serve as an indication that these instances are more lexicalised cases of coordination also in English. Further evidence for that view constitutes the

---

[9] However there are also languages which use completely different coordinators for the two classes (see Wälchli 2005: 47).

fact that it is possible with some irreversible binomials to use just one determiner, which has scope over the entire construction (Haspelmath 2004: 10), or to omit determiners throughout (Wälchli 2005: 11–12). See the following examples for an illustration:

(17) a. you can teach your child to hold the knife and fork correctly.
      b. you can teach your child to hold knife and fork correctly.

To my knowledge, no exhaustive exploration exists of how natural coordination plays out in English.[10] However, it is important to note that the typologically relevant distinction between natural and accidental coordination seems to be somewhat related to the distinction between irreversible binomials and ad hoc coordination in English, which I elaborated on earlier.[11] It is unclear at this point whether the group of irreversible binomials is co-extensive with the category of natural coordination in other languages which formally mark it. Despite these uncertainties, the clear formal distinctions between apparently similar groups in a number of languages seem to constitute indirect evidence for treating the two as distinct and emphasises the desideratum for a comparative investigation, which is one of the main aims of this book.

1.3   Why study order in English coordinate constructions?

Now that the main properties of English coordinate constructions have been described, I will address the question as to which precise characteristics render this type of construction an interesting object of study.

First and foremost, we must consider the previously stated observation that neither syntax nor semantics impose an order on the constituents, resulting in the aforementioned reversibility of constituents. The possibility of two different forms conveying the same meaning places coordinate constructions in the category of alternations or allo-sentences (Lambrecht 1994). Within this group, coordinate constructions can be argued to be of particular interest: for most alternations, the choice of the speaker is between two constructions that differ with regard to grammatical function assignment, different syntactic templates and/or different grammatical forms (see Bock 1987b: 375). For example, with the dative alternation, perhaps the most thoroughly studied phenomenon, the choice between the double object construction and the *to*-dative involves both grammatical role assignment as well as varying syntactic templates. Other cases of alternation, such as the choice between the two English comparatives or the two

---

[10] But see Wälchli (2005) on natural coordination in bare binomials in Germanic languages.
[11] A further property of natural coordination shared by English irreversible binomials is that both exhibit a tendency for non-compositional, idiomatic semantics (Haspelmath 2004: 10). I will discuss this point in detail below (see Chapter 2).

possibilities to encode future tense, furthermore involve the choice between different grammatical forms. In contrast, with coordinate constructions no changes with regard to these properties are involved, because it is merely the order of the two constituents that alternates: despite possible asymmetries in syntactic status (see discussion above), in respect of grammatical function, both coordinands are equivalent (Dik 1972: 29), as can be seen in (18).

(18)   Peter and Mary arrived late.

Both *Peter* and *Mary* are subjects of the sentence and an order alternation would not change this function assignment. Furthermore, unlike other constructions, the two alternatives do not differ with regard to lexical material. It is therefore likely that subtle differences in meaning, which are an issue with other alternations that also differ with regard to lexical material and/or grammatical function assignment, are less of a problem in the case of coordination than in other alternations. Thus, in this respect, the processing system can be investigated during linearisation in 'purer' form in coordination than in other alternating constructions.

Another criterion which sets coordinate constructions apart within the group of alternations is their frequency. A corpus count of the conjunction *and* in the ICE-GB yields 20,683 hits per million words, and the construction *NP and NP* alone, which will be investigated in the present study, occurs 6,683 times per million words. The genitive and the dative alternation, probably the two most-widely studied alternations in English, occur only around 2,000[12] and 800[13] times per million words respectively. These numbers show that coordination is a task which is performed very frequently. It may therefore be posited that it is more representative for the processing system than other alternations, underscoring the relevance of the phenomenon to an account of grammar and linguistic processing.

In summary, coordinate constructions exhibit a number of properties which set them apart, not only from the usual rules of syntax and semantics, but also within the group of alternations.

1.4   Delimiting the scope of the analysis

The question of constituent order is addressed on three linguistic levels, as exemplified by the above-mentioned expressions (see (1a–e)), thus encompassing copulative compounds, binomials and more complex phrases. By including constituent coordination in compounds (see (1a)), this work is in agreement with Olsen (2002a) and Wälchli (2005) that

[12]   Szmrecsanyi and Hinrichs (2007) manually extract all interchangeable *of-*and *s-*genitives from several electronic corpora. The frequencies in the four one-million word corpora they use vary from 1,945 to 2,204 occurrences.
[13]   Bresnan et al. (2007) identified 2,360 dative data points which may alternate between the double object and the prepositional dative in the three-million word Switchboard corpus.

coordination is not restricted to the level of syntax, but also extends to non-hierarchical compounds such as *actor-director*. The goal of this book is to provide an overview of linear order of coordinated constituents below the clausal level.

I distinguish between coordination in binomials and more complex phrases, although both can be analysed as the coordination of two phrases; bare phrases in the case of binomials, as opposed to more complex phrases. This distinction is motivated by the fact that most previous research pertains to the study of irreversible binomials. Many ordering constraints were therefore suggested for this particular type of coordination and cannot be easily extrapolated to other contexts. Investigating binomials in a separate case study therefore maximises comparability with prior research (see also Chapter 2 and Chapter 6).

Even though coordinate constructions occur with several syntactic categories, this study focuses on the coordination of nominal elements. There are three reasons for this restriction. First of all, since copulative compounds occur almost exclusively with nominal elements, it was considered best to delimit the study to this syntactic category in order to have a homogeneous sample for comparative purposes across the different levels of investigation. While there are compound adjectives like *red-white* or *bittersweet*, these seem to be restricted to the domain of colour adjectives and other isolated cases. Secondly, the coordination of nouns is the most frequent type of coordinate construction, thus providing us with a large data sample which can be considered to be representative of coordinate constructions as such.[14] Moreover, previous research suggests that differences between word classes are negligible (see Benor and Levy 2006; Mollin 2012). Thirdly, the phenomenon of *irreversible binomials* predominantly concerns coordinated nouns, and since a comparison between these and reversible cases is one of the aims, this constitutes another argument for the aforementioned restriction.

In addition to the focus on certain linguistic levels and syntactic categories, this study takes into account only the more prototypical cases of coordination in order to avoid an unnecessarily heterogeneous data sample. Hence, the investigated constructions fulfil the following characteristics:

• Both elements are independent and thus can occur on their own (this excludes coordinations with anaphoric elements, e.g. *the president and his secretary*).[15]

---

[14] A simple POS tag search of the BNC revealed the following frequencies: N *and* N (26,482), V *and* V (9,783), ADJ *and* ADJ (14,401), ADV *and* ADV (2,456).

[15] This restriction furthermore means that *Reimdoppelungen* and *Ablautverdoppelungen*, like *helter-skelter*, and *neeminy-nominy* are not considered. In these, nonce formations are conjoined (Hansen 1964; Oden and Lopes 1981), which occur only in these *Doppelungen*, thus they are not independent constituents.

- A and B belong to the same syntactic category and together form a constituent (either a word or a phrase) which has the same syntactic status as each of its parts.[16]
- The order of occurrence of A and B is reversible (except for the sample of irreversible binomials).
- Two elements A and B are coordinated (thus coordinations of more than two elements are not considered).

The last point, the focus on bipartite constructions may require some justification. A practical reason for employing this restriction is that, while coordinate constructions may contain more than two elements, those instances are rare and would make a quantitative analysis requiring large samples difficult. A further reason is that I wish to focus on those instances for which it can reasonably be assumed that both constituents are activated for production more or less simultaneously and thereby compete for first mention (see Chapter 10); whether this is true of longer coordinate constructions is doubtful, however. Besides, an inclusion of coordinations of more than two elements, by, e.g., including tripartite constructions, would limit the comparability across the different case studies, as tripartite copulative compounds do not occur and also irreversible trinomials, e.g. *lock, stock, and barrel* are extremely rare.

Regarding possible coordinators on the lexical and phrasal level, only the constructions with *and* and *or* are taken into account. Adversative *but* is not included, as it hardly ever occurs outside clausal coordination (see above). Another reason for its exclusion is that the status of *but* as a coordinating conjunction is controversial (see Dik 1972: 39).

As stated above, the main intention of the study is to analyse the constraints that govern cases of ad hoc coordination, which is why irreversibles fall outside the scope of the main analysis. Irreversible binomials are, however, investigated in Chapter 6, which compares reversible and irreversible instances.

1.5   Theoretical and disciplinary orientation

While this book addresses the specific linguistic problem of constituent ordering in the constructions delineated above, it is related to frameworks and theoretical approaches of more general concern. Therefore, a word on its disciplinary orientation is in order.

One relevant branch of research, already alluded to above, includes works on grammatical variation (e.g. Rohdenburg and Mondorf 2003) that focus on so-called *alternations* or *allo-sentences* (Lambrecht 1994), which differ

---

[16] An exception to this rule would be example (10) *John ate quickly and with good appetite* from above.

regarding form but are roughly equivalent in function. The crucial question asked in these works is '*when* and *why* speakers choose one variant over the other' (Hilpert 2008: 395). In recent years, researchers have realised that one must take into account a multitude of variables for an adequate description of a given phenomenon and cannot rely on mono-causal explanations (see Gries 2003). This necessity for multi-causal explanations has led to the rise of multifactorial quantitative analyses of linguistic data (e.g. Gries 2003; Bresnan et al. 2007). The crucial advantages of these more sophisticated statistical analyses are that they allow for a fine-grained analysis of every individual variable's strength of effect and also make a direct comparison of variables possible (for a detailed discussion, see Chapter 5). For these reasons, the present work also applies multifactorial methods. In doing so, the present work situates itself in the growing field of quantitatively oriented, corpus-based studies of variation phenomena.

For the interpretation and theoretical explanation of the results, I adopt a processing perspective; more specifically, I will draw on models from language production research in interpreting the results. Details of these models' architectures as well as their relation to the investigated phenomenon are outlined below. Any approach that couples corpus-linguistic methodology with psycholinguistic theories must address their compatibility, as corpus-based methods do not belong to the established toolkit of psycholinguistic inquiry. A combination of these two fields has even been explicitly criticised (see Branigan et al. 1995). The main point of criticism is that, regarding corpus data that has been produced in a naturalistic setting, the researcher has no control over possibly influential factors, as he or she is faced with only the result of a past production process, often devoid of pragmatic and environmental context. Therefore, any finding could be due to these uncontrolled variables. In contrast, in an experimental setting, one can carefully control for variables and provide control groups as a baseline.

While it is impossible to deny that corpus data does not compare to the controlled nature of a psycholinguistic experiment, arguments have been put forward that this fact does not invalidate it for the purposes of psycholinguistic theorising (see Gries 2005). The two most important points in favour of compatibility between the two fields are the following: First, whatever the source of linguistic data is that we work with as researchers, we can never control for all possibly confounding variables, not even in an experimental setting. Hence, the difference between experimental and corpus data is not a categorical but a gradual one. Secondly, the lack of control attributed to corpus data can also be interpreted as an advantage over experimental data. Since it has been produced in a naturalistic setting, it has higher ecological validity; i.e., results can be generalised to natural communication more easily. In turn, the lack of ecological validity is a problem with experimental approaches whose settings are often artificial.

In conclusion, I believe the caveat of corpus data mentioned by Branigan et al. (1995) is a valid one that must be taken seriously. Nevertheless, I claim that corpora represent a valuable source of data, as the drawback of limited control is a gradual one and is outweighed by the greater naturalness of corpus data. Of course, this assessment does not mean that corpus data should substitute psycholinguistic experiments; I believe that both can supplement each other in contributing to psycholinguistic theorising. In this sense, the present study is similar to others which view both experimental and corpus data as valid sources of evidence to investigate questions of language production (see, e.g., Haskell and MacDonald 2005; Jaeger 2010).

1.6   Organisation of the present study

The present study is organised as follows. In Chapter 2, previous research on ordering in coordinate constructions is presented. Chapter 3 deals with the factors that are hypothesised to influence word order in the constructions under investigation. In Chapter 4, the method as well as the data sources (corpora) are presented. The subsequent chapters form the empirical part of the book. Chapter 5 deals with constituent coordination in co-compounds. Chapter 6 is on the coordination of bare phrases and thus deals with binomials. Chapter 7 covers the coordination of complex noun phrases. Chapter 8 offers a detailed discussion of the results, discussing every individual ordering influence against the backdrop of previous research. In Chapter 9, I take a comparative approach: I contrast the results for reversibles and irreversibles, compare the results across the different levels of analysis, and take a look at possible influences of the choice of coordinator. Chapter 10 discusses the results from a processing perspective. It offers an account of the ordering process which hinges on the notions of competition and activation. The chapter also provides a processing view on the characteristics of irreversible binomials. Chapter 11 discusses the implications of the results for the study of other English alternations and for research on universal order preferences. It furthermore contains a conclusive summary and an outlook.

2 Previous research on ordering in coordinate constructions

This chapter will provide an overview of previous research and its limitations. The aim is to highlight the relationship between the present study and previous attempts. The overview does not differentiate between the different levels on which coordination is investigated (see Section 1.2). More information on level-specific research is given in the empirical chapters (Chapters 5–7).

When we consider previous attempts to investigate order in coordinate constructions, two broad approaches can be identified: the study of irreversible binomials in linguistics, and research on linearisation in psycholinguistic research on language production. Research from these two fields will be presented in Sections 2.1 and 2.2 respectively. Let me acknowledge right from the start that not all relevant works can be put neatly into one group or the other. Nevertheless, I believe that arranging previous research in such a way makes for a better understanding by providing information about the two broad paradigms relevant to the present investigation. In a second step (Section 2.3), previously pursued methodological approaches are presented. The individual factors hypothesised to underlie the ordering process, which were tested in the works cited, are presented and discussed in Chapter 3.

2.1 Research on irreversible binomials in linguistics

The first strand of research to be mentioned comprises studies on so-called *frozen* or *irreversible binomials* (IBs). As stated in the introduction, the bulk of relevant work in linguistics concerns the study of these constructions (e.g., Malkiel 1959; Cooper and Ross 1975; Müller 1997; Fenk-Oczlon 1989). Consequently, a multitude of ordering constraints has been tested with IBs. This study explores to what extent the ordering constraints at work in irreversibles also underlie ad hoc coordination. Therefore, studies from this field are directly relevant.

Irreversible binomials are expressions which are 'rigidly fixed in normal speech' (Cooper and Ross 1975: 63), and thus occur only in one particular order. Examples are given below (19a–c).

(19)   a. bed and board
        b. house and home
        c. law and order

Starting with Malkiel (1959), most works on this class concern principles determining the order within these expressions, most notably Cooper and Ross in their widely cited article on 'wor(l)d order' (Cooper and Ross 1975).

Let us focus on the characteristics of this group. Although all works agree that a binomial consists of two main constituents and a coordinator,[1] there is no consensus on the use of the term *irreversible binomial* (see Malkiel 1959; Lambrecht 1984; Olsen 2002b). Nevertheless, certain commonly agreed upon characteristics of irreversible binomials can be identified (A–C).

A   Irreversibility and formulaic character

An irreversible binomial is fixed in order and thus cannot be reversed. This criterion of irreversibility is the defining characteristic of this group (see, e.g., Cooper and Ross 1975; Fenk-Oczlon 1989) and clearly sets it apart from other cases of coordination. IBs exhibit even further formulaic properties; for example, the individual elements cannot be modified by adjectives (see Lambrecht 1984; Olsen 2002b: 183). See the following examples by Olsen (2002b: 183):

(20)   a. life and limb
        b. *dear life and precious limb

The form of irreversible binomials therefore seems to be generally invariable (see Masini 2006).

B   Conventionalisation / frequency

The expressions pertaining to the group of IBs are used with high frequency due to their conventionalised character. This property has been observed by Malkiel (1959) and has also been noted by Lambrecht (1984) and Norrick (1988). It certainly applies to the aforementioned examples (19a–c). Although not mentioned in the literature on IBs, this conventionalisation likely stems from a certain semantic relation between the two coordinated constituents. Similar to the category of natural coordination in typology (see above, Chapter 1), the constituents of IBs seem to typically denote concepts that are closely associated with each other and that often co-occur in the real

---

[1] Malkiel (1959: 113) is to my knowledge the first to have attempted to define the term binomial as 'the sequence of two words pertaining to the same form-class, placed on an identical level of syntactic hierarchy, and ordinarily connected by some kind of lexical link'. This general definition would thus encompass both reversible, as well as irreversible instances.

world. Therefore, the coordination of these constituents is in a way predictable and may lead to conventionalisation, along with a high frequency of use.

C   *Non-compositional semantics*

Expressions belonging to the group of IBs are non-compositional in meaning, such as *odds and ends, hustle and bustle, house and home*, as, for example, *house and home* does not merely denote the sum of its constituents. This criterion is certainly a matter of degree (see Lambrecht 1984). While examples (19a and b) can be considered no longer semantically transparent, example (19c) still appears to be somewhat but not completely compositional. (For a more detailed discussion of the semantics of binomial constructions, see Lambrecht 1984; Norrick 1988; Olsen 2002b; Masini 2006).

The above-mentioned characteristics, especially A and C, render irreversible binomials similar to idioms, in that their form cannot be altered and they often have a specific, non-compositional meaning. However, not all binomials necessarily exhibit all of the above characteristics. For instance, the expression *bacon and eggs* is certainly somewhat conventionalised due to high frequency (see B above). However, its form is not rigidly fixed, as it is still reversible. In contrast, expressions such as *house and home* exhibit all the characteristics. It is thus best to describe this class of expressions as being situated on a continuum ranging from a 'free' coordination of elements to completely irreversible and idiomatic cases. Despite the wealth of research on IBs, no generally accepted definition or empirically applicable operationalisation of the class exists. In Section 4.1.2, I attempt to offer such an empirical operationalisation.

Previous studies on IBs have tested an impressive range of factors supposedly underlying the order in this class of constructions – e.g., the principle that the shorter element precedes the longer one – with varying results.[2] We can hypothesise that these factors are also relevant to the constructions at the focus of this book. Caution should be taken, however, when directly applying these to the present study. As stated above, the binomial expressions dealt with in previous studies have the property of being formulaic, distinguishing them from 'regular' cases of coordination. Olsen (2002a: 184) even views the most conventionalised instances as 'completely atypical co-ordinations'. The crucial difference between the two groups, from the point of view of the language user, is that in strongly formulaic and irreversible cases such as *house and home*, the language user simply reaches for this fixed form without having to perform an online ordering process. Such an interpretation is buttressed by findings revealing that fixed constructions can be accessed faster (e.g., Gibbs and Gonzalez 1985) and can therefore be interpreted to be stored as chunks or lexicalised units in the mental lexicon (see Kuiper et al.

---

[2] A complete presentation of all factors featured in these studies follows in Chapter 3.

2007, also the research overview given in Mos 2010: chapter 1).[3] Due to their unit status in the mental lexicon,[4] they can be referred to as *complex lexical items* (Mos 2010). In contrast, such an ordering process certainly happens during ad hoc coordination, but this has been barely examined due to the aforementioned orientation of research in linguistics.

In summary, the primary limitation of relevant works in linguistics is that they have focused predominantly on formulaic IBs, leaving open the question as to whether findings can be generalised to cases of reversible ad hoc coordination. More specifically, it is not clear whether the factors proposed for IBs in fact influence the language producer when he or she is performing an online ordering process. It is this question that the present study attempts to answer.

2.2   Coordinate constructions in language production research

The second relevant field of research is psycholinguistic research on linearisation during language production. A number of papers in that field feature coordinate constructions, among other expressions. Here the works by Bock and colleagues deserve foremost attention (e.g., Bock and Warren 1985; Bock 1982, 1987a, 1987b). In order to understand their interest in coordinate constructions, a brief description of the architecture of their production model and how it deals with linearisation is necessary.

Bock and colleagues assume the existence of different stages and thus, a serial architecture of the language production system.[5] According to Levelt (1989), or Bock and Levelt (1994), syntactic processing takes place in what they term the *grammatical encoding* stage, which involves two subsequent steps: *functional* and *positional* processing. During the functional stage, lemmas – which are representations of words containing syntactic and semantic information – are assigned grammatical roles; e.g., subject or object role.[6] After that process, during the positional stage, lexemes – which are phonologically specified word forms – are serialised; i.e., their order is determined. It is crucial to emphasise that only the positional stage is relevant

---

[3] By the term 'lexicalised', I mean having unit status in the mental lexicon, similar to other lexical items (see Brinton and Traugott 2005 for other meanings of the term). For the coordinate constructions we are investigating, this means in particular that lexicalised instances are those for which an online ordering process can no longer be assumed (see the foregoing explanations). It is most likely that frequency is of key relevance for this adoption of unit status (see Mos 2010: 1.3.2).

[4] The assumption of unit status simplifies current models somewhat, as they assume a *hybrid* status of fixed expressions (see Chapter 10).

[5] For a discussion of the assumption of seriality and the different levels, see Bock (1987b).

[6] The theoretical justification for a separation between word form and lemma cannot be reviewed in detail at this point. Suffice it to say that the so-called tip-of-the-tongue state, which denotes a state wherein subjects are capable of recalling a word's meaning and syntactic information but not its form, is a key argument for this separation (Brown and McNeill 1966).

when dealing with coordinate constructions, as both constituents are assigned the same grammatical function (see Chapter 1).

The central hypothesis put forward by Bock and colleagues is that the order of constituents within an utterance is sensitive to their accessibility, as 'phrases that contain more accessible information occur[ing] early in senten-ces' (Bock 1982: 39). Accessible elements thus occur early in a given con-struction, as these can be more easily retrieved from the lexicon. Most importantly, two different forms of accessibility are differentiated, *conceptual* and *lexical* accessibility, which relate to the two stages of grammatical encod-ing. According to Bock and Warren (1985: 50) 'conceptual accessibility is the ease with which the mental representation of some potential referent can be activated in or retrieved from memory'. Thus, this form of accessibility deals with the concepts that linguistic forms denote. Conceptual accessibility is claimed to influence functional but not positional processing, and thus is only relevant to grammatical role assignment.[7]

The second form of accessibility, *lexical accessibility*, pertains to the process of retrieving word forms from memory, thus their phonological form, but not a conceptual/semantic representation; it is therefore also termed *phonological accessibility* (Bock 1987b). This pertains to characteristics such as the phono-logical length of a word. Lexical/phonological accessibility should influence the positional stage of grammatical encoding. For proponents of such a model, coordinate constructions are especially interesting, as they allow for the disentangling of the two forms of accessibility. Since both constituents are assigned the same grammatical role, serialisation should occur at the positional stage. Therefore, only lexical accessibility should influence the ordering process. In order to test this hypothesis, Bock and colleagues conducted a number of empirical studies.

Consistent with the aforementioned prediction, McDonald et al. (1993) demonstrate that *animacy*, which feeds into conceptual accessibility, yields no effect on the order of coordinated noun phrases in sentential context. Similarly, Bock and Warren (1985: 62) failed to find a significant effect of conceptual accessibility on ordering in coordinated NPs. In contrast, how-ever, McDonald et al. (1993) report an effect of animacy on order when coordinate constructions are presented without context. Bock and Warren (1985: 62) also express scepticism, conceding that 'it remains possible that there is a conceptual or semantic influence on order within conjuncts'.

---

[7] Conceptual accessibility can be further subdivided into what we may call inherent and derived accessibility. Conceptual accessibility relates to a number of dimensions which characterise the concept, which is denoted by the relevant linguistic form, such as concreteness, animacy, imageability (Bock and Warrren 1985). Derived accessibility refers to the discourse status of the referent; if the discourse is old and therefore given, its accessibility is deemed higher (see Ariel 2001). This form of accessibility is thus not inherent but derived from the particular discourse context. Both forms of accessibility are further detailed in the explanation of the hypotheses for ordering, which are tested in this book (see Sections 4.1–4.2).

Another piece of disconfirming evidence is provided by Kelly et al. (1986), who report that the more prototypical element is put first in coordinate constructions, which most likely is a conceptual effect.[8] Another relevant study comes from Bock and Irwin (1980), who found that in coordinate constructions words denoting given information precede new information, which may also be a conceptual effect.[9] Summarising these findings, it seems thus far unclear whether coordinate constructions are truly immune to conceptual accessibility effects on order.

While the sketched serial model predicts no influence of conceptual factors, it clearly claims that lexical accessibility affects order in coordinate construction. Interestingly, even the evidence for this effect is weak: while Bock (1987a) reports a positive result, McDonald et al. (1993) show that lexical accessibility does not influence word order in coordination. Similarly, Levelt and Maassen's (1981) experimental study found only a non-significant tendency in the expected direction.

This review shows that neither question, of whether conceptual accessibility or lexical accessibility influences order in coordination, is conclusively answered, casting doubt on the general assumption that accessibility affects the process. This possibility leads Branigan et al. (2008: 186–7) to assume that coordinate NPs represent highly unusual constructions that fall outside the scope of existing explanations for serialisation. The authors suggest that the usual incremental retrieval process is 'temporarily suspend[ed]' (Branigan et al. 2008: 187) in them, which is why accessibility effects are not observable (see also Tanaka 2003). However, they do not explain which process may then take over, leaving unanswered the question as to how the ordering process is to be modelled.

In conclusion, the available results from language production studies reveal two uncertainties: first, it is far from clear which factors influence ordering on the empirical level, as there are conflicting results regarding their influences. Neither conceptual nor lexical influences have been conclusively evidenced, underscoring the need for an empirical investigation. Secondly, the question as to which production model may best explain the ordering process in coordinate constructions remains unsettled. These two questions therefore constitute a shortcoming which this book tries to remedy.

2.3   Methodological approaches

In the following, previous methodological approaches to the investigation of order in coordinate constructions are presented. These are classified as

---

[8] For more on the question as to how this effect is to be classified, see Onishi et al. (2008).
[9] As this effect may be due to both lexical as well as conceptual accessibility, it is difficult to tell whether this finding is congruent with the seriality assumption (see Ferreira and Yoshita 2003).

impressionistic, experimental or corpus-linguistic. This classification is not tantamount to claiming that every individual publication can be straightfor-wardly labelled in this way, as some studies combine different methods. Nevertheless, it seems necessary for the sake of providing a general overview.

2.3.1 *Impressionistic approaches*

By 'impressionistic approaches' I refer to contributions that were largely guided by intuitive analysis of a relatively limited number of linguistic examples. Most research on irreversible binomials (see Section 2.1 above) falls into this category.

One of the main characteristics of these studies is that they employed data samples which were not produced by creating a random sample from usage data. They instead relied on introspection and therefore used data that had been collected from personal linguistic experience. The works by Abraham (1950), Malkiel (1959), Huber (1974), Lambrecht (1984), Pordány (1986), Landsberg (1995a) and also Cooper and Ross (1975) bear mentioning here.

For a second characteristic, the influence of different factors is typically demonstrated by merely listing examples that confirm the influence of the postulated variable. Counter-examples are only rarely provided. This approach brings about problems with regard to the interpretation of the results, which can be illustrated by referring to the article by Cooper and Ross (1975).[10] Through impressionistic analysis, the authors identify possible ordering principles and postulate these to be effective on the basis of a number of examples; i.e., mostly binomial pairs, which differ only with respect to this one factor. For instance, on the basis of thirteen examples (Cooper and Ross 1975: 77), among them (21), they conclude that, *ceteris paribus*, the final consonant's obstruency influences the ordering of elements, with the constituent with a more obstruent final consonant preferred in first position (see also below Chapter 3).

(21)   rock and roll

The reader is not informed of any kind of statistical analysis regarding the significance or strength of the effect. Thus, we can assume that the signifi-cance of the factor is judged impressionistically, seeing as, in the view of the authors, there seem to be few or no counter-examples.

Due to this approach, uncertainty arises as to how the validity of a specific variable is to be interpreted once counter-examples are found. This problem becomes apparent in Cooper and Ross (1975: 77), with the constraint number of final consonants. Due to the existence of counter-examples, the authors are

---

[10] The following illustration aims at informing the reader of general trends in this field of research. It should not suggest that the mentioned methodological shortcomings can necessarily be found in all aforementioned works.

uncertain as to whether their hypothesis still holds. This problem pertains to the issue of whether a given variable should be viewed as deterministic – and thus, as a rule that is obeyed without exception – or whether it is merely a probabilistic trend. The works cited often imply that the postulated variables are to be viewed as deterministic and thus, no counter-examples should be found. For instance, Pinker and Birdsong (1979: 506) judge the final consonant constraint to be falsified based merely upon a single counter-example.[11] Unfortunately, none of the works in this group takes a clear stance on the issue. This situation leads to quite a bit of confusion, which becomes apparent in a passage in Cooper and Ross (1975), wherein the authors wonder how many counter-examples need to be found to consider a variable falsified (Cooper and Ross 1975: 101).[12] However, conclusively answering these questions requires quantitative, statistical measures, which I use in this book (see Chapter 4).

In summary, it should be clear that the sketched impressionistic approach comes with methodological shortcomings that render a final assessment of the influence of the different variables impossible.

Two works on irreversible binomials stand out with respect to the aforementioned: Fenk-Oczlon (1989) and Sobkowiak (1993) present at least a limited quantitative analysis, although they also do not use random samples but mostly data acquired from previous research.

2.3.2   Experimental studies

Most of the relevant experimental studies have been conducted in the field of psycholinguistic works on linearisation. A number of different methodological approaches have been followed. Here I shall address naturalness judgement tasks, various production experiments and recognition tasks.

In naturalness judgement tasks, subjects are presented with coordinate constructions and judge their naturalness on a scale. The ordering within the test phrases differs according to the factors researchers consider relevant. In the simplest test design, subjects are presented with the two possible orderings and are to decide which one 'sounds better'. Probably the most widely cited experiment of that sort has been conducted by Pinker and Birdsong (1979), for whom four groups of subjects (English and French native speakers, as well as learners of English and French) rated which ordering of a

---

[11] What is furthermore problematic about Pinker and Birdsong's (1979) assessment is the fact that the variable was proposed for English by Cooper and Ross (1975), while the counter-example they mention is from Arabic. This rationale is surprising, as Pinker and Birdsong (1979) argue for cross-linguistic differences of ordering constraints.

[12] In Cooper and Ross (1975: 101), the authors wonder whether the identified ordering constraints may also be valid for Hindi, or whether in that language they work in the reverse direction. Faced with exceptions to this opposite trend, they wonder how many exceptions to a so-called 'swing-rule' should be allowed before one would consider it falsified: 'If they can have one exception, can they have two? Twenty? Sixty-six? If so, where is falsifiability?'

nonsense pair sounded better on a five-point-scale, testing the 'psychological reality' of several phonological and phonetic variables (Pinker and Birdsong 1979: 499). Similar experiments were conducted by Bolinger (1962), Oakeshott-Taylor (1984), McDonald et al. (1993) and Sambur (1999).

The second class are experiments in which subjects are triggered to produce a coordinate construction whose order of elements can then be analysed. These experiments mostly took the form of either a sentence recall task (e.g., McDonald et al. 1993) or an elicited utterance experiment (e.g., Wright et al. 2005). The sentence recall experiments conducted by McDonald et al. (1993) took the following form: they presented subjects with a short introductory sentence followed by a question – which together they termed a *vignette* – and then with an answer sentence that showed a certain kind of ordering. Then the *vignette* was repeated and the subjects had to answer the question. They observed whether the subjects correctly reproduced the answer or whether they varied the order of constituents. Bock and Irwin (1980), Kelly et al. (1986) and also Bock and Warren (1985) applied similar procedures. To be noted are the experiments where subjects are presented with both constituents in no immediately apparent order and are asked to produce – either orally or by marking the respective positions – the order that they consider to be most natural. Such a procedure was applied by Wright et al. (2005) and also Sambur (1999). Yet another type of experiment was conducted by Bock (1987a), wherein subjects were required to describe pictures that triggered the formulation of conjunct phrases.

The third and last group of experiments, recognition tasks, appears in only one work: Cutler and Cooper (1978) used a phoneme-monitoring task in which subjects were expected to react to a given phoneme in nonsense bipartite conjuncts that were read to them. They manipulated the make-up of the stimuli with regard to hypothesised ordering constraints (see below Chapter 4) and measured the reaction time it took the subjects to recognise the phoneme, which they then interpreted as a proxy for processing difficulty of a given ordering.

2.3.3   Corpus-linguistic approaches

Surprisingly few works have tried to tackle the present ordering problem corpus-linguistically, the method most important to this book. Corpus linguistics is commonly understood here as the study of any kind of quantitative analysis of a larger sample of usage data. The likely reason for the lack of interest in corpus-oriented research may be found in the different perspectives of the two aforementioned approaches to research that tackled the problem. Psycholinguistics traditionally places a strong focus on experimental research, and some psycholinguists even view corpus-based research as unsuitable for their aims (see discussion in Section 1.5). Regarding the second group of researchers who focused on the study of quasi-idiomatic irreversible binomials, their reason for not using corpora may lie in the fact that these IBs cannot easily be found in corpora (see Section 4.1.2 on this issue). This observation ties in with a general reluctance to use corpora in the study of idioms (see discussion in Wulff 2008). Since the present work focuses not on irreversible binomials but on coordinate constructions in general, this hindrance does not apply. On the contrary, corpus-based methods make it possible to easily acquire samples of the coordinate constructions under investigation in the current study. Despite the general reluctance to employ corpora, some relevant previous treatments deserve to be mentioned here.

A method bearing some resemblance to a corpus-linguistic approach is seen in Kelly et al. (1986), as the authors used a sample of definitions derived from a dictionary, extracted coordinate phrases from it and analysed ordering effects quantitatively. Also to be mentioned here is Gustafsson, who, in three publications on binomials (Gustafsson 1974, 1975, 1976), used binomials from a self-compiled corpus. However, as she does not focus on explaining word order within binomials but on the general properties of them, her work is not immediately relevant.

The only publication based on data from electronic corpora – and thus, employing corpus-linguistic methods in the current sense – is an article by Benor and Levy (2006). There the authors compile a random sample of binomials from three corpora and quantitatively analyse word order in them. It is this work that is most directly comparable to the current study. However, its focus is narrower because they investigate only binomials, hence the coordination of two lexical elements, and do not differentiate between reversibles and irreversibles.[13]

2.4   Limitations of previous attempts

The review of previous research revealed certain limitations. First, in linguistics we can observe a strong focus on the investigation of order in formulaic, irreversible binomials. This focus naturally raises the question as to whether results can be generalised to reversible coordination. Meanwhile, psycholinguistic studies on linearisation explicitly investigated instances of reversible coordination. However, due to the wider scope of this field, these were mostly dealt with in passing. Furthermore, the results of these studies are particularly controversial. Therefore, there is great empirical uncertainty as to what actually influences order in reversible coordinate constructions. Regarding methodology, two approaches predominate: experimental approaches, which are mostly found in the field of psycholinguistics, and

---

[13] After completion of this manuscript, Mollin (2012) published a study which is similar in orientation to the present one in that she also compares reversible and irreversible binomials. It does not, however, consider other levels of coordination, and it differs from the present study in that it does not employ multifactorial methodology.

what I termed impressionistic approaches, which are essentially introspective. Corpus-linguistic works, in contrast, are scarce. This is somewhat surprising when considering the wealth of corpus-linguistic works on other variation phenomena (see also Section 1.3).

This book will remedy a number of the shortcomings cited above. First of all, by explicitly addressing the ordering problem in reversible instances, this study will bridge the gap between linguistic and psycholinguistic approaches, thereby hopefully alleviating the empirical uncertainty regarding the influences speakers are subject to when ordering elements. Furthermore, the book will tap into the thus far little-used resource of corpus data. Compared to the introspective approach predominant in linguistics, this resource is more representative of actual language in use, as corpora contain real usage data (see Sinclair 1991). It is therefore much better suited to the investigation of the online ordering process, which is at the centre of the present study.

3   Variables and hypotheses

In the following, I provide an overview of factors that are likely to influence order in coordinate constructions, which draws on previous research. These factors are located on different linguistic levels ranging from pragmatics to phonetics. In this overview, I not only list factors that have been investigated and discussed in previous studies, but also discuss the present state of evidence for each of them and comment on its relevance to the current study. Due to the way research has evolved over the past decades, most of the works mentioned here focus on irreversible binomials (see Chapter 2). Nevertheless, other works are taken into account, mostly psycholinguistic studies on linearisation phenomena, if they investigated ordering in relevant constructions. Because of the focus in previous research on the coordination of lexical elements, some of the factors reviewed here may be of only limited applicability to the level of copulative compounds and to complex NP ordering. This issue is discussed in the following subsections on the individual factors and also in a separate section (Section 3.11).

The following review is mostly restricted to works focusing on ordering in English. However, I also consider works that formulate new claims or hypotheses for other languages that may also be immediately relevant to English. For example, Müller (1997) – although working on German binomials – is mentioned in the section on the stress pattern of binomials because he formulates new ideas from which the study of English can profit. The same approach was applied to studies focusing on constructions that do not form the focus of this book, but that address other relevant linearisation phenomena.

3.1   Pragmatic and semantic variables

This section discusses possible pragmatic and semantic influences on the order of constituents, starting with possible pragmatic influences, of which differences in *information status* can be considered for empirical analysis. With regard to conceptual and semantic factors, different suggestions have been made in previous research as to how they are to be classified. I distinguish here the three semantic factors: *hierarchical relations, conceptual accessibility* and *iconic sequencing*, roughly following the classification by Benor and Levy (2006).

3.1.1   Information status

A well-researched factor relevant for the ordering of elements – not only in coordinate constructions – is the information or discourse status of to-be-ordered elements. Constituents may denote referents that have been established in discourse already and thus constitute given information, or that refer to newly introduced referents and thus new information (see Gundel et al. 1993). It is generally agreed that language users follow what is called the 'given before new principle' (Clark and Clark 1977: 548), which is also mentioned in English grammars (e.g. Quirk et al. 1985). Differences in information status have also been termed otherwise; for example, the topic–comment distinction, or the theme vs. rheme distinction (Arnold et al. 2000). While there are certain distinctions among these different terms, I shall not attempt to disentangle the different theoretical approaches here, as all three frameworks agree that forms referring to previously established information precede forms referring to new information (see Arnold et al. 2000). Another generalisation that seems to contrast with the aforementioned suggestions is Givón's theory of Task Urgency, which states that language users 'attend first to the most urgent task' (Givón 1988: 252), which should therefore be mentioned early on. Most urgent to Givón is 'less accessible as well as less predictable information', which therefore 'tends to be placed first in the string' (Givón 1991: 43). This assumption can be interpreted as a reversal of the given–before–new principle (see Wasow 2002: 62–5 on the contrast between the two principles, also Hawkins 1994: 214–42). Since there is little empirical support (see, e.g., Hawkins 1994: 214–42) for this reverse tendency, it will not be considered further in the following sections.

In contrast, it has been shown that the given–before–new principle influences ordering in a number of alternations in English (e.g. Arnold et al. 2000; Gries 2003). Despite the wealth of research on this principle, few works explicitly apply it to coordination, probably due to the focus on structural properties of irreversibles, devoid of discourse context. An exception is Bock (1977), who shows that the prior mention of a referent has a strong effect upon its occurring in first position using a question-answer task on nine cases of order variations, including noun phrase coordination with *and*.

Based on this review of literature, the given–before–new principle is undoubtedly relevant for constituent order in coordinate constructions and is therefore investigated in the present study.

3.1.2   Focus and emphasis

Another conceivable discourse-functional effect pertains to the possibility that a particular focus or emphasis on one of the two constituents may influence the order of elements. Regarding English particle placement, Gries (2003) argues that speakers aim at putting the to-be-emphasised element in final position.

This strategy of highlighting one constituent goes along with assigning the main stress (the nucleus) to the final element and has also been referred to as end-focus (Quirk et al. 1985). The following example illustrates this phenomenon (taken from Gries 2003: 25, emphasis is mine):

(22)   What did he pick up? – He picked up *the book*.

An analogous influence is also conceivable with coordinate constructions, where the emphasised element is put in the second position. See the following (made-up) stretch of discourse for an example (words in italics are emphasised):

(23)   He brought transparencies and *what* to the meeting?
       – He brought transparencies and *pens* to the meeting.

This shows that this emphasising/focusing strategy is also intuitively plausible for coordinate constructions. Interestingly, this emphasising strategy is conflated in Quirk et al. (1985: 1357) with the principle of presenting new after given information, as end-focus refers to the 'linear presentation from low to high information status'. Such an interpretation would be congruent with example (23) above. It is unclear, however, whether the two make the same predictions in all cases. While it is therefore conceivable that this emphasising strategy yields information on ordering beyond differences in information status, it will not be considered in the empirical analyses of this book, as it is difficult to find instances to which it undoubtedly applies. The problem of identifying relevant contexts is particularly acute with the corpus resources the present study relies on. One way to go about testing a possible influence would be to use stress as an indicator, yet this requires a prosodically annotated corpora as well as an auditory categorisation of the data. Corpora for which this information is available are, however, of very limited size and would very much limit the quantitative analysis of the results.

3.1.3   *Iconic sequencing*

Iconic sequencing is the semantic-pragmatic factor most often mentioned in the literature on binomials (Malkiel 1959; Huber 1974; Cooper and Ross 1975; Fenk-Oczlon 1989; Landsberg 1995a; Widdows and Dorow 2005). It signifies that the order of elements that is perceived in the extra-linguistic world is mirrored in the order of linguistic elements. This principle also appears in language production research: Levelt (1981) relates it to an event structure which is mirrored in linguistic structure (see detailed discussion in Chapter 8). Most prominently, instances of temporal ordering fall into this category, where the temporal sequence observed in non-linguistic reality is echoed in the linguistic order of elements, e.g. in the classic expression *veni, vidi, vici*. This temporal principle is also mentioned by Givón (1991: 92) as the *semantic principle of linear order*, as seen below:

(24)   a. morning and afternoon
  b. birth and death

In addition to the temporal ordering effect, Malkiel (1959) noted that a cause–effect relation was apparent in a number of binomials pairs, which are, however, almost always inextricably intertwined. Consider the following examples:

(25)   a. shoot and kill (from Malkiel 1959)
  b. eggs and larvae (from Widdows and Dorow 2005)

Benor and Levy (2006) add a further instantiation of iconic sequencing: instances of two constituents appearing on the same scale, which already implies a certain logical order, such as:

(26)   a. eighth and ninth
  b. elementary school and high school

Similar cases are also mentioned by Allan (1987) as universal sequencing conventions. However, these bear a close resemblance to the temporal sequence tendency. For example, the sequence in (26) is a logical as well as a temporal one.

So, the three aforementioned instantiations of iconicity, viz. temporal, causal and logical iconicity, will be considered in this study. Most evidence for the iconicity constraint comes from studies on formulaic binomials. While Cooper and Ross (1975) restrict the criterion's applicability to verbs, it can obviously also apply to sequences of other word classes, at least to nouns, which form the focus of this study (see examples (24)–(26) above). Complementing the introspective evidence provided by Cooper and Ross (1975), Widdows and Dorow (2005)[1], as well as Benor and Levy (2006), show it to be effective in corpus data. It can thus be safely concluded that substantial evidence for iconic sequencing has been accumulated, showing it to be a principle that is seldom violated. Different explanations for this trend have been offered. The two opposing views boil down to whether iconicity could be viewed as a semantic property of the coordinating element (e.g. *and*) or as an independent semantic-pragmatic factor. Blakemore and Carston (2005b) adopt the latter view in arguing that the interpretation of chronological sequence is the most natural form of interpretation, and thus the presentation in such order is a fulfilment of the Gricean maxim of manner. These conflicting assumptions are examined in this study, as asyndetic coordination, which does not feature a coordinating element, is also addressed.[2] For the moment, iconic sequencing is considered a factor whose

---

[1] Widdows and Dorow (2005) focus solely on temporal ordering.
[2] Dik (1972: 271–2) also discusses this point and concludes that coordinators in English have 'just the combinatory value without any further specification of the particular relation holding between the members of the coordination'. This issue is discussed in Section 9.4

influence merits investigation. A discussion of its possible explanation follows in Chapter 9.

3.1.4   Extra-linguistic hierarchy

A further principle frequently discussed in the study of irreversible binomials applies to constituents that denote referents that are hierarchically related. The principle states that when there is such a relation, the more powerful referent precedes the less powerful one, and it has therefore been termed the *power* constraint in Benor and Levy (2006). This criterion has most often been applied to the sociocultural sphere, for example by Malkiel (1959: 145), who states that 'priorities inherent in the structure of a society' are reflected in the order of binomials, and also by Huber (1974), who terms it 'social importance' (cf. also Allan 1987). The following two examples, taken from Malkiel (1959: 138), serve to illustrate it:

(27)   a. husband and wife
        b. rich and poor

In both examples, the constituent denoting the socially more powerful referent precedes that denoting the less powerful one. As we can see, hierarchical relations may exist on different (sociocultural) scales. The most widely studied contrast is a possible gender asymmetry, since a tendency to put male referents first can be observed in English. For instance, in an experimental approach, Sambur (1999) found that the male-before-female bias is observable in the ordering of male and female names, which is a finding corroborated by Wright et al. (2005).

However, hierarchical relations are not restricted to gender. Other manifestations of the present ordering constraint can be found in examples such as *university and college*, or in the compound *director-actor*, where also the more powerful institution or person precedes the less powerful one. As all of the above-mentioned instances of hierarchies are dependent on the culture which generated them, it is likely that languages in other parts of the world may differ with regard to this constraint, for instance by a possible female-first rule (see Landsberg 1995a for a discussion of this issue).

However, we do find hierarchical relations not located in the sociocultural realm, which I also subsume under this constraint. This is the reason why it is not termed *power* here. For instance, a tendency for the greater of two (numerical) values to precede the lesser can be observed when both are located on the same scale (see Benor and Levy 2006: 239) as in:

(28)   a. kilograms and grams
        b. dollars and cents

on the possible semantic value of coordinators. Since asyndetic coordinate constructions are also examined in this work, this book provides a test case for this claim, as there should be no influence of iconicity in asyndetic constructions if it is to be attributed to the coordinator.

A hierarchical relation in terms of decreasing strength can also be observed in Ross's (1982) rule that beverages containing more alcohol precede those containing less alcohol, as in *gin and juice*, or *vodka and tonic*. What is common across these examples is a common scale on which the two coordinated elements can be located. This constraint has also been extended by Benor and Levy (2006) to combinations where a more central or important element precedes a less central one. Consider:

(29)   a. oranges and grapefruit
       b. eating and drinking   (examples from Benor and Levy 2006: 239)

I find such an extension problematic for two reasons: first of all, a hierarchical relation between the two elements is not immediately obvious. Although eating may be more central than drinking in certain contexts, I am reluctant to view this observation as a hierarchical relation between the two constituents similar to the other instances above, as the asymmetry does not seem to be inherent, but requires considerable additional context. Secondly, a *central before peripheral* rule very strongly overlaps with the prototype-first constraint, which is covered by the factor conceptual accessibility, presented below. Therefore, these cases are not considered instances of the hierarchy constraint in this book.

3.1.5   Conceptual accessibility

In the following, I examine a number of different semantic factors that are said to influence the ordering of elements for which conceptual accessibility serves as a cover term. The rationale applicable to all of these principles is that the cognitively unmarked and thus more easily accessed constituent precedes the less accessible one. Adopting an approach from language processing, I follow the work by Bock and colleagues (see Section 2.2) in choosing conceptual accessibility as a cover concept. The following is therefore also to be understood as an overview of the dimensions that are relevant to the concept of conceptual accessibility. If not noted otherwise, all of the following contrasts are considered in the empirical studies to follow.[3]

3.1.5.1   Vertical before horizontal
In formulaic binomials, the vertical dimension is claimed to precede the horizontal, as in the following examples from Cooper and Ross (1975):

(30)   a. height and width
       b. latitude and longitude

---

[3] A number of the following contrasts are subsumed under the egocentric *Me-First*-principle by Cooper and Ross (1975). This principle is detailed and discussed further below, along with other umbrella concepts.

This factor is mentioned in a number of other studies as well (Cooper and Klouda 1995; Benor and Levy 2006). Its psychological reality in terms of a difference in accessibility has been shown in psychological studies, which find that movement on the horizontal axis is harder to process than on the vertical axis (see Cooper and Klouda 1995). For instance, Farrell (1979) shows that right-left orientation of shapes is harder for subjects to identify than up-down orientation.

3.1.5.2   Up before down and right before left
Within the vertical and the horizontal planes, a preference for up before down and right before left, respectively, has been suggested (Cooper and Ross 1975; Cooper and Klouda 1995; Benor and Levy 2006), leading to ordering decisions as we can observe below:

(31)   a. rise and fall
       b. right and left

The psychological evidence for these differences is rather limited, however. Cooper and Klouda (1995) cite a study by Seymour (1969) showing that words which were presented above another object were more quickly recognised than when presented below the object. However, this study does not address possible differences between *left* and *right*. Mayerthaler argues *right* to be less marked than *left*, as 93% of any population is right-handed (Mayerthaler 1981: 12). In my opinion, however, it is less than convincing to attribute a possible conceptual difference solely to right- and left-handedness, since, apart from this biological fact, there seems to be little difference in accessibility between the two.[4] Therefore, the assumed accessibility difference between left and right is not considered in the current study, while the up-down preference is maintained.

3.1.5.3   Animate before inanimate
One of the most frequently mentioned and analysed factors in psycholinguistic works on word order, as well as in studies on binomials, is animacy (Cooper and Ross 1975; Bock 1982; McDonald et al. 1993; Müller 1997; Landsberg 1995a). It has been shown that constituents denoting animate referents precede those denoting inanimate referents as in:

(32)   people and things   (Cooper and Ross 1975: 65)

The effect of animacy has been related to conceptual accessibility in studies of language production (see, e.g., Bock 1982). Its influence on order in coordination

---

[4] Because of these doubts, I performed a corpus study in the BNC in order to check whether the proposed tendency holds in ordering. I searched for *left and/or right* in both orders, and also *up and/or down* in both orders. While *up* and *down* behave as predicted (*up and/or down*: 2,254 hits; *down and/or up*: 21 hits), the corpus study reveals no preference for *right* to be mentioned prior to *left* (*left and/or right*: 413 hits, *right and or left*: 194 hits).

is controversial; in an experimental study, McDonald et al. (1993) found that animacy did not significantly influence order of constituents in coordinated noun phrases when these were presented with context, but only when the NP conjunct was presented in isolation.

3.1.5.4   Positive before negative

Also widely cited is a preference for those constituents that denote something that is positively evaluated to precede a negatively evaluated entity or concept. It is mentioned in numerous works on binomials, but also in other studies on order of linguistic constituents (Abraham 1950; Cooper and Ross 1975; Bock 1982; Wulff 2002; Landsberg 1995a).

(33)   a. good or bad   (from Benor and Levy 2006: 238)
        b. plus or minus   (from Cooper and Ross 1975: 65)

While Abraham (1950) and Cooper and Ross (1975) show its influence in impressionistically collected examples, Wulff (2002) provides empirical evidence that, in preverbal adjective coordination, the adjective with a 'positive affective load' precedes the one with a 'negative affective load' as in *strong dangerous* (Wulff 2002: 34).

3.1.5.5   Concrete before abstract

It is generally acknowledged that there is an accessibility difference between forms denoting concrete and abstract referents, similar to the effect of animacy, resulting in orderings such as:

(34)   body and mind

Empirical evidence for this contrast exists for both healthy and aphasic speakers, mostly in the form of lexical decision and naming tasks. For an overview, as well as proposed explanations, see Ahlsén (2006: 87) and Schwanenflugel (1991a). This accessibility difference has been linked to the order of mention of linguistic elements by Bock and Warren (1985), who study whether referents which are more easily imageable (concrete) are mentioned prior to referents which are not that easily imageable (abstract). Significant effects for grammatical role assignment are found, yet mixed effects are reported for coordinate constructions. Imageability did not significantly influence order in phrasal conjuncts. Benor and Levy (2006), however, mention a concreteness effect for ordering in binomials.

3.1.5.6   Prototype first

The prototype first constraint means that the more prototypical concept precedes the less prototypical one, drawing on prototype theory as developed by Rosch et al. (1976). Example (35) illustrates this principle, as the less prototypical fruit item is preceded by the more prototypical one.

(35)   apple and lemon

Kelly et al. (1986) report evidence for this effect from a sentence recall experiment, showing that coordinate phrases 'were very sensitive to variations in prototypicality' (Kelly et al. 1986: 67). Widdows and Dorow (2005) complement this finding by presenting corpus-linguistic evidence for the constraint's effectiveness.

3.1.5.7   Basic level before superordinate or subordinate level

In a number of publications it has been argued that the constituent denoting the more general concept precedes the one with a more specific denotation. This argument has been made by Cooper and Ross (1975), Edmondson (1985), Landsberg (1995a) and also Benor and Levy (2006). I believe this effect can be described as a prior mention of basic level concepts before subordinate concepts. Example (36a) below illustrates this principle, as *flowers* is a better example of a basic-level category than *roses*. The conceptually greater accessibility of the basic level rests on the finding that it is cognitively more important and thus unmarked in comparison to other levels in the conceptual taxonomy (see Evans and Green 2006). This principle can be extended to contrasts involving superordinate categories, as these also are considered conceptually marked in comparison with the basic level. This is exemplified in (36b) as the basic-level category *houses* precedes the superordinate category *buildings*.

(36) a. flowers and roses   (from Benor and Levy 2006)
      b. houses and buildings   (from BNC data, filename CKE)

3.1.5.8   Other sub-constraints

In addition to the previously mentioned principles, other contrasts have been linked to a conceptual difference (see Cooper and Ross 1975). Among these are *friend before enemy*, *living before dead* and *solid before liquid*. I view these as being reducible to the constraints discussed above. *Friend before enemy* can be subsumed under the *positive before negative* constraint, *living before dead* is covered by animacy, and solid objects can be argued to be more concrete than liquid. Furthermore, other sub-constraints have been suggested, such as *present generation before other generation* and *proximal before distal*, as well as *own before other*. These contrasts can be explained by the first element being more frequently encountered by the prototypical speaker and can therefore be argued to constitute more accessible concepts. In summary, the following list of sub-constraints can be subsumed under the conceptual accessibility constraint:

CONCEPTUALLY MORE ACCESSIBLE before LESS ACCESSIBLE
>   animate before inanimate
>   positive before negative
>   concrete before abstract
>   vertical before horizontal

above (up) before below (down)
prototype first
basic level before subordinate/superordinate level
proximal before distal
own before other
present generation before other

Although evidence for the influence of individual contrasts varies (see above), it seems fair to say that a general influence of cognitive accessibility is well supported by previous research on irreversible binomials. However, for other, less fixed coordinated constructions, things are less clear, as psycholinguistic studies on linearisation failed to find an effect of conceptual accessibility in coordinate NPs (see Section 2.2 and McDonald et al. 1993). This uncertainty therefore asks for an empirical investigation of reversible ad hoc coordination as pursued in this book.

3.1.6   The Me-First-principle and other reductive explanations

The preceding discussion of ordering tendencies and variables raises the question as to why these are subsumed under the three above-mentioned categories, and whether they could be subsumed under just one superordinate contrast. The most well-known suggestion which argues this is Cooper and Ross's (1975) *Me-First*-principle. The authors claim that the element which is closer to the prototypical speaker is mentioned first. According to them, this speaker prototype is characterised by being 'here, now, adult, male, positive, singular, living, friendly, solid, agentive, powerful, at home, and patriotic, among other things' (1975: 67). This list certainly covers a number of variables mentioned above, mostly features of those I subsumed under the variable conceptual accessibility. After all, conceptual accessibility also makes assumptions about certain entities being more easily processed by the prototypical speaker, thereby resembling the *Me-First*-principle. As a universal explanation of all semantic factors, the latter is nevertheless problematic because the two other proposed semantic variables, iconic sequencing and extra-linguistic hierarchy, cannot be easily incorporated into it.

Turning to the extra-linguistic hierarchy constraint first, the *Me-First*-principle cannot convincingly explain the observed gender bias, because one would be hard-pressed to argue that the prototypical speaker is male, as Cooper and Ross (1975) do, since there are more females in the general population. Furthermore, numerical hierarchical relations cannot relate to *Me-First* without controversy because it seems implausible that the prototypical speaker is closer to a certain numerical value than another (see example (28) and also Benor and Levy 2006: 240). Therefore, it seems most sensible to keep hierarchical relations as a separate constraint.

The greatest problems with the *Me-First*-principle as a universal explanation arise when subsuming iconic sequencing under it: it seems implausible
that the prototypical speaker is more closely related to the first element in a
temporal sequence – as in *morning and night* – or to the first element in a
numerical sequence – as in *eighth and ninth*. Therefore, it is best to keep
iconic sequencing as a separate variable. In conclusion, regarding the evaluation of the *Me-First*-principle, I side with Benor and Levy (2006), who also
reject it as the sole explanation of semantic constraints.

Another attempt at proposing a superordinate semantic explanation is made
by van Langendonck (1995) who uses a very broad definition of iconicity to
explain all semantic factors. However, his argument also results in a 'closeness
to the speaker' principle, which is virtually the same egocentric view as found
in Cooper and Ross (1975).[5] Hence, the same problems also apply here.

A further argument against conflating the three suggested semantic variables is put forth by Benor and Levy (2006), who observe that some of the
listed semantic constraints may be in conflict with one another. For example,
eggs and larvae instantiates an iconic sequence. However, the animate before
inanimate tendency would predict the reverse order, as eggs are certainly not
as animate as larvae. Such situations are not problematic if both constraints
are understood as different variables, but create hard-to-resolve conflicts if
both are subsumed under the same explanation.

3.2   Factors related to the stress pattern of coordinate constructions

3.2.1   Rhythm

A preference for an alternation of stressed and unstressed syllables 'to
enhance rhythmic alternation' (McDonald et al. 1993: 215) has been claimed
to influence ordering decisions in coordination. This argument has been
made in works on binomials (Jespersen 1943; Müller 1997; Benor and Levy
2006), as well as in psycholinguistic studies (McDonald et al. 1993). The
effect of stress alternation is illustrated in the examples below (upper case X
marks a stressed syllable, lower case x an unstressed one). The ordering (37a)
salt and pepper is argued to be preferred, as a sequence of stressed and
unstressed syllables is produced, while the reverse ordering (37b) *pepper
and salt* would result in two adjacent unstressed syllables.

(37)   a. salt and pepper
            X   x   X x
        b. pepper and salt
            X x   x   X

---

[5] Also Landsberg (1995a) suggests a similarly egocentric interpretation of iconicity.

In studies on other alternation phenomena, the tendency to alternate stressed and unstressed syllables has been shown to affect the choice between a number of competing forms, for instance the choice between the two forms of the comparative in English (Mondorf 2009). It has been convincingly argued that this striving for contrast can be explained by an architectural feature of the language production system (see Schlüter 2005).

McDonald et al. (1993) tested the preference for rhythmic alternation by experimentally contrasting monosyllabic words with either a trochaic disyllabic, as in *doll and attic*, or an iambic disyllabic, as in *doll and antique*. The authors found an effect of stress alternation, even overruling a supposed short-before-long tendency (see Section 3.3 below). Therefore, McDonald et al. (1993) speculate whether the length criterion can be reduced to stress, as it seems only to be obeyed when rhythmic considerations also call for such an ordering (the *doll and attic* case).[6] They furthermore argue that it has only a small effect on ad hoc coordination, as their experimental results yield only weak effects for that group. They state, however, that it strongly affects frequent constructions, such as formulaic, irreversible binomials.

In summary, the principle of alternating stresses is one of the more widely discussed and investigated constraints. However, there are two questions that merit further investigation. First, most of the evidence stems from the study of formulaic binomials, thus it is unclear whether the constraint is relevant only for that group or whether it influences also ad hoc coordination, a question raised by McDonald et al. (1993). Secondly, the question as to whether rhythm may explain the widely cited short-before-long preference is an intriguing theory that warrants further investigation. Chapter 8 discusses both of these questions in light of the empirical results.

3.2.2   *Avoidance of the second constituent to bear ultimate stress*

A second variable related to the stress pattern of the overall construction is Bolinger's (1962) argument that a terminal oxytone, i.e. a final stressed syllable, is avoided in the coordination of lexemes. He investigates this claim with adjective order, as in the following test sentences:

(38)   a. It was a dull and lengthy speech.
　　　　b. It was a lengthy and dull speech.
　　　　c. His statement was frank and candid.
　　　　　(All examples from Bolinger 1962)

---

[6] This argument is also made by Müller (1997: 34) for German binomials. It is also alluded to by Jespersen (1943). Similarly, Wright et al. (2005) conflate syllable length and rhythm.

His findings indicate that speakers prefer the ordering in (38a) over that in (38b), as the latter ends in a stressed syllable (*dull*). Since the adjectives in both examples occur in attributive position and the following noun *speech* is stressed, we may suppose that this finding is an effect of the rhythmic alternation constraint holding only for that specific syntactic context. If that were the case, it would not be relevant here, as I do not investigate prenominal adjective order. However, Bolinger goes on to show that this preference still holds when the relevant adjective phrase occurs at the end of a sentence (see 34c), thus in predicative position. He argues that even in these contexts it can be explained by a striving for stress alternation as the following phrase/sentence is likely to begin with a stressed syllable. Empirical data, however, does not support such an assumption, as the typical stress pattern for the English phrase is iambic (see Schlüter 2009), hence a following phrase is likely to begin with an unstressed syllable. Thus, rhythmic considerations cannot motivate this tendency. What furthermore casts doubt on Bolinger's explanation is the fact that the test items he used not only differed in stress, but also in length, thus confounding weight effects cannot be ruled out (see (34a–c)). However, support for the effectiveness of the present constraint comes from Benor and Levy (2006), who show that it influences order in binomials, including the coordination of nouns, though employing less than ideal, monofactorial methods.[7] They argue that this tendency may be due to binomials inheriting phonological characteristics from monomorphemic words, which are usually not stressed on the final syllable. Despite its unclear motivation, this variable will be tested here with copulative compounds and bare noun phrases (binomials).

No clear predictions emerge as to the effectiveness of this ordering tendency with more complex multi-word noun phrases. Even if coordinated NPs could be shown to also typically exhibit an unstressed final syllable, this stress pattern should hold for both to-be-ordered phrases. Thus, no influence on the ordering process can be motivated. Therefore, this variable will not be tested on this level.

3.2.3   Accentuation of the second constituent and syllable weight

Previous studies argue that an observable greater accent on the second element in binomials may influence the order of elements (e.g. Müller 1997 on German irreversible binomials). Benor and Levy (2006) show this contrast in accent to hold also for English binomials, independent of their

---

[7] Monofactorial methods may invite false conclusions about the significance of a certain variable, as relations of epiphenomenality may be overlooked. Although Benor and Levy (2006) also apply multifactorial methods, for the significance values of individual variables, they solely rely on monofactorial tests. See Chapter 4 for a more detailed account of this point.

syntactic context. As syllable weight facilitates stress, they hypothesise that the constituent which contains the heavier main syllable should preferably occur in second position; however, they fail to obtain a significant effect of this variable. This possible ordering constraint may also be relevant for copulative compounds, as these also bear the main accent on the second constituent (e.g. *actor-director*, see Plag et al. 2008). Despite the lack of evidence, I will still test this variable in the empirical studies, since a possible weight contrast is based on plausible assumptions about the phonological make-up of relevant constructions.

3.3   Length and complexity

In many studies on the linearisation of constituents in English, an effect to order the lighter/shorter element before the heavier/longer element has been observed (e.g. Arnold et al. 2000; Wasow 2002), and coordinate constructions are no exception in this respect. Several length measurements are possible on the different levels of analysis, which are detailed in the following.

3.3.1   *Number of syllables*

Perhaps the most widely mentioned ordering variable in the literature on irreversible binomials is that the first element is usually shorter than the second one, measuring length in syllables. According to Cooper and Ross (1975), this principle goes back to Panini in 350 BCE, which is why it is also referred to as 'Panini's law'. This factor has been investigated impressionistically, as well as experimentally and corpus-linguistically. Most works find a strong and significant short-before-long preference (see Table 3.1 in Section 3.8). Despite the empirical support, its influence is not without controversy: Cooper and Ross (1975: 78) speculate that its applicability may be restricted to instances where the first constituent is monosyllabic and the second is bisyllabic. McDonald et al. (1993) take up this point and pose the question as to whether the length difference can be explained as being a by-product of rhythmic alternation, viz. the alternation of stressed and unstressed syllables. As mentioned above, their experiments show that length had no effect, when stress was controlled for. In contrast, Pinker and Birdsong (1979) state that length differences have an independent influence beyond just rhythmic considerations, a claim for which they provide experimental evidence. This controversial issue is addressed in Section 3.7.

A different claim is put forth by Stallings et al. (1998), who hypothesise that length considerations are relevant for phrase ordering, but not word ordering, as these processes take place during different stages in language production. This claim will be discussed in Chapter 8.

3.3.2 Number of phonemes

Several works (Malkiel 1959; Gustafsson 1974; Huber 1974) suggest that length could also be measured by counting phonemes. Sobkowiak (1993) does exactly that and finds a significant effect. Measuring length in phonemes could detect existing length differences even when length in terms of syllables is the same. For example, in the compound *actor-stuntman*, where both constituents consist of two syllables, the second is nevertheless longer by three phonemes. The reverse effect is also possible, as two constituents may be equally long counting phonemes, but may differ in number of syllables, e.g. *founder-editor*. Naturally, the two length measurements are strongly correlated; still it seems wise to consider them jointly, as there is no a priori reason as to why both of them should not be relevant. When relying on only one of them, as all previous studies have done, we run the risk of not taking into account possibly relevant length differences, as seen in the examples above. Moreover, the more fine-grained phoneme count may prove other postulated constraints to be epiphenomenal to differences in phoneme length (see Section 3.5.3 on the number of initial consonants).

3.3.3 Number of morphemes (morphological complexity)

A further possibility that has been discussed in previous research concerns whether the apparent short-before-long rule may be an effect of a possible tendency for the morphologically simpler constituent to precede the morphologically more complex one. For instance, Malkiel (1959) and also McDonald et al (1993) speculate that the number of morphemes is relevant for ordering decisions. See the examples below for an illustration:

(39) a. complete and unabridged   (from Benor and Levy 2006: 237)
      b. orange and oranges

In (39a) a monomorphemic element precedes a polymorphemic constituent, while (39b) instantiates a singular–plural contrast. Essentially, both examples show an ordering of growing morphological complexity. Since in the above-mentioned works this factor is merely mentioned but not investigated, its influence is yet to be known. It is empirically addressed in the individual case studies below.

3.3.4 Number of syntactic nodes (syntactic complexity)

Similar to morphological structure, syntactic complexity may also influence the ordering of multi-word noun phrases. Consider the following example, where a more complex noun phrase follows a noun phrase of lesser complexity (example inspired by Ferreira 1991):

(40)

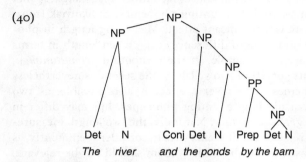

Previous research found that increased syntactic complexity leads to a higher processing load. Evidence for this relation comes from recall studies showing that syntactically more complex phrases (those including a greater number of syntactical nodes) lead to longer utterance initiation times (Johnson 1966; Ferreira 1991). Ferreira (1991) has furthermore shown that a difference in processing load stemming from differing syntactic complexity can be observed even when the length in words is the same. Hence, the processing load is sensitive to syntactic complexity independent of pure length considerations. I therefore hypothesise regarding the phrasal level that the syntactically simpler phrase precedes the more complex NP. It should be mentioned that the distinction between syntactic complexity and mere length in words is seldom made in other studies on English variation phenomena, which often employ the term *weight* as a cover term for both length and complexity (see discussion in Rosenbach 2005). This is unproblematic in many cases, as syntactic complexity and length (as, e.g., the number of words) are strongly correlated (see Wasow 1997; Szmrecsanyi 2004). Berlage (2010), however, argues that the two measurements should be disentangled, as independent effects of both are possible, an assumption which can be linked to findings by Wasow and Arnold (2003). I therefore take into account length as well as structural complexity when investigating the order of complex noun phrases, since both may yield independent influences. This issue will be discussed in light of the results obtained in Chapter 8.

3.4   Further variables related to phonological and phonetic length

A number of further phonological and phonetic criteria have been suggested to influence order in binomials by Cooper and Ross (1975). All of these relate to a greater phonological and/or phonetic length of the second constituent, demonstrating the general short–before–long preference mentioned above.

3.4.1   Vowel length

The first variable to be mentioned here states that the constituent with the 'longer resonant nucleus' follows the shorter one (Cooper and Ross 1975: 72), as in:

(41)   stress and strain   (from Cooper and Ross 1975: 72)

Pinker and Birdsong's (1979) results corroborate this effect, as subjects rated orderings of pairs which differ in this respect more natural than their reversals.[8] Wright et al. (2005) also acquired significant evidence for this effect, as it influenced ordering decisions of subjects when ordering personal names. In their corpus-linguistic study, Benor and Levy (2006) acquired mixed results for this variable, as it was only significant in certain sub-samples of their data. Oakeshott-Taylor (1984: 229) found a tendency for this factor in a naturalness judgement task, which however did not reach statistical significance.[9]

This variable vowel length is often explained by referring to phrase-final lengthening (PFL), as 'ordering long vowels after short vowels facilitates the natural process of phrase-final lengthening' (Wright et al. 2005: 537).[10] In investigating this variable, previous research focused solely on monosyllables. With polysyllabic constituents, which will also be investigated here, the question arises which syllable(s) should be taken into account. If the effect is truly related to PFL, the final nucleus is most relevant, as PFL predominantly affects the syllable before the phrase boundary (see Turk and Shattuck-Hufnagel 2007).

However, a different, phonological explanation for its effectiveness is also possible, as vowels of different lengths have different representations on the CV-tier. In phonological theory, it is generally assumed that there is an intermediate level between the syllable and the segmental level which contains coarse segmental information about whether or not a segment is syllabic (V) or not (C) (see Clements and Keyser 1983). This level has also been acknowledged by language production researchers, as there is evidence that speakers make use of it during production (see Stemberger 1990). The segments on this level can be regarded as timing units, and there is not

---

[8] A significant effect was found for native speakers, but not for foreign-language learners of English.

[9] As the author does not provide significance values, I recalculated the influence of vowel length by correlating rank orders of preference in second position (Oakeshott-Taylor 1984: Table 2) and rank order by vowel duration using Crystal and House's (1988) length measurements. Applying Spearman's Rho, the correlation coefficient is $r_{spearman} = 0.39$, $p = 0.25$ (alternatively, applying Kendall's Tau yields $r_{Kendall} = 0.2$, $p = 0.48$). This correlation coefficient differs only slightly from the value given by Oakeshott-Taylor (1984:229), which is $r = 0.33$. Most importantly, neither test yields a significant result.

[10] Gustafsson (1974) reports a phrase-final lengthening effect in a reading task of English binomials. Measuring the acoustic length of constituents, she finds that their pronunciation is lengthened in second position.

necessarily a one-to-one correspondence with the segmental level, as long vowels are assigned two slots on the CV-tier (VV). With example (41), the diphthong in the second element (*strain*) is a long (VV) vowel, as opposed to the short vowel in *stress*. This contrast may be explained by the argument of greater accent on the second constituent related to syllable weight, as a long vowel makes a syllable heavy. The constraint would thus be congruent with the variable syllable weight, as detailed above. However, it could also be argued that the second constituent should simply be longer on the CV-tier, regardless of accent, tying in with the general short-before-long assumption. If we follow the latter interpretation, we must take into account all vowels of polysyllabic constituents. In order to test all possible hypotheses, I will test vowel length considering the final syllable and also considering all syllables of a given constituent.

3.4.2   Voicing of the final consonant

Ross (1982) suggests that, in irreversible binomials, the second element exhibits a tendency to end in a voiced consonant due to the fact that a voiced coda increases the duration of a preceding nucleus.[11] This hypothesised tendency would thus tie in with the variable vowel length from a phonetic perspective.[12] Evidence for this effect is provided by Bolinger (1962). Calculating Chi-square for Bolinger's data (he does not provide a test of significance) yields the following result: if a syllable with a voiceless coda is contrasted with an open one, it is preferred in first position, while elements with voiced codas display the reverse trend.[13] The results are thus as predicted by Ross (1982). I will therefore test the prediction that emerges from Bolinger's data most naturally and that is compatible with an overall lengthening assumption of the second constituent: voiceless final consonants are preferred in the first position and voiced consonants in the second.[14]

---

[11] This is shown by Peterson and Lehiste's (1960) acoustic measurements of English syllable nuclei.

[12] Also Benor and Levy (2006) suggest taking into account the voicing of the coda consonant.

[13] Although he tested the hypothesis that the second constituent should end 'relatively open and sonorous' (Bolinger 1962: 44), his test items also varied with respect to the voicing of the final consonant. I concentrated on those data points where an open syllable was contrasted with a closed one either with a voiced or a voiceless consonant. The voicing contrast was cross-tabulated with the naturalness (yes/no) judgements provided. The statistical analysis yields a significant result: Chi-Square = 7.1, df = 1, φ = 0.11, p < 0.01. Bolinger's (1962) original hypothesis that open syllables are preferred in final position is not tested, as Bolinger's data does not corroborate such an effect. Moreover, there is no acoustic evidence that a closed syllable has an effect on the length of the preceding nucleus (cf. Crystal and House 1988).

[14] Wright et al. (2005) gather experimental evidence that a voiceless final obstruent is preferred in second position if both constituents end with a stop which would thus conflict with the aforementioned assumption. Even though their result is hard to reconcile with the present hypothesis, its influence can only be limited, as it focuses on special cases when both

3.4.3 Final consonant obstruency

Cooper and Ross (1975) suggest that in cases of contrast, the constituent ending in the more obstruent consonant is put in the first position (see also Huber 1974; Sobkowiak 1993). Ross (1982) explains this effect by a possible shortening of the preceding nucleus, thus relating it to the general short-before-long contrast. Examples (from Cooper and Ross 1975) are:

(42) a. safe and sane
       b. push and pull

This constraint ties in with Bolinger's (1962: 35) claim that the second element would end 'as . . . sonorous as possible'.

The assumed relation between consonant obstruency and phonetic lengthening/shortening of the preceding nucleus is not clear, however. Peterson and Lehiste's (1960) measurements show a tendency for sonorants to lengthen a preceding vowel as compared to obstruents, while Crystal and House (1988) fail to find such effects. Regarding the variable's influence on ordering, there is enough empirical evidence by Bolinger (1962) for it to yield an influence in the predicted direction.[15] Similarly Wright et al. (2005) provide experimental evidence that obstruent-final first names are more likely to occur in first position. Benor and Levy's (2006) results, however, show this factor to be not significant. Regarding the mixed evidence and rather weak theoretical foundation, its influence may be disputed. I will investigate it nevertheless, as it is compatible with the general short-before-long contrast.

3.5 Other phonological and phonetic variables

3.5.1 Number of final consonants

A further phonological principle Cooper and Ross (1975) propose is that the constituent with more final consonants is preferred in first position, as in:

(43) a. sink or swim
       b. betwixt and between
       c. wax and wane

In contrast, Pinker and Birdsong (1979) find evidence for the opposite effect. Subjects rated more natural orderings in which the second element contained more final consonants than the first. Ross (1980) arrives at the same

---

constituents are obstruents. The authors acknowledge that when other classes of consonants are taken into account, the opposite result is likely. Therefore, these are not considered sufficient to formulate a reverse hypothesis. Interestingly, in another study that also concentrates on stop endings, Huber (1974) suggests that final voiced stops are preferred in second position – complying with the present assumption.

[15] I conducted a binomial test using obstruency as a binary variable. Only those data points of Bolinger (1962) that showed the relevant contrast were considered. Results are highly significant (N = 477, p < 0.01).

conclusion and reformulates the original rule accordingly. This reverse hypothesis can be explained by the general tendency of short constituents preceding longer ones when measuring length in phonemes. The contrast may thus be a reflection of general weight/length relations and not an independent effect. Note that, in Pinker and Birdsong's experiment, varying the number of final consonants also altered the number of phonemes.

The question which remains to be answered is whether an independent effect of final consonants can be motivated. As noted earlier, the effect may be a reflection of the general short-before-long preference, however none of the examples in (43) exhibit a length contrast. However, effects of other constraints may be responsible. Note that all examples show the contrast in voicing of the coda I discussed (see above). Even more problematic is the fact that when there are two or more coda consonants, the nucleus almost always contains a short vowel – as seen in the examples (43a–c) – thus, the final consonants constraint is confounded with the variable vowel length. Moreover, the number of final consonants is of course also relevant to syllable weight, as more consonants increase its weight, and therefore to possible stress preferences.

In conclusion, the final consonants factor is highly correlated with a number of different constraints. Adding to the doubts regarding an independent influence is the weak empirical evidence. Benor and Levy (2006) find no significant effect of the variable.

In my opinion, it is most likely that a possible effect of final consonants is to be attributed to other variables, most importantly a general length contrast and vowel-length differences. As it is unclear exactly what the final consonants rule would measure not already covered by one of the other phonological factors – which are furthermore better motivated – it is not empirically investigated in this book.

3.5.2   Vowel quality

One of the more widely cited criteria for the ordering in irreversible binomials is vowel position. Cooper and Ross (1975) hold vowel backness to be responsible for the ordering in a number of binomials. See the following examples:

(44)   a. dribs and drabs
       b. this and that   (Cooper and Ross 1975: 71, 73)

They state that a constituent with a front vowel (lower second formant frequency) is followed by one with a back vowel (higher second formant frequency). Vowel position had also been mentioned in earlier works – in which researchers focused on vowel height and not backness – claiming, however, that the higher vowel precedes the lower one (Behaghel 1928; Abraham 1950). The importance of vowel height is also stressed by Pordány (1986), who argues that concentrating solely on vowel backness as suggested by

Cooper and Ross (1975) cannot account for all cases in his data. One data point relevant in this respect is *hook and eye*, which can be explained by vowel height – as /aɪ/ is lower than /ʊ/ – but not by vowel backness. Pinker and Birdsong (1979) discuss the difference between the two measurements and show that they are largely correlated, hence conflicting predictions are rare. The vowels /ʊ/ and /u/ in particular are judged differently depending upon which measure one applies, as they are high yet back vowels. From their data, Pinker and Birdsong (1979) conclude that vowel height has a greater influence than vowel backness, but argue that both are needed for an adequate description. They claim that the 'best' vowel pattern would alternate a 'high, front vowel with a low, back one' (Pinker and Birdsong 1979: 506).

Evidence for vowel position as an ordering constraint is mixed. In the study already mentioned, Pinker and Birdsong (1979) test the criterion in a naturalness judgement test and provide significant evidence for both measurements. Oakeshott-Taylor (1984) finds significant evidence for vowel backness (second formant frequency) but not for vowel height (first formant frequency) in an ordering experiment of nonsense monosyllabic words. He also tested an alternative measure of vowel backness (second formant frequency–first formant frequency), which, according to Ladefoged (1993), shows a better correlation with the degree of anatomic backness. However, Oakeshott-Taylor found that this measurement was a weaker predictor than second formant frequency.[16] In other studies, however, the influence of vowel position has not been empirically confirmed. Cutler and Cooper (1978) found no effect of it on ordering in a phoneme-monitoring experiment, and also Benor and Levy (2006) failed to provide significant evidence for its effectiveness. While they acquired unclear results for vowel height, vowel backness clearly did not influence ordering in the predicted way.

The theoretical explanations given for its influence also give rise to scepticism because, although widely cited, surprisingly little theoretical justification has been provided. Behaghel (1928) offers a limited explanation in arguing that when the vowel in the second constituent is /a/, the position of the tongue is close to the resting position to which the speaker returns after having produced the deviant vowel in the first constituent. Unfortunately, he remains silent on cases when a back/low vowel other than /a/ is involved. Fenk-Oczlon (1989) argues that lower vowels are also generally longer than high ones, thus vowel quality may be explained by the rule that short vowels precede long vowels. This reasoning is, however, not an explanation for

---

[16] The result is surprising as it allows the interpretation that the acoustic properties (F2) are a better predictor for ordering (or judging the naturalness of a particular ordering as in Oakeshott-Taylor's study) than the actual anatomic backness, as place of production. This could mean that the listener's perspective, for whom the acoustic properties can be argued to be more important, plays a greater role than the speaker's for whom the place of articulation is probably of higher importance. This issue is beyond the scope of this study but may be of interest for future research.

vowel quality as an independent ordering principle, but an argument for its being epiphenomenal. Thus, if vowel length were controlled for, the effect should disappear. Another argument for vowel position brought forward in the same paper is that lower vowels may sound further away than higher vowels, as Fenk-Oczlon (1989) argues that sounds that are produced further away from the speaker sound lower than sounds that are produced in her vicinity. The predicted contrast may then be explained by the semantic criterion that entities closer to the speaker tend to be uttered first (see conceptual accessibility, above). Not only is this explanation purely speculative, it again requires another variable, this time a semantic one, to explain its effectiveness. Summing up, the influence of vowel position on ordering seems to have only a weak empirical as well as theoretical foundation. As it is widely cited, I will still consider it in the following empirical investigations.

3.5.3   Number of initial consonants

Cooper and Ross (1975), as well as Ross (1982), suggest that in irreversible binomials the constituent with more initial consonants follows one with fewer initial consonants, as in the following examples.

(45)   a. sea and sky
       b. fair and square   (Cooper and Ross 1975: 75)

Cooper and Ross (1975) base this constraint on the generally observed effect that shorter constituents precede longer ones. If that is the case, then the current variable should have no effect, once we measure length relations counting phonemes. In a similar vein, Wright et al. (2005) criticise that there is no independent phonological motivation for this constraint and argue for the opposite effect, viz. that the element with more initial consonants is preferred in initial position. Their claim is based on the observation that consonant clusters are more likely in the initial position of words and phrases and they assume that coordinate expressions display similar characteristics. In an ordering experiment, they found such a tendency, but it was weak and did not reach statistical significance.[17] In contrast to Wright et al. (2005), Benor and Levy (2006) find a marginally significant effect for the second element to contain more initial consonants, thus in the direction as suggested by Cooper and Ross (1975).[18] Another work, Sobkowiak (1993), finds no significant effect in either direction. In conclusion, evidence for an effect of the number of initial consonants on ordering is weak at best. It will be considered

---

[17]   Wright et al. (2005) extend this factor to other contexts and argue that, if a constituent begins with a vowel, it should be preferred in second place. Testing this claim separately yields no significant results in their study, however.

[18]   However, this result was obtained solely from the token sample in Benor and Levy (2006). The type sample did not yield such an effect.

in the present study, testing whether it independently influences ordering decisions.

3.5.4   Initial consonant obstruency

Cooper and Ross (1975) suggest another principle concerning the initial segments of constituents. It states that the constituent with the more obstruent consonant follows the one with a more sonorous beginning,[19] as in:

(46)   a. wear and tear
        b. wheel and deal

Pinker and Birdsong (1979) test this variable experimentally using minimal pairs and acquire significant evidence for it to have an effect on naturalness judgements.[20] Benor and Levy (2006) found equivocal evidence for it and conclude that its effect can be neglected.

Wright et al. (2005) put forward a different hypothesis with regard to initial consonant obstruency. Analogous to their argumentation for the first element to have more initial consonants, they argue that there should be a greater likelihood for the first element to have the more obstruent initial segment. The argument is again based on the assumption that binomials display the same characteristics as monomorphemic words. Contrary to their expectations, and in line with the studies mentioned above, they find significant evidence that the constituent with the more sonorant beginning is placed first.[21] In conclusion, although there are conflicting assumptions, the existing evidence points to a tendency for the more sonorous beginning to be preferred in first position. However, no phonological or phonetic motivation for this preference has been given. An effect of phonetic lengthening of the vowel, similar to final consonant obstruency is unlikely, as a preceding segment does not influence the length of a following nucleus (cf. Peterson and Lehiste 1960). The hypothesised contrast is nonetheless considered in the present study, as it is widely cited and an influence cannot be ruled out on a priori grounds.

---

[19] They propose a sonority scale ranging from /h/ to stops (see also Huber 1974). Huber states essentially the same principle, but restricts its effectiveness to glides and liquids (Huber 1974: 65).

[20] This effect was found only for native speakers of English. Foreign-language learners did not give significantly different naturalness answers.

[21] Furthermore, Wright et al. (2005) put forward another, more fine-grained hypothesis regarding the initial segment and state that if both constituents begin with an obstruent of which one is voiced and one is unvoiced, the voiced consonant precedes the unvoiced one. However, their experimental study does not yield significance for this effect. Sobkowiak (1993) compares constituents beginning with obstruents and claims to have found a significant effect, such that voiceless initial segments are preferred in first position. But a recalculation of the data reveals it is not significant (Chi-square = 1.33, df = 1, p = 0.25), for data, see Sobkowiak (1993: 404). With only very limited and contradictory empirical evidence, its status is doubtful and it is therefore not considered.

3.6   Frequency

Fenk-Oczlon (1989) puts forward the hypothesis that the more frequent constituent precedes the less frequent one, which she claims can explain the ordering in many irreversible binomials. Benor and Levy (2006) also find token frequency to be a significant predictor of ordering in binomials. Fenk-Oczlon (1989) argues that token frequency is not only a relevant factor on its own, but is in fact the cause for other variables to be effective. If that were the case, then these should have no effect, if frequency was controlled for. I will elaborate on this question in Section 3.7. With regard to its theoretical grounding, it is well-established knowledge that frequency influences the accessibility of linguistic forms, as high frequency enhances lexical access (see, e.g., Levelt et al. 1999). With Fenk-Oczlon (1989) and Benor and Levy (2006) providing evidence for an effect of frequency, it is empirically well supported and will be taken into consideration in the following.

3.7   Reductive explanations

A number of suggestions have been made as to how the wealth of variables influencing the order of constituents can be reduced. It is claimed either that some variables are epiphenomenal to others, or that at least one constraint is much more influential than others.

One such claim is made by McDonald et al. (1993) who argue that the short-before-long contrast can be explained by rhythmic considerations; i.e. the alternation of stressed and unstressed syllables (see McDonald et al. 1993: Exp. 6). Crucially, in their experiment, iambic disyllables precede monosyllables, as in *antique and doll*, thereby creating a weak-strong-weak-strong stress alternation, while violating the short-before-long principle. Conversely, the length criterion is obeyed only when the rhythm factor also calls for a short-before-long order such as in *doll and attic*. The prediction that seems to follow from these findings is that the short-before-long principle is merely an epiphenomenon of the speaker's attempt to produce alternating beats.

Another reductive attempt is made by Fenk-Oczlon (1989), who aims at reducing the effects of most phonological variables to the influence of frequency. This is intuitively plausible for the length contrast, as it is well known that word length and frequency are negatively correlated. Furthermore, she argues that vowel duration can also be related to frequency, as reduced vowel length may be an effect of frequency. Similarly, a lower number of initial and final consonants may be explained as a reduction effect due to frequency.[22] She also views the variables concerning the obstruency of initial and final consonants to be linked to frequency, as more frequent words

---

[22] She assumes the first constituent to have fewer final consonants, contrary to Cooper and Ross's (1975) original rule.

rarely contain hard-to-pronounce segments. For vowel quality, a frequency account seems difficult, yet Fenk-Oczlon (1989) argues for a reduction also of this variable to vowel length, as she argues duration and backness/lowness are correlated. Moreover, she also sees a relation between semantic factors and frequency, as more prototypical constituents are also more frequent, thus conceptual accessibility may also be reduced to frequency. The only constraint which in her view cannot be explained by frequency is iconic sequencing, which is therefore still needed for an adequate description. Fenk-Oczlon (1989) tests her claim using monofactorial methods and finds that frequency can explain a greater number of data points than can other constraints. The rather bold claim that almost all other variables are epiphenomena, however, does not follow from this result, as such issues can only adequately be dealt with employing multifactorial methodology (see below Chapter 4).

A further reductive claim by Hawkins (1994) concerns the relation between the short-before-long rule and information status, which has evoked a discussion with other order alternations, viz. particle placement (Gries 2003) and Heavy NP shift (Arnold et al. 2000). Due to the apparently very general workings of these two constraints, this debate is also relevant for the present case studies. In propagating his well-known Early Immediate Constituents (EIC) principle, which hinges on considerations of weight/length, Hawkins (1994: 240–1) puts forward the rather bold statement that 'pragmatics appears to play no role whatsoever' in linear ordering, as it is weight/length considerations which dominate these decisions, leaving no room for pragmatics. However, he qualifies this statement later conceding some influence of pragmatic considerations (Hawkins 2004: 122–3). His original claim would mean for the present case studies that pragmatic factors are not needed for an adequate description of the ordering process. Interestingly, the reverse argument can also be found in the literature, as Schveiger (1995) argues that the length effect in binomials is ultimately due to given information being expressed more briefly. Both Arnold et al. (2000) as well as Gries (2003) take issue with these claims and show, both experimentally and through corpus-linguistic methods, that they cannot be upheld for the alternations in focus in their works. They demonstrate that both factors are at work independently and cannot be collapsed. Hence, this finding is also expected for the present study.

The validity and explanatory power of all reductive explanations is discussed – in light of the acquired results – in Chapter 8 of this book.

3.8   Variables and the different levels of analysis

Having reviewed and discussed the factors hypothesised to influence order in coordination, let us now turn to the question as to whether and how to apply them to the three levels of analysis focused on in the present study. I have already mentioned that some variables are not relevant for, or applicable to, all investigated constructions. Since most variables discussed stem from the study of binomials, almost all factors can be tested with these. However, not all of them are applicable to the coordination of complex noun phrases.

The variables on the semantic/pragmatic level can be applied universally to all constructions investigated. While it is more easily conceivable that, for example, iconic sequencing influences ordering on the lexical or the phrasal level, as in *egg and larvae*, it can also be detected in instances of copulative compounds, as in *invader-settler*.

The short/light-before-long/heavy tendency as a general principle can certainly also be tested with all phenomena. Syntactic complexity, however, can of course only be investigated with complex NP ordering. Meanwhile, with compounds and binomials, we can measure morphological complexity.

I turn now to variables concerning the stress pattern of the construction. Here, the variable rhythmic alternation is certainly applicable to all three levels. With the hypothesis that an ultimate stress on the terminal syllable is to be avoided, this is not the case, as it is motivated via the typical stress pattern of the phrase (see Section 3.2). Its application is therefore only justified for compounds and binomials, which are in phrase-final position, but not for coordinated NPs. As the latter consist of two phrases, one would expect an avoidance of terminal stress in both phrases. Additionally, syllable weight is only tested with coordinate compounds and binomials, as a greater stress of the second element has been put forward solely for these two levels.

Similar arguments apply to the variables associated with a greater phonological or phonetic length of the second constituent. Since these are motivated by phrase-final lengthening (PFL), their application to complex NPs is problematic, as PFL should affect the final segments of both noun phrases. A phonological effect of length on the CV-tier, viz. longer vowels in the second constituent, could be investigated on all three levels. Here it is considered only with coordinate compounds and with binomials, as it is a very fine-grained measure, whereas contrasts between constituents are likely to even out once a greater number of syllables are taken into account, as in complex phrases. Another argument for a restricted application stems from research on the architecture of the production system. It has been shown that the greater the distance between the level of decision (in the present case, the level where the ordering of the two constituents takes place) and the level of influence, the smaller the respective effect (Schlüter 2005: 285–91; cf. also Berg 1998: 26). Therefore, it can be concluded that the ordering of complex phrases is unlikely to be strongly influenced by phonological and phonetic factors.

Variables related to properties of the constituents' initial segments rely on the argument that the 'ideal' binomial should display the same characteristics as a word, and are thus based on an assumption of the word status of the

Table 3.1 *Variables and the different levels of analysis*

Variable	Copulative compounds	Coordination of nouns	Coordination of complex NPs
Information status	✓	✓	✓
Extra-linguistic hierarchy	✓	✓	✓
Conceptual accessibility	✓	✓	✓
Iconic sequencing	✓	✓	✓
B is morphologically more complex than A	✓	✓	
B is syntactically more complex than A			✓
Alternating stress	✓	✓	✓
No ultimate stress of B	✓	✓	
B has heavier main syllable	✓	✓	
B is longer than A	✓	✓	✓
Vowel length in B is greater	✓	✓	
B ends in a voiced consonant	✓	✓	
B has a less obstruent final segment	✓	✓	
B has the lower vowel	✓	✓	
B has the more back vowel	✓	✓	
B has more/fewer initial consonants	✓	✓	
B has a more/sonorous initial element	✓	✓	
A is more frequent than B	✓	✓	✓

whole construction, which cannot easily be assumed for two coordinated complex NPs. Thus these variables are also not investigated with these two coordinated complex NPs. Finally, the influence of a frequency contrast is investigated on all levels. Table 3.1 provides an overview of which factors/hypotheses are tested with the respective coordinate constructions.

4   Data and method

This chapter presents the data sources and the methodology employed in the following empirical studies. First, I describe the data acquisition process and present the data sources used. Secondly, I present the methodology and discuss problems pertaining to the application of multifactorial methods to ordering phenomena. Thirdly, I detail how the variables to be tested are operationalised and how I coded the data with regard to the ordering constraints.

4.1   Data

4.1.1   Sources of data and sampling

The main aim of this book is to determine the variables that influence the order in coordinate constructions on three levels of analysis. Order of nominal elements is to be investigated in so-called copulative compounds, coordinated nouns (*binomials*) and in coordinated complex noun phrases (see examples (1a–e) above). While specifics of the data extraction process are detailed in the respective chapters on the individual constructions, I outline the general method of data acquisition and present the utilised data sources here. Speech data was used for the present analysis wherever possible, as the ordering process is primarily viewed from a perspective of language production, which primarily focuses on the description of speech. However, on the level of compounds, written sources were also used, as copulative compounds are considerably rare, and a focus on spoken sources would have resulted in too small a data sample. With written sources the question arises as to whether the numerous phonological effects presented in Chapter 3 can be sensibly investigated in writing, which would require that phonological representations are activated also during written-language production. Schlüter (2005: 50–5) discusses this point in detail and cites studies from Aitchison and Todd (1982) and Nauclér (1983), who show that speaking and writing are connected by a shared phonological representation. Schlüter (2005: 54) therefore concludes that 'processes in speaking and writing are largely parallel' and that phonological preferences can be detected in written texts. This book follows this conclusion. Let me point out that this is not

Table 4.1 *Data sources used in the present study*

Construction	Data source(s) used
Copulative compounds	Data provided by Olsen (2001a, 2001b) and Corpus of Contemporary American English (COCA)
Coordination of nouns	Spoken section of the British National Corpus (BNC) (except for irreversible binomials)
Coordination of complex NPs	Spoken section of the International Corpus of English – Great Britain (ICE-GB)

tantamount to stating that phonological effects are completely congruent in both modalities: one crucial difference between writing and speaking is the rate of delivery that is expected from the language user, since there is generally much more time available in writing than in speech. This point is taken up during the discussion in Chapter 8.

One further aspect that guided the data acquisition process should be mentioned. As explained above, it is the aim of the present study to investigate ordering in real usage data, focusing on those instances for which an online ordering process can be assumed. Therefore, I excluded formulaic irreversibles from the main analysis and focused on reversible instances, as the former can be assumed to be lexicalised and an online ordering process is therefore unlikely (see Chapter 2). However, Chapter 6 compares ordering influences between irreversibles and reversible cases using a sample of formulaic, irreversible binomials created for this purpose. Details of the empirical operationalisation that this distinction necessitates are given below. Except for the exclusion of irreversibles, I aimed at creating random samples from usage data. The data sources presented in Table 4.1 are used for the present analysis.

On the level of compounds, I use the data provided by Olsen (2001a, 2001b), which she acquired from corpus data, and I supplemented her sample with data from the *Corpus of Contemporary American English (COCA)*. For the lexical and the phrasal level, data was acquired from the spoken sections of the British National Corpus and the ICE-GB. The data sources thus encompass data from both American and British English. My general aim was to use solely spoken data from representative, well-balanced corpora, which led to the choice of the BNC and the ICE-GB. Due to the low frequency of copulative compounds, a very large corpus had to be employed. Since to my knowledge the largest accessible corpus is the COCA, which contains American English, I considered this linguistic variety as well. While this selection may not be ideal, it should not be cause for great concern, since it seems unlikely that the two varieties differ greatly with regard to a process as basic and general as order in coordination. Specifics of the data extraction process are given in the relevant empirical chapters (Chapters 5–7).

4.1.2   Identifying irreversible cases in corpus data

As mentioned above, in previous works in linguistics researchers focused strongly on irreversible constructions (e.g. Malkiel 1959; Cooper and Ross 1975) or did not differentiate between irreversible and reversibles in their investigation (Benor and Levy 2006). In contrast, this book pursues a distinction between the two groups, as the main objective is to identify the influences language producers are subject to in online ordering decisions; i.e., in those constructions that do not have unit status in the mental lexicon. Furthermore, I address the question as to what extent these influences may be similar to those determining the fossilised order in irreversible constructions. Irreversible, formulaic constructions are predominantly found on the lexical level, but are also possible on the other two investigated levels, as illustrated in the following examples.

(47)   a. hunter-gatherer
        b. (at) the top and the bottom

Additionally, (47a, b) show a pronounced tendency to occur in only one order. Thus, the issue of teasing apart irreversible, lexicalised and regular cases of coordination is relevant for all investigated phenomena. In order to do so, we need criteria for the identification of irreversible cases. While this sounds straightforward and easy, it is not quite so simple from an empirical, corpus-based perspective. Thus far, researchers have circumvented this operationalisation problem by making this decision intuitively. However, since such an introspective approach relies on highly subjective assessments, it is not pursued here.

In order to arrive at an empirically applicable operationalisation, let us recall the most important characteristics of irreversible binomials. The most apparent one is of course their irreversibility. Certainly the most obvious way of testing this characteristic is to test whether a given coordinate construction occurs only in one order in a large corpus, and thus is practically irreversible. For example, this holds true for the expression *odds and ends*, which occurs fifty-four times in the BNC, but not at all in the reverse order *ends and odds*. The result would be that this is a lexicalised, irreversible binomial, which complies with previous intuitive judgements. However, the question arises as to whether conversely constructions should be classified as reversible, even if reversals are found only very rarely in a given corpus? An example is *husband and wife* (406 hits in the BNC), which was mentioned as an irreversible by Malkiel (1959), but violates a strict test, as rare cases of *wife and husband* (9 in the BNC) do occur. Should we therefore view this data point as an example of reversible coordination? I argue no, as it is possible that speakers still produce the reverse of a lexicalised construction in rare cases, e.g. for rhetorical effect. A famous example of such a reversal is Samuel Beckett's collection of dramas entitled *Ends and Odds*, a word play on the irreversible binomial *odds and ends* that certainly does not render the latter reversible.[1] Thus, it seems wise to leave some room for these exceptions and refrain from applying an overly strict irreversibility measure. I therefore apply the heuristic measurement that one ordering must make up more than 90% of all cases, in order for the construction to count as irreversible.

The second characteristic mentioned above (see Section 2.1), is the conventionalisation and a concomitant high frequency of use of formulaic binomials. This characteristic can of course be easily measured using corpus data by taking into account the token frequency of the coordinate construction. This measurement ties in with general assumptions that frequency affects the mental representation of multi-word phrases (see Mos 2010; Arnon and Snider 2010). The frequency criterion is also relevant for testing the aforementioned irreversibility criterion. If we just focused on reversibility without considering frequency, misleading results would be obtained for instances of low frequency. For example, the coordination *viola and harp* occurs three times in the BNC, but never in reverse order, still it would be wrong to classify it as irreversible, as a reversal is certainly possible. Chances are high that it is simply not found in the data due to chance, as the coordinate construction contains two elements that are rarely combined. Only when a certain frequency threshold of the construction is surpassed can we assume that the corpus finding of irreversibility is not due to chance. For these two reasons, a frequency threshold of 10 per 100 million words had to be surpassed to qualify as a formulaic, irreversible binomial.

Although the present operationalisation results in a cut-off point that divides linguistic examples into two categories, I do not wish to propagate a binary view on formulaicity or lexicalisation. On the contrary, as has been shown for other fixed expressions, we are most likely dealing with a continuum of free and fixed coordinations (see Wulff 2008). Nevertheless, in order to distinguish between the two groups, for which an (at least gradually) different storage and therefore processing is likely, some kind of operationalisation is necessary. However, I am the first to admit that the one suggested here is no more than a heuristic measurement that does not necessarily mirror cognitive and psychological reality adequately. Yet it is a step forward, as so far irreversible binomials have been identified intuitively, without empirical support.

Using this operationalisation, we can exclude formulaic irreversibles and focus on reversible cases of coordination. Furthermore, a comparison of fixed, and possibly lexicalised, constructions and reversible cases is made possible. This comparison is carried out solely on the lexical level, as it is here that we find a large number of irreversible, formulaic instances. With copulative compounds and NP coordination, things are different: there are simply not enough cases of formulaic irreversibles for a meaningful

---

[1] I thank Britta Mondorf for bringing this example to my attention.

comparison (see the respective empirical Chapters 5–7 and the discussion in Section 9.2).

4.2   Method

Regarding the methodology, the present study assumes that for any coordinate construction across the three levels investigated, both ordering options are possible, and the likelihood for either option can be expressed as a function of several variables.[2] The method applied is thus a multifactorial quantitative analysis, more specifically, logistic regression. Multifactorial approaches are the tool of choice when investigating variation phenomena, in particular logistic regression analysis (see Szmrecsanyi 2006; Hilpert 2008). This method thus seems to be an obvious choice, but its application nevertheless gives rise to various problems in the case of symmetrical ordering phenomena, which warrant a separate discussion. In the following, I first address in brief the advantages of multifactorial over monofactorial approaches before turning to a discussion of logistic regression analysis applied to coordinate constructions.

4.2.1   Advantages of multifactorial over monofactorial approaches

The problems of monofactorial accounts and the advantages of multifactorial approaches in researching language, and especially variation phenomena, have been discussed in detail elsewhere (see, e.g., Gries 2003; Bresnan et al. 2007); an in-depth discussion is therefore not necessary here. However, two methodological issues are worth mentioning, as they are particularly relevant for the present investigation.

The first of these concerns possible correlations between variables that may tempt researchers to make false assumptions about their effects. This situation is easily conceivable for the present investigation. For example, the variable frequency – i.e., a highly frequent constituent precedes one of lesser frequency – is likely to be correlated with the short-before-long rule, as frequent items are usually short. This observation may invite assumptions as to the reduction of one variable to another, as in our case suggested by Fenk-Oczlon (1989), who argues for considering only frequency in order to predict orderings in irreversibles. Monofactorial analyses cannot easily disentangle correlations (see Bresnan et al. 2007), thus they are not capable of deciding whether both properties of the to-be-ordered constituents exert significant influences, or whether some may truly be epiphenomenal to others

---

[2] Of course, for irreversible constructions, no such option exists for the language user, as only one order is possible. Statistically the question can still be tackled the same way as with reversible constructions. The corresponding linguistic question would then be, why did the ordering lexicalise in this order and not in the reverse.

and therefore superfluous for an adequate description. Hence, researchers applying solely monovariate methods run the risk of either assigning significance to all variables – although some of them might in fact be epiphenomenal to others – or are tempted into overly reductive explanations, by more or less intuitively choosing only one variable which is then argued to be more relevant than others.[3] Multifactorial methods can control for variables and therefore avoid these pitfalls more easily, as multiple variables are tested in concurrence. If, for example, it turned out that both length and frequency were significant in one and the same model, it is likely they could not be reduced to each other.[4]

The second advantage of multifactorial approaches, which is particularly relevant for the present study, pertains to the possibility that these provide us with information about the relative strength and importance of individual variables. The strength of a variable in the present case denotes how often it is violated in the data, with those variables yielding strong effects being seldom violated. The importance, or relevance, of a variable pertains to what share of the data can be explained by it. A comparison of ordering influences on this level yields crucial information about the varying influences of ordering constraints, which are of theoretical relevance when interpreted from a language production perspective (see Chapter 10).

4.2.2   The statistical analysis of ordering phenomena

Most statistical analyses investigate the relationship between one or more independent variable(s) and usually one dependent variable. When studying variation phenomena, the dependent variable is usually the choice between two competing constructions, thus the variable is usually a binary one. For example, with the English comparative, the dependent variable can take on two values, one that corresponds to the analytic form (e.g. *more proud*) and another that corresponds to the synthetic form (e.g. *prouder*). Similarly, for particle placement the binary choice is either the construction featuring the particle after the verb (e.g. *She picked up the book*) or the particle after the direct object (e.g. *She picked the book up*). In these two examples, we can unambiguously assign every data point a value of the dependent variable, as there are choices between two alternating constructions which can be easily

---

[3] See also Gries (2003), who discusses these problems with regard to assumptions as to which variables govern particle placement in English, particularly the part where Hawkins' EIC principle is discussed (Gries 2003: 146–52).

[4] This is, however, only true as long as we do not deal with very strong correlations among the predictor variables. In such a case, which is known as *multicollinearity*, multifactorial models yield false coefficients and are thus no longer reliable. Hence, while multivariate models are theoretically better geared towards avoiding the false conclusions noted above, this holds true only as long as multicollinearity is carefully controlled for. This is something we do during the model-building and fitting process. See Section 4.2.3 for details.

distinguished from each other. In coding the data, researchers usually code one value of the dependent variable as a success (1) and the other variant as a failure (0). In the example above, the synthetic comparative could be a 'success' and therefore coded (1), while the data point *more proud* would be a failure and hence receive the coding (0).

At first glance, it seems that the situation is the same for order in coordinate constructions, as two ordering variants are generally possible: either AB (e.g. *salt and pepper*) or its reversal, BA (e.g. *pepper and salt*). As long as we merely investigate a single type in the data – for example, the coordination of the two lexemes *salt* and *pepper* – the determination of the dependent variable would be unproblematic, as we could treat one ordering (AB) as a success and the reversal (BA) as a failure. However, the situation is not that simple, as what we are really interested in is not just the coordination of two particular elements (e.g. *salt and pepper*), but the coordination of many types. The problem arises when we now tackle another data point such as *apples and lemons*, as it is now unclear which value we may assign to the attested order. If we just chose one value for a given data point (e.g. 'success' for *apples and lemons*), we would have to argue what this order has in common with another instance to which we assigned the same value (e.g. *salt and pepper*). However, there is no particular feature that the two have in common which would qualify the two data points for membership in the same category. Thus, it seems impossible to consistently assign successes and failures, which was the strategy employed in other cases, as there are no two clear-cut categories to which all data points can be unambiguously assigned. How can we resolve this dilemma? After all, since the language user really has two options to choose from, there must be a way to come to terms with the problem statistically. Let us turn to a discussion of suggested solutions.

4.2.2.1   Linear Discriminant Analysis

One possible solution has been put forward by Wulff (2002, 2003), who studied the order of prenominal adjectives (e.g. *big, yellow ball* vs. *yellow, big ball*) and who has to be commended for putting forward the first multi-factorial approach applied to a similarly problematic ordering phenomenon. The method she employs is Linear Discriminant Analysis (LDA), which is a multifactorial approach that calculates for each item the probability of which category it belongs to. In the case of Wulff's work, the decision would be whether a given adjective should be classified as a first- or second-position adjective, given the available independent variable values. Wulff circumvented the problem of determining a dependent variable for every instance of coordination by locating the dependent variable not on the level of the construction as a whole, but on the level of the to-be-ordered constituent. After all, it can be unambiguously decided for every adjective, whether it is in first or second position. There is a problem with this approach, however: in

Wulff's study, LDA assigns every constituent to either position A or B, without considering the values of the second constituent; values of a given adjective are merely compared to the overall means of relevant variables. Consider the example *big, yellow ball* again. Here, LDA would, on the basis of all factors involved, assign the adjectives *big* and *yellow* either position A or B, by comparing their properties to the overall variable means. Let us consider the constraint that the short constituent precedes the long one, which also affects prenominal adjective order. The mean length of the adjectives in Wulff's dataset is between six and seven phonemes (see Wulff 2002: 56). LDA would then compare both adjectives to this mean and assign both to position A, because, with a length of three and four phonemes respectively, both are shorter than the average adjective. The method thus fails to capture the fact there is still a meaningful length difference, as *yellow* is longer than *big*. Differences between the constituents are thus not captured if both their values are either below or above the mean value. Therefore, the method leads to a certain number of classifications whereby both adjectives of the same usage event are assigned to the same position. Such classifications are of course illogical. Since only one of the two adjectives can ever occupy either position, LDA produces implausible results.[5]

An alternative strategy that avoids this problem would be to predict position based not on a comparison to mean values, but on the differences between the two constituents. Thus, length would not be coded in absolute values, but the relative difference between the two constituents would be coded, resulting in the values +1 and −1 for *big* and *yellow* respectively, if we count length in number of phonemes. Hence, if there were a length difference, one constituent would be coded with a positive value and the other with a negative value, avoiding the outcome that both would be in the same category when compared to a mean value. There is a problem with this solution, however, in that it violates an important prerequisite of multi-factorial approaches: almost all of these quantitative analyses require the data points to be independent, thus any data point must not be influenced by any other. This, however, is not fulfilled with this strategy, as the variable values of one constituent would be the mirror image of those of the constituent with which it co-occurs, harshly violating the criterion of independence in the data. In summary, circumventing the problem of defining a dependent variable by using the position of the individual constituent as a dependent variable is problematic, because it violates the fundamental prerequisite of independence in the data and/or may produce the result that co-occuring constituents are assigned the same position.

[5] What is furthermore problematic about LDA is that its prerequisites are seldom met in linguistic study, as LDA requires input data that is normally distributed (see Backhaus et al. 2008), which cannot be ensured with most linguistic data.

4.2.2.2   *Logistic regression without intercept*

The second study which is immediately methodologically relevant to the present one is Benor and Levy's (2006) article on binomials because the authors also run a logistic regression analysis. This method is addressed in more detail, as it will also be applied in the present study.[6] I will first outline the general properties of logistic regression, before turning to its application in the particular case of order in coordinate constructions. Crucially, logistic regression predicts a binary outcome, e.g. a linguistic choice, given a number of independent variables, and is able to quantify the influence of each individual variable. Imagine for a moment that we had a binary dependent variable, coded for successes (1) and failures (0). The mathematical outcome of logistic regression (z) is a so-called fitted value, which, when logistically transformed, is a value between 0 and 1 that predicts the probability of a success. Values above 0.5 can thus be understood as predicted successes, while values under 0.5 are predicted failures. The underlying formula is the following:

$$z = \beta_0 + \beta_1 x_1 + \beta_2 x_2 + \beta_3 x_3 + \ldots + \beta_k x_k$$

On the right-hand side of the equation, the characters x_{1-k} refer to (a principally unlimited number of) values of independent variables, while β_{1-k} refer to the coefficients that are assigned to them. These coefficients refer to the strength and direction of a certain variable's effect. When one of the coefficients β_{1-k} is assigned a positive value, the respective variable influences the outcome towards the value 1, meaning success, while a negative value contributes to the dependent variable taking on the value 0, meaning failure. If the coefficient is close to zero, its effect is small, while a large value of the coefficient, no matter if it is positive or negative, corresponds to a large effect. In addition, the formula contains another term, β_0, which refers to the so-called *intercept*. This is a constant term, which should be viewed as a baseline for z to which the effects of the independent variables are then added. It is necessary because we also want the model to make realistic predictions of successes or failures; if all independent variables take on the value 0, as in such a case, it would be the only numerical value left in the formula.

The variable z on the left-hand side of the equation is thus the sum of the contributions of all independent variables plus the intercept. It takes on values between $-\infty$ and $+\infty$ which are transformed into values between 0 and 1 through the application of the logistic function. Large positive values of z result in predicted values close to 1, while large negative values lead to predicted values close to 0.

As logistic regression predicts a binary choice – thus either a success or a failure – how does this method help us with our problem of assigning a binary

---

[6]   See also Levy forthcoming: 123–4 for a description of the method.

dependent variable? Benor and Levy (2006) suggest an application of the method that circumvents this problem. Instead of having a binary dependent variable, they treat the dependent variable as having only one level – thus, always a success – and code it (1) in all cases. The independent variables influencing the ordering are then tested as to whether they correctly predict the success and, thus, the observed ordering. In order to do so, they are given a positive value (+1) whenever they correctly predict the ordering and a negative one (−1) when they predict the reverse. They are coded (0) when they are inapplicable. In the case of the binomial *salt and pepper*, the variable corresponding to the short-before-long constraint receives the coding (1), since *salt* is shorter than *pepper*; a data point for which the length factor is violated – such as *pepper and salt* – would receive the coding (−1).

Let us discuss the mathematical consequences of this solution. If a variable such as the short-before-long rule is more often obeyed than violated – thus receiving more (1) codings instead of (−1)s – it is assigned a positive coefficient (one of the β_{1-k} values in the formula above), as then the overall formula would correctly predict more successes (1)s – and thus correctly predict observed orderings – than make false predictions. Similar to other applications of logistic regression, the model would still make predictions which lie between 0 and 1 (so-called fitted values). These fitted values can be interpreted directly; i.e., values of greater than 0.5 are successful predictions and values smaller than 0.5 are false predictions.

What is problematic about a dependent variable with just one level is the *intercept* or constant term in the model (β_0 in the equation above). Remember that with logistic regression, we see a prediction of a success when z takes on a very high value, as then it is transformed into a value close to 1 through logistic transformation. With a dependent variable that has merely the level 1, it would thus be the goal of the model to produce only high values of z, as the regression formula would then produce solely correct predictions (see Levy forthcoming: 124). If we let the model automatically assign values to coefficients and intercept, the following would occur: the intercept would be set at a very high value and all coefficients would be assigned values of close to zero. This way the formula would predict solely fitted values of 1 and thus be correct in its predictions. However, it would do so by making false assumptions about the data. Remember that the intercept should give us a baseline probability if all independent variables are zero. It is certainly not logical to assume that this baseline is always a success, in cases when none of the hypothesised ordering constraints apply. In contrast, in such cases we would assume that either order is equally likely, thus the correct baseline should be 0.5, corresponding to a 50% chance of predicting the observed order correctly. The value of z that corresponds to this prediction is zero, thus it would make sense if the intercept also took on the value zero. Benor and Levy (2006) therefore remove the intercept from the model, which is tantamount to assigning it the value zero. This way the problem of an arbitrarily high intercept that neutralises the effect of all independent variables is avoided. This approach addresses the problem of determining the dependent variable without violating the prerequisite of independence in the data, as every construction, and not every constituent, is treated as one data point. I will therefore apply this general methodology in the empirical studies to follow.

4.2.3   *The method applied: logistic regression with scalar variables*

This study has much in common with Benor and Levy's (2006) methodology; however, it departs from it in several important ways. First of all, regarding the sampling process, a distinction is made between formulaic and non-formulaic reversible constructions, as described in detail above, and also between different coordinating conjunctions. Secondly, the independent variables are treated in a more refined way. In Benor and Levy's approach, every ordering factor can take on the values −1, meaning violated, 0, meaning inactive, or 1, meaning obeyed. This procedure means that all variables are treated as nominal, which does not, however, adequately mirror the complexities of linguistic reality. Many of the variables and constraints hypothesised to influence order are in fact interval/scalar variables, hence treating them as if they were nominal results in a loss of information.[7] Allow me to illustrate this loss with an example. In the data points *salt and pepper* and *salt and margarine*, the shorter constituent precedes the longer one. The corresponding variable would thus receive the coding (1) in both cases if treated as nominal. It is obvious, however, that in the first example the length difference is smaller (one syllable) than in the second (two syllables). Hence, we would hypothesise that the variable should have a larger effect in the second example. Corroborating findings come from studies on other alternations: e.g., both Hawkins (1992) and Rosenbach (2005) show for other ordering alternations that a greater difference in length between constituents results in a greater effect on ordering decisions.[8] The present study captures this difference, in allowing for scalar relational values which express the difference between the two constituents regarding a certain variable. The coding process of scalar variables is illustrated in the following for the short before long constraint; see Table 4.2.

In the first row, the constraint is coded (+1), as *pepper* is one syllable longer than *salt*. The value is positive, because the short constituent precedes the

---

[7] In this respect, the approach by Benor and Levy (2006) is similar to earlier VARBRUL approaches, which were predominant in sociolinguistics and which also did not allow for the accommodation of scalar variables (cf. Gries and Hilpert 2010: 304).

[8] Hawkins investigates the length differences of prepositional phrases (Hawkins 1992: 205), while Rosenbach (2005) examines the length difference between possessor and possessum in the English genitive alternation.

Table 4.2 *Coding of scalar variables*

Item	Short before long (LENGTHSYL)
salt and pepper	+1
salt and margarine	+2
pepper and salt	−1

longer one and the constraint is thus fulfilled. With *salt and margarine*, the coding is (+2), as the length difference is two syllables. *Pepper and salt* is coded (−1), as the short-before-long tendency is violated, since the first constituent *pepper* is one syllable longer than *salt*. All scalar variables were coded this way. Nominal variables are coded (−1), i.e. violated, and (+1), i.e. fulfilled. When a particular constraint does not apply to a given data point it is coded (0). For example, the above variable *iconic sequencing* would be coded (0) because there is no iconic motivation for ordering in these cases. While similar to the approach taken by Benor and Levy (2006), this method is more fine-grained, as it allows for the inclusion of scalar variables without information loss.

Another important characteristic of the methodology used concerns the actual model-building procedure, more specifically the so-called model fitting stage. In model fitting, I aim at *minimal adequate models* – i.e. models that do not include non-significant variables – while featuring all variables that yield significant effects (Gries 2009). This strategy stands in contrast to other approaches that include all variables without considering significance (e.g. Szmrecsanyi 2006 and crucially Benor and Levy 2006); that is, so-called *maximal models* (see Crawley 2005: 104). The latter method of keeping all tested variables in a model even if these are not significant carries the risk of model overfitting, i.e., assigning relevance to random noise. Furthermore, since in a multifactorial analysis all constraints or variables are entered into one common equation, every change of one variable also affects the results of all others. Therefore, it is risky to keep variables of negligible or uncertain influence in a model, as they may distort the values of other relevant variables. A further argument for minimal models is that these comply better with the principle of Occam's razor by not including variables which are not necessary for an adequate description of the data.

With regard to model fitting, I proceeded in a step-wise fashion of variable exclusion: first, a maximal model was built which included all hypothesised factors. Starting with the least significant one, I removed non-significant variables from the model, until only significant factors were left. Thus only those variables that yielded significant influences were kept in the regression models.

A more general issue pertaining to logistic regression is the potential problem of multicollinearity. Multicollinearity arises when independent variables are highly correlated. In such a case, regression analyses may yield unreliable results. This is cause for concern in the present study, as some of the variables may be highly correlated. This study therefore carefully controls for multicollinearity in all regression models.

4.2.4   Key notions in regression modelling

Multivariate logistic regression has been described in detail elsewhere (Pampel 2000; Szmrecsanyi 2006). Thus, only the most important notions, which are crucial for an understanding of the reported results, are briefly presented here.

4.2.4.1   Predictive accuracy

This notion pertains to how well the model predicts the dependent variable, hence the attested orderings in the data. Every individual model in this study reports a percentage indicating to what extent the data is predicted accurately. This value is to be viewed in relation to the baseline, which denotes the accuracy with which a model operating on chance alone would 'guess' orderings correctly. This baseline is 50% in all cases, as the null-hypothesis states that the order of the two coordinated elements is completely free to vary, which means that each order is equally likely.

4.2.4.2   Significance values of variables (p)

The p-value informs us, for every tested factor, whether its influence is significant or whether ostensible tendencies in the data are merely due to chance. Generally, a value of $p < 0.05$ denotes a significant contribution of the respective variable, while higher values mean that the null-hypothesis – i.e., that the respective variable exerts no influence on ordering – cannot be refuted. Often values of $p < 0.1$ are also considered to still be of relevance, as values between 0.05 and 0.1 are thought to denote marginal significance.

4.2.4.3   Measures of effect size

Effect size indicates the strength of an individual factor's influence. While p denotes whether the factor makes a meaningful contribution at all (or whether its influence is merely due to chance), effect size tells us about whether its effect is a small or large one. For instance, while it is conceivable that both *length* and *conceptual accessibility* influence ordering significantly in a given sample (thus p-values would be below 0.05 for both of them), it could be the case that one of the two is violated more often than the other and its effect size would then be smaller in comparison. Two measures of effect size are used in this study: coefficients and odds ratios. Coefficients denote the values in the regression formula explained above (see Section 4.2.2.2). Its values range from $-\infty$ to $+\infty$ and are to be interpreted as follows: high positive values indicate that the factor is obeyed in a majority of cases under investigation and that it contributes strongly to the observed orderings;

conversely, values close to zero denote a small effect; high negative values indicate that a factor is violated in a majority of cases. However, a direct interpretation in terms of the probability of a certain outcome is not possible. Its advantage in comparison to other measures of effect size is that the coefficients are on a common linear scale, which makes it possible to compare directly their magnitude numerically.

Odds ratios, the second measure of effect size to be reported, range from zero to +∞. Their value denotes the number by which we would multiply the odds of an event (i.e., the probability of occurrence of a certain ordering), if the relevant factor is obeyed (i.e., when the predicted contrast between the two constituents holds). Odds ratios of higher than 1 indicate that the investigated factor influences ordering in the predicted way; the higher the value, the stronger the effect. Odds ratios between 0 and 1 mean that the relevant factor influences order in the opposite direction; the closer the value is to zero, the stronger the (negative) effect. For example, if for the frequency contrast we found an odds ratio of greater than 1, this would mean that frequency influences ordering in the predicted way; i.e., the more frequent element occurs in first position. However, if we found an odds ratio between 0 and 1 for frequency, this would indicate that a tendency for putting the least frequent element first was found.[9]

4.3   Operationalisation and data coding

In the following, the general operationalisation and coding procedures are described, i.e., how the data was coded with respect to the hypothesised ordering influences. The terms in parentheses are abbreviations used for the individual factors for easier handling in computerised statistical analysis. Specific requirements of the individual case studies are detailed in the relevant empirical chapters (Chapters 5–7).

4.3.1   Pragmatic and semantic variables

4.3.1.1   Information status (INF)
For an investigation of this constraint, it is necessary to determine the information status of the referents denoted by the two coordinated constituents in order to detect possible differences between the two. Information status is notoriously hard to operationalise, as it is not always obvious which referents are established in the discourse and which are new. This problem becomes especially acute when dealing with corpus data, as there is usually little information about the situational/pragmatic context. In this work, a referent is viewed as given when it has been mentioned previously in the discourse context, similar to a comparable corpus-based study (Gries 2003).

---

[9] For further details on this and other effect size measurements in logistic regression, see Pampel (2000).

The previous context was delimited to 100 words prior to the mentioning of the relevant construction. The variable was treated as nominal. If the referent of the first constituent was mentioned in the prior context, in contrast to the referent of the second constituent, the variable was coded (1), as this situation represents a given-before-new ordering. If the reverse order was found it was coded (−1). If both or none of the constituents' referents were mentioned in the prior context, the variable was coded (0). As speakers may refer to the same referent using different forms, the coding was done manually and co-referential forms were also taken into account. It is acknowledged that this operationalisation is just a rough approximation of differences in information status, yet possibly the best to be achieved with corpus data.

A further challenge occurs when coding this variable on the phrasal level, since complex noun phrases, e.g. *the computer I bought yesterday*, may contain more than one referent. In such cases, only the main referent of the NP was considered, which is denoted by the head noun, e.g. *computer*.

4.3.1.2   Iconic Sequencing (IconSeq)
Iconic sequencing was coded as fulfilled (1), if the order of elements mirrored the order in extra-linguistic reality, or violated (−1), if the order was reversed. In cases where there is no particular extra-linguistic order, it does not apply and was therefore coded (0).

4.3.1.3   Extra-linguistic hierarchy (Hierarchy)
In case of a hierarchical relation between the referents denoted by the constituents, those cases were coded (1) where the referent that is ranked higher preceded one of a lower rank. Conversely, if that constituent was mentioned last, the constraint was coded violated (−1). When there was no hierarchical relation apparent between the two constituents, as in the majority of cases, the factor did not apply and was coded (0).

4.3.1.4   Conceptual accessibility (ConAcc)
Conceptual accessibility was judged applicable if one of the oppositions described in Section 3.1.5 was found. If the constituent denoting the more accessible concept preceded the one of lesser accessibility, it was coded adhered to (1), in the reverse order it was coded violated (−1).

4.3.2   Factors related to the stress pattern of coordinate constructions

4.3.2.1   Rhythmic alternation (Rhythm)
This ordering constraint was coded fulfilled (1) if the observed ordering resulted in an alternation of stressed and unstressed syllables, but the reverse order would have not. It was considered violated (−1) when the attested order resulted in a series of either unstressed or stressed syllables in adjacency, but the reverse would have not. If both the attested as well as the reverse order would have resulted in either a perfect alternation of stressed and unstressed syllables or

both in a violation of it, the factor was considered inapplicable and thus coded (0). Consider the following examples from all three levels of analysis:

(48) a. advisor – counsellor
          x X x   X   x
      b. pen and paper
          X   x   X x
      c. the wealthy men and poorer people
          x   X x   X   x   X x   X x

All examples above (48a–c) were coded (1), as a perfect alternation of stressed and unstressed syllables can be observed, while the respective reversals (e.g. *counsellor-advisor*) would have led to sequences of (at least) two unstressed syllables. With binomials and complex NPs (48b, c), the coordinating conjunction had to be taken into account as an unstressed buffer element, of course. Sequences of stressed syllables or lapses within the constituents were ignored, as solely the stress pattern difference between the two possible orders was deemed crucial.

4.3.2.2 *Avoidance of ultimate stress (ULTSTRESS)*
This factor was judged adhered to (1) if the constituents were ordered in a way to avoid terminal stress and considered violated (−1) if the observed ordering exhibited terminal stress, but the reverse would have not. If, as in the majority of cases, both constituents did not bear stress on the terminal syllable, it was considered not to apply and was therefore coded (0). Consider the examples (48a–c) above: with (48a), *advisor-counsellor*, it was coded (0), as neither ordering features a terminal stressed syllable. With *pen and paper*, however, it was coded (1), as putting *pen* in second position would have resulted in terminal stress.

4.3.2.3 *Syllable weight (SYLW)*
This constraint states that the second element's main syllable is hypothesised to be heavier. This contrast was treated as a nominal one, and thus coded (1) if the hypothesised heaviness contrast held and (−1) if it was violated. If neither syllable exhibited a difference in terms of syllable weight, it was coded (0). Syllables with long vowels (VV), a filled coda position (VC), or both (VVC) were considered heavy syllables, while syllables with a short vowel and no coda (V) were considered light.

4.3.3 *Length and complexity*

4.3.3.1 *Number of syllables/number of phonemes (LENGTHSYL/LENGTHPHO)*
These factors were treated as scalar variables, as length differences between constituents can vary (see Section 4.2.3 above). Different measurements of length were applied in the individual case studies. On the level of compounds

and binomials, length was measured in number of phonemes and number of syllables. As both operationalisations measure essentially the same contrast and are therefore highly correlated, they cannot both be included in one model. To avoid this problem, the following operationalisation strategy was applied. The number of syllables of the two constituents was counted and the difference between the two was calculated (see also above Table 4.2). The difference in phonemes, however, was only coded when the constituents exhibited no length difference in syllables. For example, with *actor-stuntman*, the variable was coded (0) on the level of syllables, as both constituents consist of the same number of syllables. However, *stuntman* is longer than *actor*, counting phonemes (eight as opposed to five segments), therefore it received a coding of (3) on this level. This strategy allows for the detection of length effects in a more fine-grained way than previous studies. The drawback to this solution is that these measurements were only considered when there was no length difference in syllables, yet it is more plausible to assume that all levels are always effective during language processing. The alternative would have been to design an artificial length/complexity index consisting of all factors. This was not done for two reasons: first, it would have required making arbitrary assumptions about the influence of each level, as so far their relative influence is unclear; secondly, and most importantly, it would have led to results that cannot be traced back to a particular level of influence, making it hard to interpret.

A different strategy was applied with complex NPs. Here the length of both phrases was measured in syllables and words. Counting phonemes was considered too fine-grained on this level. This decision ties in with research by Stallings et al. (1998), who claim that during the ordering of phrases, speakers process only coarse length information, such as number of words, but do not have access to fine-grained phonological properties. Furthermore, in many studies on other variation phenomena, length in number of words is the most widely used operationalisation of weight (e.g. Rosenbach 2005), which is why it has been taken into account here as an additional measurement.

4.3.3.2 *Morphological complexity (MORPHCOMPL)*

This variable was treated as a nominal one and was coded as follows. If the morphologically more complex constituent followed the less complex one, it was coded (1), meaning 'adhered to', while the reverse order was coded (−1), signifying a violation. If there were no differences in complexity, it received the coding (0). As it is naturally strongly correlated with syllable length, it was only considered when the length in syllables was equal between both constituents to avoid collinearity.[10]

---

[10] No serious correlation between the difference in phonemes and morphological complexity could be detected in cases where there was no difference in number of syllables.

4.3.3.3   Syntactic complexity (SYNTCOMPL)
With the coordination of complex noun phrases, their syntactic complexity was
also taken into account. Operationalisation details are given in Chapter 7.

4.3.4   Further constraints related to phonological and phonetic length

4.3.4.1   Vowel length (VLENGTHTOTAL/VLENGTHFINAL)
It has been hypothesised that the constituent with the longer vowel should be
preferred in second position. In previous studies, this variable had been
applied solely to monosyllabic constituents. With polysyllables, the question
arises as to which nuclei should be considered. Three different possibilities can
be theoretically motivated. First, when relating the contrast to a greater accent
of the second element, which is plausible as a long vowel contributes to syllable
weight, the main stressed syllable's nucleus should be focused on. However,
this contrast is already measured through SYLW (see Section 4.3.2.3).
Secondly, when considering phonological length on the CV-tier of the constituents as a whole, all vowels have to be considered. The third option is
relating a possible effect to phrase-final lengthening (PFL). Since PFL effects
are strongest in the final syllable of polysyllabic words (cf. Turk and Shattuck-
Hufnagel 2007), it is the final syllable which is most important. The latter two
measurements, the length contrast of the final vowel as well as that of all
vowels, were considered. In coding vowel length, a two-way phonemic distinction was applied, following Benor and Levy (2006: 245).

> Short vowels: æ, ɛ, ɪ, ʌ, ʊ
> Long vowels: ɑ, e, i, o, u, ɔ, ɜ (in American English furthermore: Vr)

Diphthongs were uniformly treated as long vowels. Two measurements were
conducted: first, the lengths of the final vowels were compared, and the
difference was coded as a nominal variable. Thus, when the second constituent contained the longer final vowel compared to the first, the constraint was
coded (1), and in the opposite case it was coded (−1). Furthermore, in order to
measure the CV-tier, all vowels of every constituent were coded as either long
or short and assigned a value (0) for short and (1) for long. These values were
then summed up for every individual constituent, with the result being a
vowel-length scale for each constituent. The difference between these two
scales was then calculated. As this value is highly correlated with the number
of nuclei and collinearity would arise if it was investigated alongside
the length measurements, it was only coded when both constituents had
the same number of nuclei, thus did not differ in number of syllables. As the
total vowel length scale (VLENGTHTOTAL) and the final vowel contrast
(VLENGTHFINAL) were of course correlated as well, since the final vowel
also contributes to overall vowel length, both cannot be entered jointly into
one model. Therefore they were entered separately, testing for significance
independently.

Table 4.3 *Hypothesised ordering preferences with regard to voicing of the final consonant*

First constituent	Second constituent
Ends in a vowel	Ends in a voiced consonant
Ends in a voiceless consonant	Ends in a vowel
Ends in a voiceless consonant	Ends in a voiced consonant

4.3.4.2   Voicing of the final consonant (VOICFINC)

Recall that we hypothesised that a contrast in voicing of the final consonant may influence the ordering process due to its lengthening/shortening effect on the preceding nucleus. Voiced endings therefore should be preferred in second position, while voiceless endings are claimed to occur more often in first position. The contrast also applies, if one of the constituents features an open syllable (see Table 4.3).

This factor was coded as a nominal variable: when there was a contrast as hypothesised, it was coded adhered to (1), and in the reverse order, it was coded violated (−1). Cases of constituents ending in two consonants were also taken into account. If both of them were either voiced or unvoiced (*band* vs. *artist*), they were coded accordingly. If the two consonants differed with respect to voicing, the variable was judged inapplicable.

4.3.4.3   Sonority of the initial and final consonant (SONINIC/SONFINC)

It has been hypothesised that the second constituent preferably ends in a more sonorous consonant, due to phonetic lengthening. As it is unclear what effects may ensue if one constituent ends in a vowel or in more than one consonant, this constraint was considered only when both constituents ended in exactly one consonant. The variable was treated as a scalar one, using the following eight-point sonority scale.

h > j > w > r > l > nasals > fricatives > stops
(sonorous ————————————→ obstruent)
8 > 7 > 6 > 5 > 4 > 3   > 2   > 1

The final consonants of both constituents were coded accordingly and the value of the first constituent was subtracted from that of the second. The hypothesised contrast (the final consonant of the second element is more sonorous) thus yields a positive value.

Initial segments received the same treatment. However, since the phonological motivation of this variable is unclear, it was universally applied, including when the relevant constituent contained an initial consonant cluster. It was not applied, however, when the constituent began with a vowel, because it should not be conflated with the initial consonants factor (see

Section 4.3.4.4). This variable was also treated as a scalar one, subtracting the value of the second constituent from the first, as the original hypothesis put forward by Cooper and Ross (1975) states that the first constituent exhibits the more sonorous beginning. Such a contrast results in a positive value through the applied operationalisation.

4.3.4.4   Number of initial consonants (INIC)

The number of initial consonants of every constituent was coded and the difference between both was calculated, subtracting the value of the first constituent from the value of the second constituent, as the first element was claimed to have fewer initial consonants.

4.3.5   Other phonological and phonetic variables

4.3.5.1   Vowel quality

As mentioned above (see Section 3.5.2), there has been a controversy about whether height or backness is the most relevant measure of vowel position for ordering in binomials. Thus, several measures of vowel position were applied helping to determine empirically which one performs best against the data.

4.3.5.2   First and second formant frequencies (F1/F2)

Vowel height and backness were coded using the F_1 and F_2 frequencies of the constituent's main stressed vowel. The frequencies were obtained from studies on American and British English, respectively (see individual cases studies in Chapters 5–6). The variable was treated as a scalar one, calculating the difference between the two constituents' values. The result was divided by 100 to arrive at interpretable unit sizes for statistical analysis. Corresponding to a front > back succession, the first constituent should have a higher F_2 value than the second, and for F_1 the lower value should precede the higher one, which corresponds to a high > low sequence. Therefore, for F_2 the value of the second constituent was subtracted from the first and vice-versa for F_1.

4.3.5.3   Ladefoged's measure (LADE)

Ladefoged (1993) suggests the difference between the two formant frequencies (F_2–F_1) as an alternative measure of vowel backness. According to him, this measure is better correlated with actual, anatomic backness, i.e. position of the tongue. Therefore, it was also taken into account. The F_2–F_1 difference was calculated for the primary stressed syllable's vowel for each constituent and treated in the same way as the F_1 and F_2 values. As high values of this measure correspond to front vowels, we would expect a decrease of this value from the first to the second constituent. Since Ladefoged's measure is derived from F_1 and F_2, it is problematic to insert it into the same model with other measures of vowel position. Thus, I proceeded in a step-wise fashion: the variables for F_1 and F_2 were entered into one model simultaneously and their influence was assessed. They were then removed from the model and

replaced by Ladefoged's measure in a second step. The measure that performed best against the data was kept in the model in case it yielded a
statistically significant result.

4.3.6   Frequency

Across all case studies, the token frequency of the two constituents was
measured and treated as a scalar variable. As we predicted that the more
frequent constituent would precede the less frequent one, the frequency of
the second constituent was subtracted from that of the first one, resulting in a
positive value if the constituents displayed the predicted order of decreasing
frequency. The frequency values for the individual constituents were obtained
from relevant corpora (see individual case studies, Chapters 5–7). Before
calculating the frequency difference, the values were logarithmically transformed, as we know from lexical decision experiments (e.g. Scarborough
et al. 1977; Gordon and Caramazza 1982) that subjects do not react to frequency
in a linear fashion. Scarborough et al. (1977) show that there is an equal increase
in performance (reaction time) for every tenfold increase in frequency.[11]
Therefore, the obtained frequency values were logarithmically transformed
to the base of 10.

---

[11] Scarborough et al. (1977) find that reaction time improved by 50 ms in a lexical decision task
for every tenfold increase in frequency.

5   Order of compound constituents

In the following sections, the coordination of constituents within copulative compounds is investigated.

5.1   Background and previous research

This chapter focuses on those copulative compounds in whose formation 'two or more nominal predicates are coordinated at the morphological level' (Olsen 2002b: 250). Examples from English are:

(49)   a. poet-doctor
       b. teacher-researcher
       c. singer-songwriter

Semantically, 'copulative compounds encompass a coordinative relationship between the two constituents such that both concepts are attributed simultaneously' (Olsen 2001a: 279). Thus, in (49a) a *poet-doctor* denotes an individual who is both a poet and a doctor (see also Plag 2003: 146). On the semantic level, copulative compounds should thus be distinguished from determinative compounds, as they do not express a determiner–head relation, but a symmetrical relation between the component parts.[1] Syntactically, however, they can be analysed as being right-headed, since only the final element inflects when pluralised (see Plag 2003: 147):

(50)   writer-directors

Further characteristics that distinguish this class of compounds are their considerably lower frequency[2] and their deviant stress pattern, as, unlike the

---

[1] Structurally, these compounds are described by Mortensen (2003: 6) as follows: '[e]ach construction of this type must have two and only two daughters. Neither of these daughters may depend syntactically upon the other and both daughters must always be of the same syntactic type. The compound as a whole is always of this syntactic type as well.' This statement is strongly reminiscent of the definition of coordinate constructions that I apply (see Section 1.2.1), which thus serves as another argument for their inclusion in the current investigation.

[2] Arnaud (2002) as cited in Renner (2008) estimates they make up no more than 2% of all English compound types in the *Oxford English Dictionary*. Based upon a smaller sample, Berg (2009) arrives at a similar value.

majority of determiner compounds, they bear main stress on the second constituent. The examples below from Plag et al. (2008: 761) illustrate this difference.[3]

(51)   a. geologist-astrónomer
       b. trúck driver

Copulative compounds have alternatively been termed *appositional compounds* by Wälchli (2005) who, despite using a different term, applies a semantic description similar to Olsen's because, according to him, these 'are referentially intersective, as both coordinants denote a single referent' (Wälchli 2005: 76).[4] Within the general class of coordinate compounds, Renner (2008) distinguishes three types on semantic grounds: *additional*, *hybrid* and *multifunctional*, which he defines thus:

(52)   a. *multifunctional*:   (an) XY is (an) X who/which is also (a) Y
       b. *hybrid*:   (an) XY is midway between (an) X and a Y
       c. *additional*:   (an) XY is (an) X plus (a) Y

An example of the *multifunctional type* is *hunter-gatherer* because it denotes an individual who is both a hunter and a gatherer. This type is therefore endocentric and both constituents can be analysed as heads. An example of the *hybrid* type is *jazz-rock* because this music genre lies between jazz and rock and thus, this type is exocentric. An example of an *additional* coordinate compound is *fridge-freezer*, as the combination of a fridge and a freezer is denoted. This type is also exocentric. Sometimes the multifunctional type is also termed appositional and the hybrid type is termed copulative (Kortmann 2005). Since all types exhibit the crucial property of being reversible, all three types are considered in this book. Similar to Olsen (2001a), I use the term 'copulative compounds' as the class to be investigated here, which encompasses all three sub-categories.

A crucial difference between coordination in syntax and the compounds investigated in this chapter is that coordinate constructions in syntax usually denote two referents, while copulative compounds 'are limited to the denotation of a single ontologically coherent individual' (Olsen 2001a: 301), a characteristic Renner (2008) terms *homoreferentiality*. An exception to this principle concerns copulative compounds in embedded contexts. Typically, these are copulatives in determiner position, as in:

---

[3] In a large-scale corpus study, Plag et al. (2008) confirm the almost uniform exceptional stress pattern of co-compounds. It must be noted, however, that this criterion is, along with all other criteria determining stress, a probabilistic and not a deterministic one. Thus, there are exceptions to it.

[4] Wälchli (2005) uses this term to allude to their similarity to coordinative appositions in syntax, which also denote only a single referent and which are thus similar to copulative compounds; e.g., *The owner and editor of the Daily Post was a member of the club* (example from Quirk et al. 1985: 760–1).

(53) a. man–wife team
      b. producer–customer relationship

In (53a, b), the copulative denotes at least two referents. These embedded forms are not considered here because they constitute a different class with regard to their semantics and inclusion could lead to a problematically heterogeneous sample. Embedded copulatives are more reasonably analysed as determiner-head constructions, therefore it is not unproblematic to focus on the compound modifier part, since an influence of the head on the ordering cannot be ruled out (see Plag 2003:146–7 on the difference between the two classes).[5]

The most important feature of copulative compounds for the current investigation is that the order of constituents is reversible (see Olsen 2001a; Renner 2008), as in:

(54) a. writer-director
      b. director-writer
      c. producer-manager
      d. manager-producer

Reversibility pertains to all nonce-formation and low-frequency compounds which are not lexicalised in a particular order. Exceptions are high-frequency irreversible instances such as *hunter-gatherer* and *singer-songwriter*, which are thus excluded from the analysis (see Section 5.3). These irreversible copulatives are analogous to formulaic, irreversible binomials in the domain of lexical coordination, as their order is fixed and they can be hypothesised as having unit status in the mental lexicon.

5.2   Specific aims and hypotheses

Already Malkiel (1959) has observed a similarity of this class of compounds to cases of lexical coordination (binomials), but to my knowledge no studies on constituent order in copulative compounds exist to date. Therefore, the most general question to address in this chapter is whether and to what extent coordinate compounds are subject to the forces believed to influence order, as outlined above, and whether the effects are comparable to the other levels of analysis. Possible inter-level correspondences are particularly interesting with copulative compounds, as it can be assumed that these developed out of syntactic constructions (cf. Olsen 2001a).[6]

---

[5] Wulff (2002) found such an influence for pronominal adjective ordering, as some adjectives are preferred in head-adjacent position.
[6] In tracing back the origin of copulative compounds in Sanskrit, Olsen (2001a) argues that they stem from syntactic coordinate constructions and have been reanalysed as morphological objects in English, and are now productive lexical templates. Thus, 'the implicit coordinative relation between the two concepts conjoined in a morphological copulative is related to, and at the same time contrasted with, the syntactic coordination of noun phrases'

As mentioned above, I distinguish between ad hoc formations and highly frequent, probably lexicalised instances. Interestingly, according to Olsen (2001a: 297–8), factors underlying constituent order in other constructions, particularly those that determine order in irreversible binomials, are not at work with copulative compounds, as 'nonce-formations seem to be completely free as to which order is used for the constituents'. Thus, here as well the question as to whether regular, reversible cases of coordination are subject to the same influences as formulaic constructions is immediately relevant (see Section 1.1).

Olsen (2001a) further argues that if an ordering preference can be found at all, it would be determined by pragmatics. She predicts that, if one of the two constituents is 'under focus' (p. 297), then this constituent occurs in final position. She argues this prediction to be a reflection of copulative compounds' relation to determinative compounds, whereby the most important element, the head, is also in the final position. It seems that what Olsen means by 'under focus' is largely congruent with the concept of topic of the relevant context (cf. Olsen 2001a: 297). In that case, her hypothesis stands in contrast with the hypothesised order from low to high information status (see Section 3.1), as the topical constituent tends to have lower information status because it is usually given and should therefore occur early (see also Dressler 2005: 275). I will discuss the influences of both possible pragmatic ordering constraints in light of the results obtained for order in copulative compounds (see below, Section 5.5).

5.3   Data extraction

For the creation of a sample of copulative compounds, I took as a starting point two lists of copulative compounds provided by Olsen (2001a, 2001b) that are compiled from corpus data.[7] I excluded from these all tripartite compounds. Furthermore, I did not consider data points where my interpretation was not a coordinate, but a determinative one. This resulted in an exclusion of all instances, including kinship terms, such as:

(55)   lawyer-son

Example (55) is ambiguous between the two interpretations *son of a lawyer* and *lawyer and son* and is therefore not kept for further analysis.

(Olsen 2001a: 280). This view is in accordance with empirical data on the compounds' diachronic inheritance of structural relations from syntax (cf. Gaeta 2008). According to the assumption 'today's morphology is yesterday's syntax', Olsen (2001a) claims that syntactic modifier-head relations motivated determinative compounds, while asyndetic syntactic coordinations caused copulative compounds. For a detailed discussion of the syntax–morphology correspondence in compounds, see Gaeta (2008) and also Wälchli (2005).

[7] Her lists are based on the corpus *Tipster Research Collection Vol. I* (1994), annotated by Gerhard Heyer and Uwe Quasthoff at the University of Leipzig (Olsen 2001b: 32).

This selection process resulted in a sample of 204 compounds kept for further analysis. In a second step, I conducted a corpus search to expand the sample. As copulative compounds are relatively rare (see Section 5.1), I employed the large 385-million-word *Corpus of Contemporary American English* (COCA).[8] This corpus contains 20 million words from every year ranging from 1990 to the present. It is divided equally into the sub-corpora spoken, fiction, popular magazine, newspaper and academic, and is contin-ually updated.[9] Since copulative compounds are not annotated in that corpus, and thus cannot be searched for directly, I developed a number of criteria for suitable search strings. The most conspicuous characteristic of copulative compounds is that they are hyphenated; thus, I decided to search for hyphenated words. Moreover, I extracted the most frequent constituent endings from Olsen's lists. The most productive group of copulative compounds consists of coordinations of two terms of profession or characteristic, as in the examples *writer-director* or *teacher-researcher*. Second in terms of frequency are combinations of objects, e.g. *fighter-bomber*. With both groups, the large majority of constituents end in the agentive morphemes *-er* or *-or*. Other frequent endings are *-ian* (e.g. *musician*), and *-ist* (e.g. *artist*). I therefore searched for all bipartite hyphenated words whose constituents ended in either *-er*, *-ian*, *-ist* or *-or*, in any possible combination, resulting in sixteen different search strings. Concordances were created using regex search protocols. An example search string is given below.

(56)   *[any number of any letters] -er [any number of any letters] -or*

The resulting concordances were manually cleaned from false hits: only those instances that do not occur in embedded position were kept (see Section 5.1) and all hits where a possible determinative interpretation was likely were not considered. Cases where the first constituent is ambiguous between adjectival and nominal interpretation as in *racist-preacher* were also excluded.

The total sample of copulative compounds, including the COCA results, as well as the examples by Olsen, amounts to 661 different types. Since the aim of this book first and foremost is to investigate the factors that influence the ordering decision of a speaker in a particular production event, a token sample was created. Therefore, concordances for all 661 types in both possible orders were created from the COCA corpus. If types from Olsen's lists did not occur in the corpus, they were entered into the token sample with a frequency of 1, as Olsen's lists contain data points whose use is attested (see footnote 7). The token sample contains 1,394 data points. Highly frequent, possibly lexicalised compounds whose order is irreversible,

---

[8] Accessible via http://www.americancorpus.org/
[9] All corpus searches were conducted during three days of the first two weeks of April 2009 in order to ensure that no updates in corpus contents would skew the results.

Table 5.1 *Samples of copulative compounds*

Sample	Number of tokens (N)
Complete sample	1,394
Sample including contextual information (COCA sample)	1,286

such as *singer-songwriter* and *hunter-gatherer*, were excluded in accordance with the criteria laid out above (see Section 4.1.2). This resulted in an exclusion of sixteen formulaic, irreversible types. The token sample was then coded with regard to the variables discussed above (see Section 4.2). The resultant data frame was then submitted to logistic regression analysis, as explained in Section 4.2.3, using the statistics software R.

5.4   Operationalisation details

Certain specific requirements arose during the operationalisation of variables with the sample of copulative compounds, which pertain to the following variables:

Information status (INF)

This variable could of course only be investigated when contextual information was available, thus for types that actually occurred in the COCA corpus. With data points from Olsen's lists, which did not occur in the corpus, it could therefore not be coded. Thus, two separate samples were created, one containing only those hits for which contextual information was available and another one including all compound tokens, for which the INF ordering constraint was not considered. See Table 5.1 for an overview.

Vowel quality (F1, F2, LADE)

Vowel height and backness were coded using average F1 and F2 frequencies of American speakers provided by Kent and Read (2002).[10] These values were coded for the primary stressed vowel of the individual constituents. The difference between the vowels in both constituents was calculated and divided by 100 to arrive at interpretable unit sizes for the quantitative analysis. The result of this calculation was entered into the data frame

---

[10] Their values were obtained by averaging over six representative studies measuring vowel values of North American speakers, including Peterson and Barney's classic study (1952).

for every data point. Vowel quality based on Ladefoged's measure (see Section 4.3.5.3) was calculated for the primary stressed vowel of every constituent and submitted to the same calculation.

Frequency (FREQ)

The frequency of every constituent was retrieved from the COCA corpus, standardised to a frequency value per 1 million words and then transformed logarithmically to the base of 10 (see Section 4.3.6). Then the difference between the two constituents' values was calculated and entered into the data frame.

5.5   Results

In the following, the results of the logistic regression analysis are given in the form of a table (Table 5.2). As explained in Section 4.2.3, minimal adequate models are aimed at, hence non-significant variables are not included. Since two samples were submitted to regression analysis (see Section 5.4), two separate models, one for each sample, are reported here.

The following variables have been excluded from both models during the model-fitting process, as significance values exceeded even marginal significance ($p > 0.1$). These variables are therefore missing from the tables above.

HIERARCHY, ULTSTRESS, VOICFINC, F2, LADE, SONINIC, LENGTHPHO

Table 5.2 *Results of the regression analysis for two samples of copulative compounds (minimal adequate models)[a]*

Variable	Complete sample			COCA sample		
	Coefficient	Odds ratio	p	Coefficient	Odds ratio	p
INF	NA	NA	NA	0.64	1.90	***
CONACC	0.65	1.92	*	0.74	2.09	*
ICONSEQ	2.33	10.29	***	2.11	8.25	***
RHYTHM	0.39	1.47	***	0.36	1.43	**
SYLW	0.52	1.69	***	0.58	1.79	***
MORPHCOMPL	n.s.	n.s.	n.s.	0.53	1.70	**
LENGTHSYL	0.66	1.94	***	0.70	2.02	***
VLENGTHFINAL	0.34	1.40	*	0.51	1.67	**
INIC	0.23	1.29	***	0.28	1.31	**
F1	0.07	1.08	**	0.06	1.06	*
FREQ	0.32	1.38	***	0.36	1.43	***
N		1,363			1,174	
df		1,352			1,162	
% correct		69.41			72.49	

[a] The variables are referred to here in abbreviated form (see also previous chapter). A complete list of the abbreviations of variables along with their expanded forms can be found in the appendix.
* = $p < 0.05$, ** = $p < 0.01$, *** = $p < 0.001$, n.s. = not significant

The variable MORPHCOMPL was found to be significant only in the COCA model.

The resultant minimal adequate models predict about 70% of the observed orderings correctly (69.41% and 72.49% respectively). By merely guessing the ordering, we would arrive at a correctness rate of already 50%. Thus, our models allow us to classify about 20% more cases correctly, but still make incorrect predictions for 30% of the data.

A look at the results table reveals that nine or ten variables 'survived' the selection process, all of which predict order in the hypothesised direction, as can be inferred from the positive coefficients of the predictors. I will briefly discuss the results of these factors in the following. A thorough discussion of all results, including those variables which yielded non-significant results is provided in the general results section (see Chapter 8).

Starting with the pragmatic level, it can be observed that differences in information status (INF) significantly affect ordering in the COCA sample. When a constituent is given, the odds for it being mentioned first increase by 90%. Information status thus exerts the same influence on copulative compounds as has been hypothesised for other contexts, thus there is a preference for the order from low to high information status. This result shows that Olsen's assumption that it would affect co-compounds differently due to their (possible) right-headedness is not supported by the data. Olsen's suggestion that only the pragmatic level would influence ordering is also not supported by the data, as INF is by no means the only variable that affects ordering. However, including INF increases the overall predictive accuracy, as the model for the COCA sample has a better model fit compared to the one for the other sample, in classifying about 3% more of the data correctly.

Of the semantic variables, two out of three are statistically significant and therefore remain in the minimal adequate models. Iconic sequencing (ICONSEQ) with an odds ratio of 10.29 or 8.25 respectively is the semantic predictor with the largest effect size. These very high values show that, if there is a temporal or causal sequence in extra-linguistic reality, this is almost always mirrored in the order of compound constituents. In the samples, there are only four types where this constraint is violated, among them *editor-writer*, as a text has to be written first before it can be edited. Also conceptual accessibility (CONACC) influences ordering decisions significantly. When a constituent is more accessible than the co-occurring one, the odds for occurring in first position rise by 1.92 or 2.09 respectively. Only the semantic factor of extra-linguistic hierarchy (HIERARCHY) does not significantly contribute to the observed distribution and therefore is not retained in the models. This non-significant result may be a consequence of the very small number of only thirty types in which hierarchical relations were actually observable. This low number is due to the fact that, in copulative compounds, extra-linguistic hierarchies are only rarely involved, as these usually coordinate two terms of profession.

Turning to factors related to the stress pattern of copulative compounds, RHYTHM exerts a significant influence on ordering decisions, with odds ratios of 1.47 and 1.43. Language users try to order constituents such that they show a sequence of alternating stresses. In contrast, no evidence is found for the avoidance of ultimate stress of the second element (ULTSTRESS). The syllable weight (SYLW) of the main stressed syllable, however, is a significant predictor. Heavier syllables are preferred in the second constituent, the odds ratios being 1.69 and 1.79 respectively.

Regarding the length of compound constituents, a clear short-before-long preference can be found. For length in number of syllables (LENGTHSYL), we observe an increase of the odds of 94% or 102% for the found ordering, for every syllable that the first constituent is shorter. The number of phonemes (LENGTHPHO) does not, however, influence ordering. Remember that we coded the difference in number of phonemes and number of morphemes only when both constituents had the same number of syllables. In such cases, MORPHCOMPL influences ordering as expected because the morphologically more complex element is preferred in second position (odds ratio of 1.70). This is, however, only true in the COCA sample, while in the other sample it is found to be not significant.

For another length measurement, the length of the constituents' final vowels (VLENGTHFINAL) is also a significant predictor, and is therefore retained in the minimal model. Its effect is hypothesised thus: constituents with short final vowels show a preference for first position, while those with longer vowels are preferred in second position. The odds ratios are 1.40 and 1.67 respectively. Alternatively, when we enter the length difference of all vowels (VLENGTHTOTAL) into the model, this variable yields a non-significant result. Furthermore, the constituent with more initial consonants is preferred in second place (INIC), with odds ratios of 1.29 and 1.31 respectively.

Of the different measurements of vowel quality, F1 is the only predictor retained in the models, while the other measures, F2 and LADE, yielded non-significant results. If a constituent's first formant frequency is 100Hz lower than that of the second one, its odds for occurring in first position change by 10% or 9% respectively. There is thus a tendency for high vowels to precede low ones.

Lastly, the variable frequency (FREQ) also influences ordering decisions and is therefore retained in both minimal adequate models. For every log10-step difference that a constituent is more frequent than the other, its odds for occurring in first position change by 40% or 51% respectively; i.e., if a constituent is ten times more frequent than the other one, its odds for occurring in first position rise by that value. I checked for collinearity of the model (see Section 4.2.3), by calculating the condition number κ (Baayen

2008: 198–200). With condition numbers of $\kappa = 2.74$ (model for complete sample) and $\kappa = 2.63$ (model for the COCA sample), there is no collinearity to speak of.

5.6   Interim summary

Overall, the results show that the order of constituents in copulative compounds is influenced by an array of factors. The ordering of compound constituents is therefore far from random, or 'completely free', as Olsen (2001a: 297–8) suggested. The influential factors range from the pragmatic to the phonological level. We can thus conclude that language users are susceptible to a wide variety of influences during the production of reversible copulative compounds.

6   Order of bare noun phrases (binomials)

6.1   Background and previous research

This chapter addresses the coordination of bare noun phrases, i.e., individual nouns that form an overall NP. This type of construction matches the definition of a 'binomial', and therefore this empirical part is most closely related to research on irreversible binomials. As pointed out in Chapter 2, it is this class of constructions that were the focus of most relevant works. Two examples of the type of construction to be investigated are given below:

(57)

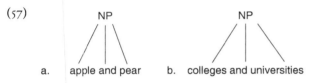

    a.   apple and pear   b.   colleges and universities

Binomials such as (57a, b) are dealt with in a separate empirical chapter here, although syntactically they are similar to more complex NPs (see Chapter 7), since in both cases two NPs are coordinated. I still distinguish these two constructions for two reasons. First, as mentioned above (see Chapter 2), most relevant research focuses on irreversible binomials. Therefore, many of the ordering constraints suggested in previous research are motivated by the particular structure of a binomial, as they pertain to subtle phonological differences between the two lexemes, or to the stress pattern of a binomial as a whole (see Chapter 3). In order to be able to test these ordering constraints, it is necessary to investigate a separate sample of binomials, which is then directly comparable to previous research. Secondly, with more complex NPs there is another influence that needs to be taken into account, viz. the syntactic complexity of an NP, which is not relevant to the order in binomials because they lack an internal syntactic structure.[1] This potential influence constitutes an argument for a separate case study of more complex NPs (see also Chapter 7).

---

[1] On the issue of branching direction, see Section 1.2.

6.2   Specific aims and hypotheses

The primary aim of this book is to investigate the factors influencing ordering decisions. Addressing this question with binomials is especially interesting, as these constructions have been most extensively studied in previous research (see above) and it is thus possible to directly compare the results to previous findings. The second aim of this chapter, as well as of the book as a whole, is to investigate the relation between irreversible, probably lexicalised constructions (irreversible binomials) and cases of reversible coordination. As most previous research focused on irreversibles, we do not know whether the forces identified for them are also at work in ad hoc coordination, which I assume is an online process. Conversely, the comparison allows for an investigation as to whether irreversible instances are fossilised coordinates whose order is influenced by the same forces as in 'normal' coordination, or whether different influences are at work. These questions are empirically addressed in this chapter. A theoretical discussion on the relation between irreversible and reversible binomials is given in the main discussion part (Chapter 9).

6.3   Data extraction

In order to test the relation between fixed, possibly lexicalised constructions and cases of ad hoc coordination, samples of each group were created. For the sample of reversible binomials, the spoken part of the British National Corpus (BNC) was chosen. The BNC is annotated for word class to make a noun search possible. I created concordances using the two search strings *Noun and/or Noun*, relying on the part-of-speech tagging of the BNC.[2] The resultant data sample was then manually rid of false hits in order to include only data points where the two nouns alone made up the overall noun phrase without additional constituents. Thus, instances of greater complexity and instances of both nouns belonging to different phrases were excluded. Repetitions such as *years and years* were not considered. Binomials whose second constituent was a semantically empty extension, e.g. *and things* or *and stuff* were excluded, as these cases are not reversible. Furthermore, proper nouns such as names of corporations/bands/products or other entities that

---

[2] In creating this sample, we must determine which string instantiates a word (or bare phrase) or a complex phrase. The problem with making the distinction between compound and phrase is that we are dealing with a continuum here, where compound and phrase are the endpoints of a scale. Thus, any linguistic motivation for classifying the data would result in a somewhat arbitrary cut-off point. I therefore apply the same strategy as in other studies and include only those examples that are words graphematically, similar to previous studies (e.g. Fenk-Oczlon 1989; Benor and Levy 2006). The drawback of this strategy is that its application results in a loss of possibly positive results. However, its gain is that the present work is straightforwardly comparable to previous research.

are practically irreversible – e.g. *Guns and Roses* – were excluded. Coordinations of personal names – e.g. *Peter and Emily* – were excluded because their ordering could be influenced by idiosyncratic factors.

The sample of formulaic binomials was acquired by applying the operationalisation detailed in Section 4.1.2. Thus, only instances with a strong bias for one ordering and a certain token frequency were selected. Since the application of these two criteria requires a large corpus in order to yield reliable results, the entire BNC was used for the identification of irreversibles. The identified irreversible binomials were then removed from the sample of reversible coordination with one additional consideration. Types with a high token frequency, whether reversible or not, were not considered because their lexical unit status cannot be ruled out, since even when a certain construction does not exhibit a strong tendency towards one ordering, it is still conceivable that a language user has both orderings stored as units in the mental lexicon. Therefore, all instances of coordination that surpass the frequency threshold of 10 per 100 million words were not considered in the sample of non-formulaic, reversible constructions.

I created four sub-samples, differing on the two dimensions reversibility (reversibles vs. irreversibles) and choice of coordinator (*and* vs. *or*). During the process of data acquisition, I found that the sample of irreversibles containing the coordinator *or* was too small for further analysis, as it contained fewer than fifty types. This finding corresponds to the fact that, in previous studies, irreversible binomials almost always featured the coordinator *and*. Of the 342 irreversible binomials mentioned in Cooper and Ross (1975), only 35 feature *or*.

There is also the question as to whether types or tokens should be considered for the empirical analysis. The general aim of this book is to investigate which factors influence the language user when in the process of coordinating two elements. For the investigation of this process, every individual instance of coordination is relevant and thus calls for a token sample. This is why such a sample was used for reversible binomials (one sample each for the coordinators *and*/*or*, respectively). However, this is not the case regarding irreversible, formulaic constructions, whereby I assume that no online ordering process takes place anymore. With irreversible binomials, we are primarily interested in the question as to which factors led to the lexicalised order we find. Thus, we are concerned with the structural level but not with every individual instance of language use. Using a token sample here would create the problem that very few high-frequency types dominated the sample, e.g. *black and white* (token frequency of 1,049 in the BNC) or *goods and services* (token frequency of 643 in the BNC); however, these would not necessarily be representative of the lexicalisation process as a whole. Therefore, with formulaic irreversibles, a type sample was used for the empirical analysis. In order to be able to compare reversibles and irreversibles, an additional type sample of reversibles featuring *and* was created from

Table 6.1 *Samples employed for the analysis of binomials*

No	Sample	Number of cases (N =)
1	Irreversible binomials (*and*)	259 types
2	Reversible binomials (*and*)	1,109 types
3	Reversible binomials (*and*)	1,130 tokens
4	Reversible binomials (*or*)	560 tokens

the corresponding token sample. Table 6.1 above lists the four samples that were analysed.

Samples 1 and 4 represent exhaustive samples of the respective corpora (the whole BNC for 1, the spoken section of the BNC for 4), as all hits that remained after the filtering process were kept for further analysis. With samples 2 and 3, only every other hit was considered to arrive at a manageable sample size.

6.4   Operationalisation details

Specific requirements for the operationalisation of variables for the case study of binomials pertain to the following factors:

Information status (INF)

Differences in information status need of course to be investigated for every individual instance of language use, and thus can only be coded with token samples. This variable was therefore considered only with these samples and left out of the analysis with the type samples.

Vowel quality (F1, F2, LADE)

Similar to the previous empirical chapter (Chapter 5), the three measures F1, F2 and LADE were taken into account. Since the samples are acquired from a British English corpus, the formant frequencies were taken from Steinlen (2002) on that variety.[3] I calculated the average formant frequency of values that were obtained in the five different contexts Steinlen considered.

Frequency (FREQ)

The frequency of every constituent was retrieved from the spoken section of the BNC and treated as described in Section 4.3.

---

[3] Steinlen (2002) investigated the phonetic qualities of vowels over different phonological contexts, thus providing more representative values than previous studies.

6.5   Results

Minimal adequate models were created that contain only statistically significant factors (see Chapter 4), one for each investigated sample, see Tables 6.2
and 6.3 below.

The individual steps of variable exclusion are not reported here;
however, variable exclusion was done in the same manner as described

Table 6.2 *Results of the regression analysis for type samples of binomials
(minimal adequate models).*

Variable	Irreversible binomials			*and* sample (types)		
	Coefficient	Odds ratio	p	Coefficient	Odds ratio	p
INF	NA	NA	NA	NA	NA	NA
CONACC	1.69	5.43	**	0.45	1.56	*
ICONSEQ	3.13	22.8	**	1.46	4.32	**
HIERARCHY	1.92	6.8	***	0.74	2.10	**
RHYTHM	0.97	2.65	*	n.s.	n.s.	n.s.
ULTSTRESS	n.s.	n.s.	n.s.	0.27	1.31	+
SYLW	1.73	5.66	***	n.s.	n.s.	n.s.
LENGTHSYL	1.02	2.78	***	0.16	1.18	*
SONFINC	0.37	1.45	*	n.s.	n.s.	n.s.
FREQ	0.74	2.09	*	0.12	1.12	+
N		259			1,109	
df		251			1,103	
%correct		84.2			60.6	

*** = p < 0.001, ** = p < 0.01, * = p < 0.05, + = p < 0.1, n.s. = not significant

Table 6.3 *Results of the regression analysis for token samples of binomials
(minimal adequate models)*

Variable	*and* sample (tokens)			*or* sample (tokens)		
	Coefficient	Odds ratio	p	Coefficient	Odds ratio	p
INF	1.09	2.98	**	1.46	4.33	***
CONACC	0.44	1.55	*	0.94	2.55	**
ICONSEQ	1.44	4.22	**	2.38	10.8	**
HIERARCHY	0.53	1.70	*	n.s.	n.s.	n.s.
ULTSTRESS	0.24	1.27	+	n.s.	n.s.	n.s.
LENGTHSYL	0.16	1.17	*	0.28	1.32	**
SONINIC	0.06	1.06	*	0.13	1.14	**
FREQ	0.13	1.14	+	0.27	1.31	*
N		1,130			459	
df		1,122			453	
%correct		62.7			69.1	

*** = p < 0.001, ** = p < 0.01, * = p < 0.05, + = p < 0.1, n.s. = not significant

above (Section 4.2.3), eliminating non-significant variables in a step-wise fashion.

These have been conducted in the same fashion across the different models. Non-significant and therefore excluded factors are abbreviated (n.s.) in the tables above. The abbreviation NA ('not available') means that the respective variable was not available for that sample and this applies to the variable INF in the two type samples.

The values for predictive accuracy reveal that the statistical models predict between 60% and 84% of the orderings correctly. There is a striking difference between the model of irreversible binomials (84%) and the other samples (~60–70%), which is a point that is discussed below (see Section 9.2).

Turning to the coefficients of the variables in the models, we see that they all have positive values, showing that these factors influence ordering in the predicted direction. If we look at the influence of individual constraints, we observe that differences in information status (INF) influence ordering significantly in binomials with *or* and *and*. The odds ratio is 2.98 for binomials with *and* and 4.33 for those with the coordinator *or*.

Turning to other pragmatic/semantic factors, ICONSEQ is highly significant in all samples, and it is the semantic factor with the highest effect size across the board, ranging from an odds ratio of 4.22 in the samples with the coordinator *and* to an odds ratio of 22.8 in the sample of formulaic binomials. CONACC also influences ordering significantly across all samples. The odds ratios for that variable range from 1.55 in the samples featuring *and* to 5.43 in the sample of irreversible binomials. Results are mixed for the constraint HIERARCHY. While it is significant for binomials with *and* including irreversibles, it does not reach significance in the sample of binomials with *or*. Its effect size is moderate with coordinations featuring *and*, with an odds ratio from 1.7 (tokens) to 2.1 (types), and considerably stronger in irreversibles (odds ratio 6.8). In summary, with regard to the effects of the semantic constraints, there is a conspicuous difference between irreversible, formulaic binomials and reversibles, as effects are considerably stronger with formulaic binomials, reflected in considerably higher coefficients and odds ratios.

A mixed pattern emerges for the variables related to stress pattern of the binomials. While the striving for stress alternation (RHYTHM) is only significant with irreversibles (odds ratio = 2.65), the avoidance of a stressed ultimate syllable (ULTSTRESS) is significant for coordination with *and*, but not with *or*. Stress avoidance of the ultimate syllable (ULTSTRESS) yields odds ratios between 1.27 (*and* tokens) to 1.31 (*and* types). Syllable weight (SYLW) significantly influences ordering in the predicted way, such that a heavier main syllable is preferred in the second element in the sample of irreversibles (odds ratio = 5.66).

Two variables that exert a significant influence across all samples are LENGTHSYL as well as FREQ. The tendency to order elements with few syllables before constituents with more syllables leads to an increase of the odds from 17% (*and* tokens) to 178% (irreversible binomials) for the observed ordering to occur for every one-syllable difference. The trend to put the more frequent constituent in first position yields odds ratios ranging from 1.12 (*and* types) to 2.09 (irreversible binomials).

Furthermore, SONINIC influences ordering decisions in token samples: constituents are ordered such that a word with a more sonorous beginning is preferred in first position. Odds ratios of this effect are 1.06 for the *and*-sample and 1.14 for coordination with *or*. The tendency of elements with a more sonorous ending to occur in second position (SONFINC) is significant only in the sample of irreversibles (odds ratio = 1.45). Collinearity is not an issue with any of the four models, with very low condition numbers, $\kappa < 4$.

6.6   Interim summary

The results of the empirical analyses of binomials show that their order is influenced by a variety of factors. However, not all influences claimed to be relevant for order in binomials are retained in the minimal models, as non-significant results were obtained for a number of variables.

Two findings are particularly noteworthy. First, the models of irreversible binomials and reversible, ad hoc coordination cases vary considerably. The statistical models are better able to predict ordering in formulaic binomials compared to reversible instances. Furthermore, the effect size of a number of factors is considerably higher in the former group. Secondly, differences between coordinate constructions with *and* and *or* can be detected, as some factors are only relevant with one coordinator but not the other. Both of these issues are discussed in detail below (Chapter 9).

7   Order of complex noun phrases

In this chapter, coordination is investigated in noun phrases which are more complex than binomials. I focus on constructions wherein two NPs constitute a superordinate NP and at least one of them is more complex than a single lexical item, and thus contains more than one lexical node. Consider the following example sentences:

(58)

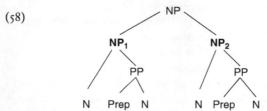

Students had not met *people with disabilities or people in wheelchairs.*

(59)

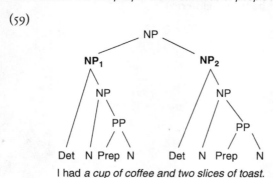

I had *a cup of coffee and two slices of toast.*

In both (58) and (59), the two coordinated phrases contain more than one lexical constituent and have an internal syntactic structure. These two instances are of course merely two random examples chosen for illustrative purposes. In the actual sample on which this investigation is based, a multitude of different phrases have been considered, encompassing much more complex phrases, which may also include embedded clauses.

7.1 Background and previous research

Above I elaborated on the differences between binomials, viz. the coordination of bare phrases, and the coordination of more complex phrases (see Chapter 6). From a production perspective, a further difference between the two is that different levels of serialisation are to be distinguished within complex coordinate phrases, in contrast to binomials. With binomials in a minimally complex syntactic model, the language user can be assumed to solely linearise two lexical units below a phrase node through coordination. With branched NPs, however, additional ordering operations must be carried out. Consider the examples (58–59), where the language user has to perform serialisation tasks on (at least) two levels. On the phrasal level, the language user must order the two coordinate NPs (marked in italics), which is the ordering operation at focus here. On the lexical level, within the two NPs, lexical elements are ordered with the help of hierarchical syntactic structures (cf. Bock 1987b). While this latter serialisation process is not directly investigated here, it may influence the process of coordination we are interested in. It is certainly possible that the presence of a syntactic structure below the coordinated NPs affects their ordering, since it is generally agreed upon that syntactic nodes are mentally 'present' during production, and 'evidence for phrase structure organisation in speech is very strong' (Bock 1987b: 354; see also Cooper and Paccia-Cooper 1980; also Berg 2009: section 2.3.2).[1] This possibility is explored in this chapter.

A further important difference between binomials and the present case study is that, in some language production studies, word and phrase ordering are viewed as distinct processes, as they 'may pertain to different parts of the syntactic world' (Stallings et al. 1998: 411). This assumption is based on a view of different stages in the production process, where phrase ordering belongs to an earlier stage than word ordering and it is thus not clear that effects in one stage carry over to the other.[2] We turn to this issue in light of the results obtained.

There are few studies in linguistics that specifically address the coordination of complex phrases, possibly due to the strong focus on the lexical level, viz. the properties of irreversible binomials. The situation is not much different in psycholinguistic works on linearisation. Some studies are based upon coordinate noun phrases; however, these include solely NPs of the structure determiner-noun (e.g. McDonald et al. 1993), while more complex phrases have rarely been taken into consideration. Two studies that investigate the order of complex coordinate phrases are Levy (2004)

---

[1] In the cited works, differences regarding the psychological status between different syntactic node types are discussed. This issue is not explored here for reasons of brevity.

[2] Unfortunately, the authors do not clarify at which stage exactly the two are located, but remain indecisive between the late functional and early grammatical stage (Stallings et al. 1998).

and Temperley (2005) who, however, focus solely on length relations and find that a short-before-long preference can also be detected on this level.[3]

7.2   Specific aims and hypotheses

Similar to the previous empirical case studies, the main goal is to identify the factors that influence speakers when ordering constituents. Since only a handful of works have focused on the order of complex phrases, the guiding question is whether the variables that were motivated largely for the class of binomials also influence the phrasal level.

In that regard, it is noteworthy that Stallings et al. (1998) argue that phrase and word ordering belong to different stages in production (see above, Section 7.1). More specifically, they speculate that the phrase length in number of words may be relevant for phrase ordering, but not length of individual words, as phonological information is only accessed after the ordering decision is carried out (Stallings et al. 1998: 411). Based on this assumption, we may hypothesise that the number of words a phrase contains should be a relevant predictor for order, but not the syllabic length of words making up the phrases, which is an assumption tested below.

As mentioned above (Section 7.1), the syntactic complexity of the to-be-coordinated NPs will be considered an additional factor under investigation.

7.3   Data extraction

As the current investigation requires the search for a specific phrase structure, a parsed corpus, the *International Corpus of English-Great Britain* (ICE-GB), was selected for data acquisition. It contains one million words of written and spoken British English from different genres and registers. Only the spoken part of the corpus was used, containing 638,000 words, as speech data is preferable for the current investigation (see Section 4.1). A fuzzy tree fragment (FTF) search was carried out, allowing for a search for syntactic trees or parts of syntactic trees, using ICECUP 3, which is the concordancing program of the ICE-GB. Two separate searches were conducted: one for coordinated noun phrases containing the coordinator *and*, and one for noun phrases coordinated by

---

[3] One issue addressed by these works is whether length effects are dependent on sentential context. Both studies assume dependency relations between syntactic units, which may affect the order within coordinate constructions. In contrast to the dominant short-before-long preference, Levy (2004) and Temperley (2005) argue for a long-before-short preference in sentence-initial contexts. This preference is not borne out by their empirical analyses, however, as they find a short-before-long tendency across all contexts. Hence, while it may be premature to discard an influence of sentential context altogether, no evidence has yet been found for such an effect. See also Temperley (2007: 317–18) on this issue.

or. The search was limited to coordinated NPs that together form a superordinate NP.[4] The data was then cleaned of hits that were not suitable for further analysis, removing, for instance, those data points that were incorrectly tagged syntactically. Moreover, all constructions had to fit the criterion of reversibility (see Section 1.4). Irreversible instances were excluded, applying the criteria laid out above (see Section 4.1.2). As the spoken part of the ICE-GB is too small to retrieve reliable frequency information, these tests were conducted using the BNC. This process resulted in the exclusion of a handful of irreversible instances, e.g. *the top and the bottom*. Furthermore, instances were excluded in which the second constituent was an extender phrase, such as *and that sort of stuff*, and *and so on*, which can occur only in second position. Data points in which the second phrase was dependent on the first and a pro-form referring back to the first constituent were also excluded – e.g. *the president and his secretary* – as these are also not reversible. Instances which contained the adjective *other* in the second constituent, as in *the green house and other renovated buildings* also failed the reversibility criterion and were therefore not considered. By the same token, numerals, such as *one hundred and eight*, and expressions of time periods, such as *a week and a half* or an *hour or two*, were weeded out. Moreover, those instances in which the two noun phrases were embedded into a larger NP were excluded – e.g. *the ex-captain and former test selector Wilfred Wooler* – to prevent influences of the following phrasal head. Syntactically ambiguous phrases were also not considered.

After the cleaning process, the two resultant samples (featuring *or* and *and* respectively), were coded for relevant variables, entered into data frames and submitted to logistic regression analysis, as explained in the main Methods part (Chapter 4).

7.4   Operationalisation details

With regard to possibly influential ordering constraints, for the most part the same variables as in the preceding empirical chapters are considered, with the exception of phonological factors that relate to properties on the segmental level. Now that we are moving up within the linguistic hierarchy, it is unlikely that effects on the segmental level exert a strong influence. As has been shown elsewhere, the further away the level of influence is situated from the level of investigation, the smaller its effect (Schlüter 2005: 285–91). Moreover, many phonological factors are motivated via the assumption of

---

[4] The ICE-GB tagger assigns the coordinators *and* and *or* either the POS tag 'conjunction' [*conjunc*], or alternatively the tag 'connective' [*connec*]. The latter is assigned in case of appositional conjuncts, i.e. when the forms denote just one referent (see also Section 1.2). Both tags were considered in order not to exclude potentially relevant hits. All matches were manually checked and cleaned from false hits.

ideal word structure (e.g. INIC, SONINIC, see Chapter 3); it is therefore unclear whether and how these variables should be tested with larger units, such as multi-word phrases.

With regard to the following variables level-specific requirements for data treatment arose:

Syntactic complexity (SYNTCOMPL)

With the present case study, an additional variable is the syntactic complexity of the two coordinated NPs. I operationalised syntactic complexity by counting the syntactic nodes of the relevant phrases, similar to Ferreira (1991). This measurement brings about the problem that it is highly correlated with the number of words of the individual phrases, as phrases consisting of more words would automatically also have the higher node count (cf. Szmrecsanyi 2004). Such a measure would thus conflate syntactic complexity and a simple length measure, since with corpus data it is not possible to hold length constant. I therefore normalised the number of nodes – including lexical nodes, but excluding the governing NP – with respect to length by dividing it by the number of words of the phrase, i.e., lexical nodes. The result is a length-independent complexity index of the phrase. In counting the nodes, I relied upon the syntactic analysis of the relevant phrases provided by the ICE-GB (see Nelson et al. 2002). For a perfectly flat structure, which consists of solely lexical nodes, this calculation would yield a complexity value of 1, while intermediate nodes between the top NP and the lexical nodes increase the complexity index above 1. Example (60) below serves to illustrate the calculation. The first phrase has a length of three words and consists of three (lexical) nodes which results in a complexity index of $3/3 = 1$. The second phrase is six words long and consists of eight nodes, thus the complexity index is $8/6 = 1.33$. Hence the length-adjusted complexity of the second phrase is higher.

(60)

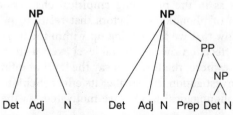

They had *the greatest jobs* and *the biggest house on the property*.

Frequency (FREQ)

As we are focusing on phrases in this chapter, the calculation of frequency was not as straightforward as in the previous case studies, where we dealt merely with the frequency of individual lexical items. For complex phrases, it has been shown that not only are the individual words of which they consist stored, but they are also stored as multi-word strings (for example, see Krug 1998; Arnon and Snider 2010), whose mental representation is dependent on their frequency of usage. In fact, an entire branch of research is emerging dedicated to these *n*-gram frequencies and their cognitive relevance. For this reason, the variable frequency was operationalised as the *n*-gram string frequency of the complete phrases. So far, the longest phrases for which frequency effects have been shown are 4-grams (cf. Arnon and Snider 2010). Therefore, string frequency was only considered when the phrases did not exceed the length of four words. In other cases, the frequency difference was coded (0). By applying this operationalisation, I do not claim that the frequency of other units, such as the individual word frequencies, is irrelevant. In fact, it is likely that frequency information of different *n*-grams and on multiple levels of abstractness is also important. This would mean that for a four-word phrase, the frequency values of all words, all 2-grams, 3-grams and the 4-gram are relevant (cf. Arnon and Snider 2010). Furthermore, speakers may also be sensitive to frequency information on coarser syntactic levels. Which level is most relevant to the processing system is still an unresolved question (see also Mitchell et al. 1995) and it is therefore unclear how these different levels should be integrated into a single frequency measure. Thus, I only use string frequency here, which should be understood merely as a feasible heuristic. Since no corpus of a suitable size could be found, and since longer phrases occur rarely even in large corpora, the web concordancer *Webcorp* was used and the search was limited to webpages with the .uk suffix.[5] Similar to the coding procedure in the previous chapters, frequency was measured logarithmically to the base of 10 and the difference between the values of the two phrases was calculated.

7.5 Results

The model-fitting process resulted in the deletion of one predictor in both samples, which was RHYTHM, for which significance values considerably higher than the 5% level were obtained (p > 0.4 for the *and* sample and p > 0.9 for the *or* sample). All other predictors were found to be statistically significant and are hence included in the minimal adequate models. See Table 7.1 below.

Even a cursory look at the results reveals that all variables yield positive coefficients, which means they influence ordering in the predicted directions. Regarding model-fitting, 71% (with the coordinator *and*) and 74.5% (with *or*)

---

[5] All webcorp searches were conducted on 3 December 2009 in order to reduce the probability of varying frequencies due to changing web content.

Table 7.1 *Results of the regression analysis for samples of complex NPs (minimal adequate models)*

Variable	Phrases coordinated by *and*			Phrases coordinated by *or*		
	Coefficient	Odds ratio	p	Coefficient	Odds ratio	p
INF	0.60	1.83	***	0.96	2.60	***
CONACC	0.98	2.65	***	0.99	2.69	*
ICONSEQ	2.28	9.78	***	2.16	8.71	***
HIERARCHY	0.61	1.85	*	1.83	6.24	*
SYNTCOMPL	1.67	5.31	***	1.99	7.31	***
LENGTHSYL	0.10	1.11	***	0.14	1.15	**
FREQ	0.21	1.23	+	0.64	1.90	**
N	837			333		
df	830			326		
% correct	70.97			74.47		

*** = p < 0.001, ** = p < 0.01, * = p < 0.05, + = p = <0.1

of the observations are correctly predicted, which is an accuracy comparable to the other case studies.

In the following, I discuss the results of the individual constraints, starting with the conceptual/semantic factors. With regard to effect size, ICONSEQ is the strongest predictor, with an odds ratio of 9.78 and 8.71 respectively. CONACC also influences ordering in a significant way, but its effect is considerably weaker. The odds ratios are almost the same for *and* and *or*, with values between 2.6 and 2.7. The variable HIERARCHY is significant in both samples; however, there is a considerable difference in strength of effect between the two samples. In the sample containing phrases linked by *and*, the odds ratio is 1.85, and HIERARCHY is thereby the weakest of the semantic predictors. With *or*, it yields an odds ratio of 6.24, which shows it is almost similar in strength to ICONSEQ. Differences in information status (INF) were also found to yield significant effects with odds ratios of 1.83 (with *and*) and 2.60 (with *or*) respectively.

Of the non-semantic variables, SYNTCOMPL exerts a significant influence such that more complex phrases are preferably placed in second position. The odds for first mention change by 5.31 (with *and*) and 7.31 (with *or*) for a one-unit difference on the complexity scale. Regarding length, a short-before-long preference can once again be observed. For every syllable by which a phrase is shorter than the co-occurring one, the odds for it being in first position increase by 11% with *and* and by 15% with *or* (see LENGTHSYL above). A significant effect of length is also obtained when we measure the length difference in number of words. However, this alternative operationalisation results in a slightly lower predictive accuracy of the corresponding models compared to the models that contain LENGTHSYL.

This result contrasts with the claim by Stallings et al. (1998) that speakers are only sensitive to coarse length information, viz. the number of words, but not their intrinsic length when ordering phrases. Since considering phonological information improves accuracy, we may conclude that language users do in fact process such information.

Lastly, differences in string frequency of the NPs (FREQ) yield a significant effect in the *or*-sample and a marginally significant one with the coordinator *and* ($p = 0.06$). These results show that the more frequent phrase is indeed mentioned early. With every log-10 difference, the odds for first mention change by 1.21 in the *and*-sample and by 1.88 in the *or*-sample. Again, collinearity is no cause for concern with low condition numbers for the two samples ($\kappa = 2.1$ for the *or*-sample and $\kappa = 2.09$ for the *and*-sample).

7.6   Interim summary

The multifactorial analysis reveals that the ordering of noun phrases is influenced by a number of factors also shown to be effective on other levels of analysis (see Chapters 5 and 6). It follows that language producers are influenced by a host of different factors also on the level of phrasal ordering. The syntactic complexity (SYNTCOMPL) of phrases also influences the ordering process, with more complex phrases exhibiting a tendency to occur in second, phrase-final position; a result that supports findings for other English alternation phenomena (cf. Wasow and Arnold 2003; Berlage 2010).

8   Results

In this chapter, I discuss the results acquired from the three individual case studies, addressing the hypothesised constraints collectively (Section 8.1) before then turning to discussion of their individual influence (Section 8.2). The findings are thus contrasted with previous research. I also discuss the validity of reductive explanations that were outlined above (see Section 3.7) in light of the obtained results (Section 8.3).

8.1   Overview of results obtained

Before discussing the results in detail, I give an overview of what has thus far been discovered about the effects of hypothesised constraints. Bear in mind that it is the main goal of this book to investigate which variables are needed for an adequate description of order in coordinate constructions of three different types. The individual case studies revealed that not all constraints yield significant results and some effects vary across different case studies or samples. An overview of the results is given in Table 8.1.

This overview of the results reveals interesting patterns. Most importantly it shows that some factors are of an almost universal effectiveness, while others yield no significant results in any of the case studies.

One of the conspicuous results is that the pragmatic and semantic constraints are of an almost general effectiveness and thus influence order in almost all investigated samples. HIERARCHY is the only factor of this group that does not feature in all statistical models. Length/weight differences (LENGTHSYL) and frequency differences (FREQ) were also found to influence ordering decisions across all samples.

Other variables yield a more mixed pattern or are generally missing from the models due to non-significant results. For instance, the variables related to the stress pattern of the constructions (RHYTHM and SYLW) have been found to influence only irreversibles and copulative compounds, except for ULTSTRESS, which is retained only in the model of reversible noun coordinates with *and*. The other phonological factors, viz. VLENGTHFINAL, INIC, SONINIC and SONFINC, yield significant results only in one or two samples. Ordering constraints pertaining to vowel quality (F1, F2, LADE)

Table 8.1 *Overview of results*

Case study	Sample	ICON SEQ	HIERARCHY	CONACC	INF	RHYTHM	SYLW	ULT STRESS	LENGTH SYL	LENGTH PHO	MORPH COMPL	SYNT COMPL	VOIC FINC	VOIC INIC	SON INIC	SON FINC	VLENGTH FINAL	F1	F2	LADE	FREQ
Coordination of compound constituents	Complete Sample	*	–	*	n.t.	*	*	–	*	–	–	n.t.	–	*	–	–	*	*	–	–	*
	COCA sample	*	–	*	*	*	*	–	*	–	*	n.t.	–	*	–	–	*	*	–	–	*
Coordination of bare NPs (binomials)	Irreversibles	*	*	*	n.t.	*	*	–	*	–	–	n.t.	–	–	*	–	–	–	–	–	*
	and (types)	*	*	*	n.t.	–	–	*	*	–	–	n.t.	–	–	–	–	–	–	–	–	*
	and (tokens)	*	*	*	*	–	–	*	*	–	–	n.t.	–	*	–	–	–	–	–	–	*
	or (tokens)	*	–	*	*	–	–	–	*	–	–	n.t.	–	–	–	–	–	–	–	–	*
Coordination of complex NPs	*And*	*	*	*	*	–	n.t.	–	*	n.t.	n.t.	*	n.t.	n.t.	n.t.	n.t.	n.t.	n.t.	n.t.	n.t.	*
	Or	*	*	*	*	–	n.t.	n.t.	*	n.t.	n.t.	*	n.t.	n.t.	n.t.	n.t.	n.t.	n.t.	n.t.	n.t.	*

n.t. = not tested; * = statistically significant effect; – = not statistically significant

were found to not significantly influence the ordering process, with the exception of F1, which yielded a significant result with compounds. Thus, these factors do not appear to be of general importance for the ordering process.

Having discussed the statistical significance of the individual constraints, I now turn to a comparison of the different effects. I approach this issue from two perspectives. First, I discuss how strong a particular effect is compared to others. This strength is dependent on how often a given constraint is adhered to, as opposed to how often it is violated. In statistical terms this means a comparison of *effect sizes* (see Gries 2009: chapter 4).

A second perspective is to investigate which factors allow us to best predict orderings, which is referred to as the *coverage* of ordering constraints. This is a different issue, as there may be constraints that are hardly ever violated and thus have a large effect size (e.g. ICONSEQ) but do not apply to many data points. Such variables therefore predict order in only a small share of the sample and thus have low coverage. In contrast, constraints that allow for a large number of correct predictions have a high coverage and are therefore of great importance for the empirical analysis. This second analysis is therefore also termed a comparison of *overall importance* (see Szmrecsanyi 2013: 82).

First I turn to the question of differing strengths (effect sizes) of constraints. In order to compare these, we may use the effect size measures provided by the statistical models calculated in the empirical chapters (Chapters 5–7). When dealing with nominal/categorical variables, as for instance with the semantic variables in the present study, this can be done by a simple comparison of their coefficients. For instance, with the token sample featuring *and* we find that ICONSEQ with a coefficient of 2.34 has a stronger effect than CONACC with a coefficient of 0.95.[1] However, such a comparison is not immediately possible with scalar variables (LENGTHSYL, FREQ, SYNTCOMPL, SONINIC, SONFINC), as the coefficients only indicate the effect of every one-unit change of the respective variable. For example, on the phrasal level with constructions containing the coordinator *and*, for LENGTHSYL we obtain a coefficient value of 0.1, which corresponds to an odds ratio of 1.11. This means that for every syllable by which a constituent is shorter than its coordinand, the odds of it being placed in first position change by 1.11 or 11%. However, this value cannot be directly compared to the results of the variable frequency in the same model (coefficient = 0.21, odds ratio = 1.23), since both variables run on different scales, viz. the length difference in syllables and a logarithmic frequency difference respectively. This problem of limited comparability also arises

---

[1] The coefficient values are on a common linear interval scale which makes it possible to directly compare their magnitude numerically, which is not the case with other measures of effect size such as odds ratios (cf. Pampel 2000).

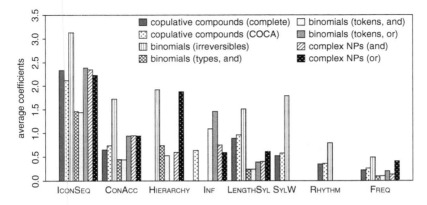

Figure 8.1 Average coefficients of ordering constraints across samples

with the comparison of nominal values to scalar ones. One way of coming to terms with it is to calculate a mean effect size, which indicates the effect the variable exerts on average when it is active in the ordering process. In order to arrive at this value, I calculated the mean of all values of a given variable for cases when it was not 0, hence when there was actually a difference between the two constituents regarding the contrast the variable denotes.[2] The calculation is based on absolute values, so that positive and negative values do not cancel each other out. This way, the procedure is also applicable to nominal variables because their absolute value is always 1, since they can only take on the values +1 or −1, when active. The resultant mean was then multiplied by the original coefficient β_x in the model. For example, as the average length difference in syllables for complex NPs coordinated by *and* is 4.01 syllables, a multiplication with the coefficient yields a value of 0.40324. These mean coefficient values were calculated for all significant variables and are reported in the bar chart in Figure 8.1.[3]

Perhaps the most conspicuous result is that across all samples iconic sequencing (IconSeq) is the variable that exerts the strongest effect;

---

[2] If we took the mean of all values, some variables which are only effective in a small number of cases, e.g. IconSeq, would yield very low values, which would then not be representative of their true effect.

[3] This method of normalising coefficients for comparative purposes deviates from standard procedures. These usually involve subtracting the mean from every value and dividing it by one or two of the variable's standard deviations (see Gelman and Hill 2007; Gries 2009). However, this is not done here because mean-centred coefficients, which result from the aforementioned procedures, are problematic in the present case due to a missing intercept in the model (see Chapter 4). As positive values in our data signify an adherence to and negative ones a violation of a particular constraint, a subtraction of the mean would render the coefficient values impossible to interpret.

i.e. when there is an extra-linguistic temporal or logical ordering, it is almost always reflected in the order of constituents.

In most samples, second in terms of effect size are the other semantic constraints, as well as differences in information status (INF).[4] This result ties in with other studies that also observed a dominance of semantic factors (Cooper and Ross 1975; Müller 1997; Benor and Levy 2006). This finding is discussed in greater detail when turning to a processing interpretation of the results (see Chapter 10).

The factor pertaining to the length difference between the two constituents (LENGTHSYL) and the constraints related to the stress pattern of coordinate constructions (RHYTHM, SYLW, ULTSTRESS) yield medium effect sizes. The other phonological constraints (VLENGTHFINAL, INIC, SONINIC and SONFINC) are found at the lower end of the effect-size spectrum.

The variable with the lowest average effect size in all models is frequency (FREQ). The varying strengths of effects naturally raise the question as to what motivates these varying influences. An explanation and an attempt to model these outcomes will be provided in Chapter 10, which addresses the results from a perspective of language production.

Now that we have an idea of the different constraints' average strengths of effect, let us turn to the second dimension of comparison: the exploration of the overall importance of constraints. Are the variables with the greatest effect size also the ones that allow us to make a large number of correct predictions? This does not necessarily have to be the case, as some of the variables such as CONACC may only seldom be violated and thus yield large effect sizes. However, they apply only to a small subset of the data, as in most cases no difference with regard to conceptual accessibility is observed. The effect sizes of other variables may be considerably weaker, but they are almost always effective, hence they allow for correct predictions in a greater number of cases. In order to address this question quantitatively, several alternative regression models were built, which contained only one variable or a small selection of constraints. Figure 8.2 illustrates the percentage of correct predictions of these models. The columns display the percentage of correct predictions of models containing only the listed variable(s).

If we focus on the leftmost columns featuring models containing only the variable ICONSEQ – the constraint leading in terms of effect size – we observe that a monofactorial model that considers only iconic sequencing predicts only between 4% and 10% of the data correctly, depending on the sample. Even the three semantic factors, when considered together, explain a share below 25%. Only with irreversibles is the number higher, as here they explain

---

[4] Except for the COCA sample of copulative compounds, where LENGTHSYL features in second place.

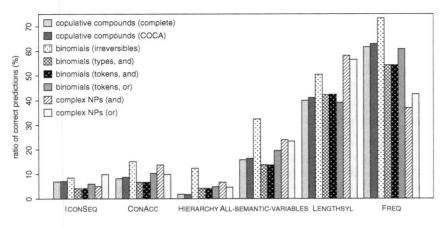

Figure 8.2 Percentage of correct predictions of alternative models

32.4% of the data (for a comparison of reversibles and irreversibles, see Section 9.2). This is due to the fact that, in most cases, the two constituents do not differ with regard to these constraints. Leading in terms of overall importance are LENGTHSYL and FREQ; length and frequency differences between the constituents alone enable correct predictions in 38–75% of cases. Thus, if we had to rely on just one or two constraints, these two would be the safest bet. But would it then be possible to rely solely upon length and frequency differences for an exhaustive explanation of ordering? The answer is no, because if semantic/pragmatic differences hold between the elements, they usually overrule effects of FREQ and LENGTHSYL, as the comparison of average effect sizes showed. Therefore, we cannot simply leave them out of the equation. This issue relates to a possible reduction of certain variables to others, an issue I will discuss in detail below (see Section 8.3). What becomes apparent is that the variables that yield the greatest effect size are not the ones that also explain a large percentage of the data. For example, we found that the semantic variables generally exert the strongest effects on ordering, yet they explain only a meagre share of the data, as they do not apply to a large portion of the data. In contrast, frequency differences that yielded only a small effect size allow for the highest percentage of correct predictions, as this variable always applies, because it is virtually never the case that two constituents are of the same frequency. These results suggest that there is a negative correlation between overall importance and effect size. However, to my knowledge there is no causal relation between these two measures, and thus there is no straightforward explanation for this pattern. Another conspicuous result of a comparison across samples is that with both measures the values are highest for the group of irreversibles (see Figures 8.1 and 8.2). I will address this result below (Section 8.2).

8.2   Results of individual constraints

In the following, I will discuss the results of all tested constraints individually and thus, metaphorically speaking, turn from the forest to the trees. In doing so, I will compare the results obtained to previous findings.

8.2.1   *Pragmatic and semantic variables*

8.2.1.1   *Information status (INF)*

Differences in information status between to-be-ordered constituents could be shown to influence ordering across all case studies, as INF yielded highly significant results along with positive coefficients in all samples in which it was tested. Hence, language users produce an order from lower to higher information value in coordinate constructions. This finding ties in with works on other order alternations, e.g. *particle placement* (Gries 2003) and *Heavy Noun Phrase Shift* (Arnold et al. 2000). It furthermore corroborates experimental research on coordinate constructions, which yielded similar results (Bock 1977; Bock and Irwin 1980). In explaining this tendency, it has been claimed that a constituent that refers to a given referent is more accessible (Levelt 1989: 99–100), and is therefore produced early, by virtue of the *Accessibility Hypothesis* (see above Section 2.2). Bock and Irwin (1980) reason that this effect plays out on two levels, as it may be related to the referential as well as lexical availability of the relevant constituent. Referential availability means that the concept corresponding to the given referent is more readily available for the further production process, as compared to concepts corresponding to newly introduced referents (see also Gries 2003: 49–52). However, since in most cases it is the same word that is repeated when mentioning the referent a second time, lexical availability can be assumed to also be relevant in a majority of cases. This two-level argumentation means that both the accessibility of a certain concept as well as the availability of the corresponding (lexical or morphological) form may explain the given-before-new tendency. This point is treated in greater detail when discussing factors from a processing perspective (Chapter 10). The relation of the present constraint to length/weight differences, discussed in previous research (Hawkins 1994, 2004), is detailed further when I address reductive accounts (see Section 8.3).

8.2.1.2   *Iconic Sequencing (ICONSEQ)*

The tendency to linguistically mirror the order of an extra-linguistic sequence is very strong in all empirical case studies. Across all samples, if there is either a temporal or a logical order, this is almost always reflected in the order of linguistic constituents. Such orderings fall under what Levelt (1989: 138) terms the 'Principle of natural order', which states that we 'arrange information for expression according to the natural ordering of its content'. Levelt specifies this principle for sequences of temporal order, for which a chronological order is deemed natural. Other ramifications of the principle have not been detailed, yet it seems sensible to assume that it also applies to causal and other logical relations that imply a certain sequence, as these are closely related to temporal sequencing (see also the examples I mentioned in Section 3.1.3, e.g. *elementary school and high school*). In Levelt's (1989) model of language production, natural order affects the macroplanning of the utterance in the so-called *message generation* stage. This stage is part of the conceptualisation process, where it is the goal of the speaker to produce a preverbal message, which is then later expressed using linguistic forms. This natural order has also been related to the Gricean *Maxim of Manner* (Grice 1989) which among other things states 'be orderly', an imperative under which adherence to the chronological principle can be subsumed (see Blakemore and Carston 2005b: 576). The logic is that a cooperative speaker would obey natural order, as it is easier to process for the listener. This interpretation locates the iconicity principle on the level of pragmatics. However, it has also been suggested that an iconic order of elements may be part of the semantics of the coordinating conjunction, which is a suggestion I will address below (see Section 9.3).

8.2.1.3 *Extra-linguistic hierarchy (HIERARCHY)*

This constraint, which predicts that the constituent that is ranked higher in any sort of hierarchy is mentioned first, yields mixed results. It significantly affects the ordering of complex NPs but is not effective in compounds. On the lexical level, it is found to be significant in all samples, excluding those coordinated by *or*. This naturally raises the question as to why this constraint is significant in some but not all samples.

Let us first turn to the investigation of copulative compounds. A likely explanation for the non-significant effect in that sample is the fact that it simply does not apply to many copulative compounds, as hierarchical relations only rarely hold between the two constituents, which usually denote a profession or characteristic of the referent. In only thirty compound types could a hierarchical relation be detected. In eighteen the ordering constraint is adhered to and in twelve it is violated. This 60% adherence rate may emerge as a significant trend once a larger sample is considered. A small sample size may also explain why HIERARCHY does not exert a significant influence on binomials with *or*.

Nevertheless, HIERARCHY is included in most models on the lexical and phrasal levels as a significant predictor. These findings tie in with previous research that revealed a significant effect of similar constraints in binomials (Malkiel 1959; Benor and Levy 2006). It is still not entirely clear why language users exhibit this ordering preference. Cooper and Ross (1975) view the rule as being based on the *Me-First*-principle, as higher-ranking concepts may be more similar to the prototypical speaker. This would be a possible explanation for some hierarchical relations, as entities closer to the speaker may be more accessible and therefore mentioned earlier. This interpretation renders the constraint in close proximity to the variable ConAcc. Such an account, however, leads to certain problematic assumptions regarding the properties of the prototypical speaker, especially with the gender bias, a problem I have mentioned earlier (see Section 3.1). Another explanation is that a hierarchical order reflects the extra-linguistic relations of the two entities in a better way and is therefore easier to process, again by virtue of Grice's maxim of quality. One of the two referents precedes another one in a given hierarchy, a relation thus reflected in the linguistic order of elements. It may even be possible that this constraint also falls under what Levelt termed *natural order* (see Section 8.2.1.2), as the boundaries of the latter principle have not been specified. If, however, hierarchical relations similarly determine order during the message generation stage, it is surprising that this constraint is violated a lot more often than IconSeq (see average effect sizes in Section 8.1 above). The relation of the two constraints to the principle of natural order certainly deserves a more thorough investigation, which should probably involve a comparison of the two effects in an experiment.

8.2.1.4   Conceptual accessibility (ConAcc)
Across all case studies, differences in conceptual accessibility were found to significantly influence ordering; i.e., the conceptually more accessible element precedes the less accessible one.

This result corresponds to and at the same time contrasts with previous research. In a corpus-linguistic study, Benor and Levy (2006) obtain a significant result for this variable on the order in binomials. However, McDonald et al. (1993) test the effect of animacy – one important contributor to conceptual accessibility – on the order of noun phrases in sentential contexts and obtain a negative result (see Section 2.2). Since the results of this variable are of special relevance for the evaluation of language production models, they will be discussed in greater detail in Chapter 10.

8.2.2   Variables pertaining to the stress pattern of coordinate constructions

8.2.2.1   Rhythm (Rhythm)
The principle of stress alternation was found to significantly contribute to the modelling of the ordering process in copulative compounds and in irreversible binomials. In other samples, however, it was found not to be effective. In order to understand this discrepancy, let us examine the explanations given for its effect. These explanations usually make reference to the architecture of the speech production system. During production, nodes that correspond to linguistic forms, or features of linguistic forms, are activated. After having been activated, these nodes undergo a refractory

phase during which they cannot easily be activated again (for an example, see MacKay 1987). Therefore, language users are assumed to avoid such repeated activation by not producing similar forms in close adjacency. One of these avoidance effects is the tendency to alternate stressed and unstressed syllables (Schlüter 2005: 260–77).

But why is this tendency not effective on all investigated levels? Let us address this question by examining every case study individually. Turning first to complex-phrase ordering, remember that we did not expect it to yield a strong influence on that level in the first place. This is because most noun phrases begin with an unstressed syllable (see Schlüter 2009) and thus, combined with the unstressed coordinator, either order would create a lapse. Only if one of the two phrases starts with a stressed syllable can it possibly yield an effect. However, a look at the data shows that this is only seldom the case, as the RHYTHM constraint is active only in *c.* 25% of data points and thus, there may not be enough instances to reach significance. If the speaker's ordering choice was influenced by rhythmic considerations with complex phrases, this would mean that he or she would already know about the stress pattern of both NPs when making the ordering decision. Such an assumption, however, is unlikely. Across different models, it is assumed that language production is incremental to some degree (see Levelt 1989: 24). Hence, the articulation of a word may already begin before the phonological forms of other words of the sentence have been accessed. It is thus likely that the speaker performs a phrasal-ordering decision before the relevant stress patterns are processed (see Stallings et al. 1998: 411). While it has been shown that rhythmic considerations can indeed influence higher-level processes, such as the morphology or syntax of an utterance (Schlüter 2005), rhythmic influences are restricted by the time constraints speakers are subject to, as 'decisions at higher layers cannot be held in unlimited suspense' (Schlüter 2005: 289; see also Berg 1998: 122–3). Levelt (1989: 385) states that in fast speech 'rhythm rules are the first to be disturbed'. While it is still unknown what the time window is at which a reordering of phrases due to rhythmic considerations may still occur, it is likely that it is exceeded in many cases involving complex phrases. Schlüter's (2005) results correspond to this assessment, as none of the rhythm effects she reports require 'looking ahead' over several words, and in Levelt (1989), speech-production model adjustments to avoid stress clashes normally do not involve a 'preview' of more than a single word.[5] This assumption of a limited 'look-ahead' may thus

---

[5] According to Levelt (1989) speakers adjust rhythmic structure by beat movement and through cliticisation. Due to the serial architecture of his model, ordering decisions of words should not be influenced by rhythmic considerations, as these take place on different levels. Further below we interpret our findings in a spreading activation model, which allows for these influences (Chapter 10).

explain why the phrasal level is unaffected by rhythmic considerations, but an effect is observable with copulative compounds, because in compounds the distance between the two constituents is shorter, as no conjunction intervenes.

Another explanation for the results may pertain to the fact that with compounds we did not restrict ourselves to speech data, and the language producer is not under the same time pressure in writing as in speech. This difference is mentioned by Schlüter (2005: 289–91), who argues that in writing the language user is more inclined towards satisfying rhythmic considerations due to having more time available to perform the necessary look-ahead. Turning to the case studies of binomials, we would not expect to find rhythm effects at all because at least a two-words look-ahead is required here, and we need to take into account the intervening coordinator. Corresponding to that assumption, binomials are unaffected, with irreversibles being the only exception. This finding tallies with McDonald et al. (1993: 222), who state that rhythmic considerations 'because of their fragility ... may be most evident in language that is used repeatedly, such as frozen conjunctions'. For more formulaic constructions such as irreversibles, a certain planning or ritualisation process can be hypothesised such that their creation involves a collaboration of speakers until the best-to-process order is chosen, a process that cannot be assumed for cases of ad hoc coordination. This argument ties in with the aforementioned explanation pertaining to look-ahead under time constraints, as it seems sensible to assume that time constraints are not effective to the same degree due to a collaborative planning process with formulaic irreversibles.

In conclusion, the capricious workings of the RHYTHM constraint can be sensibly explained by the varying amount of planning time available to the language user in the production of the different constructions investigated.

8.2.2.2   *Avoidance of ultimate stress (ULTSTRESS)*

The tendency to avoid a stressed ultimate syllable, put forward by Bolinger (1962), was found to influence ordering solely with lexical coordinands linked by *and*, where it reached marginal significance. These results correspond and at the same time contrast with those by Benor and Levy (2006: 253–4). The authors found a significant effect for binomials with *and*, which thus corresponds to the present findings. However, they argue that the avoidance of final stress may be inherited by the typical stress pattern of words, which crucially does not feature terminal stress. As formulaic irreversibles and compounds are undoubtedly closer to word status, it comes as a surprise that it is not effective in these but in ad hoc constructions. What is furthermore puzzling is that ULTSTRESS is effective with *and* but not with *or*. Since the present constraint is only very weakly theoretically motivated and is effective only in two out of six investigated samples where it reaches only marginal significance, it would be tempting to declare it a spurious finding of no greater relevance. However, whether this conclusion is warranted must be clarified by future research.

8.2.2.3   Syllable weight (SYLW)

A heavier main syllable was hypothesised to be preferred in second position, due to greater stress on the second constituent in copulative compounds and coordinated nouns (see Section 3.2.3). This expectation is borne out with compounds and irreversible binomials, but not with the ad hoc formation of binomials. A reason for these results may be the existence or non-existence of stress templates for the respective constructions: copulative compounds show a very stable pattern of stress on the second element (see Plag et al. 2008) which can explain why syllable weight has an effect on their internal order, as having a heavy syllable in second position facilitates this stress pattern. A stress template has also been argued to exist for irreversible binomials, which, according to Müller (1997), is inherited from the typical stress pattern of equally long monomorphemic words. He views this inheritance as a symptom of lexicalisation. In contrast, Benor and Levy (2006) claim that in English both fixed binomials as well as regular coordinations of lexemes bear greater accent on the second element. One interpretation of the current findings is that a stress pattern or template exists solely for irreversibles, or is at least much more pronounced with them, due to their conventionalisation. As the coordination of a sequence of words becomes more conventionalised and thereby lexicalised, it is more likely to be affected by stress preferences, which exist in the form of a pattern/template for irreversible, word-like binomials. Conversely, less conventionalised constructions, such as ad hoc coordinations, are not yet affected. Such a development would render lexicalised irreversibles similar to copulative compounds, which are also characterised by a stable stress pattern.

8.2.3   Length and complexity

8.2.3.1   Phonological length (LENGTHSYL/LENGTHPHO)

The length difference between the two constituents is probably the variable that has received the most attention in the research on irreversible binomials. Corresponding to its importance in previous research, it has been found to yield a significant effect across all case studies.

The short-before-long effect is also a well-known factor in language production research, because it can be directly explained by notions of accessibility, as phonologically shorter forms are believed to be easier to access (e.g. Bock 1987b). However, the finding of a robust short-before-long tendency stands in contrast with a widely cited study, McDonald et al. (1993), which fails to find evidence for this effect on conjunct order in its production experiments and speculates that it may only be found in language that is used repeatedly, for example, in irreversible binomials (McDonald et al. 1993: 222). In contrast, the present results show the length constraint yielding strikingly robust effects across all case studies. The null-result McDonald et al. (1993) obtained could, however, be an effect of their experimental design, which was a recall experiment testing whether length led to a shift of constituent order during recall. Since the NP conjunctions they tested were rather short – all of them were of the structure DET NP *and* DET NP, such as *the manager and the keys* – it may be that subjects had little trouble in remembering their internal order, which may have led to the non-significant effects of length. A re-analysis of their data does in fact lend some weight to this suspicion: there is a trend for subjects to prefer a short-before-long order in NP conjuncts, yet reversals occurred only very rarely (only 7.6% of the NP conjuncts were reversed in their Experiment 1).[6] It is thus possible that in McDonald et al. (1993) the tendency to put short words before longer ones did not reach significance due to the experimental design.

The results we obtained furthermore contrast with assumptions by Stallings et al. (1998), who hypothesised length to influence solely phrase ordering but not word order, as both pertain to different stages in production (see Chapter 7). Our findings, however, indicate a convergence between the phrasal and the lexical level and not a divergence, as the effect persists in binomials and more complex phrases.

In addition to measuring length in number of syllables, I investigated whether the number of phonemes also affected ordering. Contrary to expectations, this variable was not found significant in any of the investigated samples. A closer look at the data reveals, however, that in the case of binomials, the second constituent is longer by between 0.02 (lexical coordination with *and*, types/tokens) and 0.05 phonemes (irreversible binomials, as well as coordination with *or*), even in cases of equal syllabic length. Thus, the phoneme difference is as expected, but it is too small to reach significance. The reasons for that result may well lie in the layered operationalisation I applied, taking into account phoneme length only when syllable length was the same. It can be concluded that phonological length influences the process of ordering elements in coordination. However, the intricate relation between the syllabic and the phonemic level still needs to be further explored. For this, larger samples would be needed, featuring constituents that differ only with regard to one of the two dimensions of length measurement (number of syllables or number of phonemes), while the other is held constant.

---

[6] The data in Experiment 2 yields a reversal rate of 8.75%. It must be noted, however, that the trend to shift NP conjuncts to create a short-before-long order is slight. In Experiment 1, 9% of the conjuncts that were presented in a long-before-short order were shifted, while the ratio of shifted conjuncts was 6.3% for those that were presented in a short-before-long order. (For Experiment 2, the numbers are 9.3% and 6.3% respectively.)

Table 8.2 *Morphological complexity (binomials)*

Configuration	irreversibles	*and* (types)	*and* (tokens)	*or* (tokens)
Second constituent is more complex	46	215	221	81
First constituent is more complex	14	158	160	43
Both are equally complex	199	736	749	332

8.2.3.2   Morphological complexity (MORPHCOMPL)

Morphological complexity influences ordering significantly with compounds, but yields non-significant results with binomials. With copulative compounds, the morphologically more complex constituent is preferred in second position. In interpreting the non-significant effect on the lexical level, we must bear in mind that, due to its correlation with the syllable count, it has only been considered if the two words consist of the same number of syllables, in order to prevent collinearity. Thus, we cannot rule out a possible effect that may simply not manifest itself in the limited number of examples. If we look at the morphological complexity criterion on the lexical level, we see that a clear tendency for the second element to be more complex can be observed (Table 8.2).

These tendencies are not included in the statistical models in their entirety, as in most cases of course the number of syllables also differs. It is possible that an even larger sample of coordinate constructions would yield an independent effect of morphological complexity. Summarising, the evidence for an effect of morphological complexity is equivocal. While with copulative compounds we find conclusive evidence that the language user seems to prefer an order of growing morphological complexity, this is not the case with binomials. The affirmative finding may be viewed as another reflection of a general short-before-long or light-before-heavy tendency.

8.2.3.3   Syntactic complexity (SYNTCOMPL)

Syntactic complexity, measured as the number of nodes of to-be-ordered NPs, exerts a significant influence on ordering (see Chapter 7, above). The phrase that contains more syntactic nodes is preferred in second position, independent of its length in words.

This effect beyond mere length relations has implications for an ongoing debate about how complexity effects are best measured. In most studies, complexity has been operationalised by using a word count of the relevant phrase as a proxy (cf. Arnold et al. 2000). This procedure is justified by Szmrecsanyi (2004: 1031) who claims that when operationalising syntactic complexity, 'researchers can feel safe in using the measure that is most economically [*sic*] to conduct, word counts', as node and word count are

Table 8.3 *Average coefficients of length and syntactic complexity*

	LENGTHSYL	SYNTCOMPL
Coordinator *and*	0.4	0.45
Coordinator *or*	0.61	0.59

highly correlated (similarly Wasow 1997).[7] The results obtained in this study cast doubt on such an operationalisation. If we use a length-normalised measure of the number of syntactic nodes per constituent, this index significantly influences speakers *in addition* to length considerations. To further investigate this issue, I built alternative regression models, which measured the length of constituents in words, not in syllables, which still yielded the result that both length and syntactic complexity jointly influence ordering. In other words, just relying on a word count results in a loss of explanatory adequacy, as both variables are needed for an adequate description. These findings tie in with empirical studies conducted by Wasow and Arnold (2003) and Berlage (2010), who also argue for a separate consideration of the two parameters. In the case study of NP ordering, both variables influence ordering with almost identical mean effect sizes (see Table 8.3 above).

This finding relates to Berlage (2010), who attempts to answer the question as to whether length or syntactic complexity is the more important factor in driving speaker's choices in a number of syntactic and lexical alternations. Berlage (2010: 237) finds that the strengths of the two measures vary with every individual case of variation and concludes 'that the relative strength of each syntactic parameter depends on some additional factors not yet explored'. It is unclear at the moment how our results may contribute to such an attempt, as both parameters have virtually identical (mean) influences on the order variation explored here. Nevertheless, a further exploration of the varying influences of these factors should also take into account the present findings.

The present findings of a shorter/lighter element preceding a longer/heavier one are strongly reminiscent of other observations and theoretical accounts, for example Behaghel's (1928) *Law of Growing Constituents*. Also worth mentioning is the principle of *End Weight*, which also states that heavier elements should follow lighter ones (Quirk et al. 1985). This principle can undoubtedly be related to the present analysis, as it denotes 'the placing of more complex ... units towards the end of the noun phrase' (Quirk et al. 1985: 323), which is exactly what we find.

---

[7] Still, Szmrecsanyi (2004: 1033) concedes that counting nodes would be the 'structural measure which is psychologically most real'.

8.2.4   Further variables related to phonological and phonetic length

8.2.4.1   Vowel length (VLENGTHFINAL/VLENGTHTOTAL):
Vowel length, although widely cited in the literature on binomials, was found to influence ordering only in the sample of copulative compounds. Remember that we investigated this constraint applying two different operationalisations: first, the difference in length of the final vowels was calculated, and then the length of both constituents on the CV-tier was measured, normalising for number of nuclei. Let us discuss each operationalisation in turn.

Remember that we motivated the length difference of the final vowel referring to phrase-final lengthening (PFL). VLENGTHFINAL was found to significantly influence copulative compounds, yet it yielded non-significant results in other samples. A possible explanation for these null results is that relating vowel length and PFL may have been premature. PFL means that forms preceding a phrase boundary are phonetically lengthened and thus stretched longer than they are usually articulated. If this process influences the ordering process, those constituents which can be more easily lengthened may be preferred in second position. However, this is, strictly speaking, not what we tested, as we solely investigated the length of vowels, but not their 'stretchability'. Thus, it may be the case that the connection often made in the literature between PFL and vowel length (e.g. Wright et al. 2005), which led us towards considering the final vowel, is too simplified, which could be an explanation for largely non-significant results of this variable.

Turning to the vowel lengths of all nuclei, we see that it does not yield a single significant result. Thus, no evidence for a short-before-long preference on the CV-tier was found. Remember, however, that in order to avoid collinearity, we coded VLENGTHTOTAL only when length in syllables was the same. Thus, it is possible that an existing influence did not reach significance due to the small number of cases for which we tested the constraint.

8.2.4.2   Voicing of the final consonant (VOICFINC)
A difference between the two constituents with regard to voicing of the final coda was not found to significantly influence ordering in any of the investigated samples. Based on observations by Ross (1982), I hypothesised that the phonetic duration of the second constituent's final nucleus is longer than that of the first due to phrase-final lengthening (PFL). Since voiced codas lengthen a preceding nucleus, an effect of VOICFINC could be expected. However, reservations as to this variable's motivation via PFL once again apply. Strictly speaking, I did not investigate the possibility of lengthening a vowel or the whole constituent, which may be the more relevant character-istic for PFL (see discussion of vowel length in Section 8.2.4.1). Voiced codas lengthen a preceding nucleus regardless of position, but it is not clear if they

themselves or their preceding vowels are also more stretchable than voiceless ones, which may be the more relevant property. Pertaining to this issue, in a recent study Turk and Shattuck-Hufnagel (2007) tested several word shapes and their being affected by PFL. While they found that the phrase-final rime is most strongly affected by it, they do not report an influence of voicing of the coda on lengthening.[8] Thus, it seems likely that voicing has no effect on the possibility of lengthening a phrase-final rime, which could be an explanation for it not influencing ordering decisions significantly. However, more research on this issue is clearly necessary.

8.2.4.3   *Sonority of the final consonant (SONFINC)*

A difference between constituents with regard to the obstruency of the final segment is a significant predictor only in the sample of irreversible binomials. With these, the element featuring the more sonorous ending is preferred in second position. This finding ties in with Cooper and Ross's (1975) study of irreversibles.

The result also tallies with Wright et al. (2005), who claim that binomials should exhibit the same phonological properties as monomorphemic English words. They conducted an analysis of the CELEX database and showed that these are much more likely to end in obstruents than to begin with one. As the irreversibles investigated in this study can be assumed to be more strongly lexicalised than other coordinate constructions that were studied, we may conclude that these also take on more properties of words than cases of ad hoc coordination. This is an interpretation congruent with the findings.

However, an explanation in terms of phrase-final lengthening is also possible. Turk and Shattuck-Hufnagel (2007) find that the coda of the phrase-final rime is the segment that is most strongly lengthened. It is conceivable that lengthening is more easily possible with sonorants than obstruents, which also includes stops.[9] Thus, a sonorous ending may lend itself well to PFL and thereby influence order.

In conclusion, my finding complements the observations made by Cooper and Ross (1975) and Wright et al. (2005), suggesting that SONFINC is a constraint primarily affecting lexicalised constructions. It therefore seems that the prototypical phonological make-up of the English word is inherited by word-like irreversible binomials. Such an explanation fares better in light

---

[8]   Although Turk and Shattuck-Hufnagel (2007) do not explicitly address this variable, their test sample features the present voicing contrast. However, their article does not mention any conspicuous findings regarding its influence.

[9]   It must be acknowledged, however, that there is no acoustic evidence for that possibility, thus it remains speculative at this point. Turk and Shattuck-Hufnagel (2007) test words ending in sonorants as well as obstruents. As they do not reveal their results per item, it is unclear whether differences between the two classes regarding lengthening were observable. Other studies on PFL do not rigorously test different word shapes, and thus do also not shed light on this point.

of the results obtained as compared to relating this constraint to PFL, which cannot explain why the effect is limited to irreversible binomials.

8.2.5   Other phonological and phonetic variables

8.2.5.1   Sonority of initial consonant (SonInic)

While sonority differences between the initial consonants have been found to significantly influence the ordering within binomials in both token samples, negative results have been obtained for the other samples. Thus, with ad hoc formations of binomials, an initially sonorant element is preferred in first position, which is a result tying in with previous studies (Cooper and Ross 1975; Pinker and Birdsong 1979). Since there is no phonological motivation for the effectiveness of this variable, we can only acknowledge this finding. In contrast with the present results, Wright et al. (2005) claim the first element to have the more obstruent beginning, based on observations of the typical phonological make-up of English monomorphemic words. Their claim, however, is not borne out by the data, neither with lexicalised irreversibles nor with other constructions.

8.2.5.2   Number of initial consonants (IniC)

The number of initial consonants significantly influences order only in copulative compounds. Here it is the constituent with fewer consonants that is preferred in first position, corresponding to Cooper and Ross's (1975) original hypothesis. Interestingly the finding cannot be explained by the first element being phonologically shorter than the second. There is even a negative correlation between the short-before-long preference measured in phonemes and the number of initial consonants. If we control for length by creating a sub-sample of compounds in which both elements have the same number of phonemes, the trend still holds: fewer initial consonants are preferred in first position. This finding contrasts with the assumption by Wright et al. (2005) that the first element should have more initial consonants, reflecting phonological characteristics of monomorphemic words. An explanation for this result can be found in the mental node theory by MacKay (1987: 25–7). He argues that, for words with initial consonant clusters, utterance initiation takes longer due to a more complex serialisation process in the syllable onset. In order to ensure an uninterrupted production process, it would thus be advantageous to produce the constituent with the less complex onset earlier. This point is detailed when discussing this variable from a processing perspective in the following chapter.

8.2.5.3   Vowel quality (F1, F2, LADE)

Vowel quality was found to significantly influence order only within copulative compounds. Here it is the order of high vowel before low vowel (F1) that yields a significant result, while the other two operationalisations of vowel quality did not reach significance. Remember that previous studies yielded equivocal results and offered only a weak theoretical motivation for this variable. Interestingly, in previous research the workings of this variable have been shown foremost with asyndetic constructions and in coordinations of monosyllables, and thus in constructions where there is little distance between the two crucial vowels. These findings point to the possibility that vowel height matters only when the two vowels are closely adjacent. If the sequence of a decreasing vowel height is advantageous to the language producer, it would make sense that this effect is strongest if little linguistic material intervenes between the two stressed vowels. My results tally with this observation to the extent that, with copulative compounds, there is little distance between the two constituents, as compounds lack an intervening conjunction. This possible interaction of the constraint with the type of construction investigated should be considered in addressing its yet insufficiently explored theoretical foundation.

8.2.6   *Frequency*

The tendency to order constituents of a higher frequency before less frequent ones was found to be statistically significant across all case studies. Since frequency is generally related to ease of access from the mental lexicon, this finding ties in well with an explanation in terms of accessibility of coordinated elements. Claims pertaining to a possible extraordinary importance of frequency such that other variables can be reduced to it (see Fenk-Oczlon 1989) are addressed below (see Section 8.3).

8.3   Revisiting reductive explanations

In this section, the previously mentioned attempts to reduce the number of variables to the workings of others are discussed in the light of the results obtained (see Section 3.7). McDonald et al. (1993) mentioned the possibility that for irreversible constructions the striving for stress alternation may explain the widely observed short-before-long tendency, as in their data short-before-long was only adhered to in cases that also exhibited stress alternation. Müller (1997) puts forward a similar explanation for German binomials. In contrast, Pinker and Birdsong (1979) caution against a conflation of the two, as their findings indicate that length is active independently of rhythmic considerations. Remember that corresponding to the hypothesis of McDonald et al. (1993), we found RHYTHM only to be effective with irreversibles and copulative compounds (see Chapters 5 and 6). However, since for the two groups both LENGTHSYL as well as RHYTHM were retained in the minimal adequate models, it seems that both are actually needed for an adequate description and none can be explained by the workings of the other. The calculation of the overall importance of the two variables also does not indicate that RHYTHM may explain the short-before-long tendency, as RHYTHM explains only a limited number of cases (47.5% of irreversibles, 19.8%/12.4% of copulative compounds), while length is active in a greater number of cases and makes correct predictions for these (see Figure 8.1, above). McDonald et al. (1993) tested their claim only with orderings of monosyllables contrasted with either iambic or trochaic disyllables (see Section 3.7). A closer look at this sub-group in the data reveals that iambic disyllables do not occur in conjunction with monosyllables in our sample of irreversibles. Thus, the question as to which ordering constraint is dominant with them cannot be answered, as the relevant contrast does not occur in the data. Therefore, McDonald et al.'s (1993) observation may be true for a sub-sample of coordinate constructions, which is empirically largely irrelevant for the present case studies. The results obtained indicate that, for an adequate and complete description of ordering within irreversibles and compounds, both constraints should be kept.

The most far-reaching reductive attempt has been put forward by Fenk-Oczlon (1989), who argues that frequency is *the* variable ultimately responsible for most phonological constraints and also for all semantic factors, except for iconic sequencing. This essentially means that other variables are epiphenomenal, thus mere by-products of frequency. Let us have a look at the results obtained through the regression modelling process in order to discuss this rather sweeping claim. To start off, the good news for Fenk-Oczlon's explanation is that the tendency to put highly frequent elements in first position is significant across all investigated constructions and was therefore kept in all minimal adequate models reported. Thus, the frequency of to-be-ordered constituents is undoubtedly important for the linearisation process. For her sample of freezes, Fenk-Oczlon (1989) claimed that it can account for 84% of all data points. The models that contain only this one constraint, which I calculated above, also inspire optimism regarding the relevance of this constraint, as in a majority of samples frequency is the variable that makes the largest share of correct predictions. For the case studies of binomials, which compare best to her data, these monofactorial models yield a slightly lower value of correct predictions for irreversibles (73.5%) than Fenk-Oczlon's results and considerably lower values for the other samples, ranging from 54 to 60% (see Section 8.1).[10] Nevertheless, since the models containing only this one variable do not seem to be much less accurate in their predictions than the models containing more constraints, it is tempting to agree with Fenk-Oczlon. But my results do

---

[10]   Regression models containing solely the FREQ constraint were built and the percentage of correct predictions was calculated. The exact results are: type sample (*and*) 54.2%; token sample (*and*) 54.2%; token sample (*or*) 60%. On the phrasal level, results are coordinator (*and*) 37.2%, or 42.5%; with copulative compounds 61.7% (complete sample), 63.1% (COCA sample).

not quite confirm her assumption of epiphenomenality of other variables. While models containing frequency as the only constraint may not be that far off the mark, my minimal adequate models show that other variables yield significant results and do improve model fit, as I ensured through the applied model-fitting procedures (see Chapter 4). As a case in point, not a single one contains only the factor iconic sequencing as the only semantic constraint, a prediction following from her claim. All models also contain CONACC and most of them also contain HIERARCHY as significant semantic variables. Furthermore, phonological constraints are also retained, most importantly LENGTHSYL, which is highly significant across all case studies. There is therefore no indication that frequency is the superordinate variable that renders most other constraints epiphenomenal and would therefore be the only variable needed for an adequate explanation. However, since Fenk-Oczlon's assumptions are based on plausible assumptions regarding correlations between frequency and the variables length and conceptual accessibility, let us take a closer look at the relationship of the relevant variables to frequency. A testing of the correlation of frequency and length in syllables in the largest sample of binomials (token sample with *and*) reveals that, although there is a negative correlation, it is not very strong ($r_{pearson} = -0.18$), which does not indicate a complete dependence of the two variables.[11] This low value may be explained by the fact that a rather homogeneous class of words (content words of the same word class) was considered. In contrast, note that Zipf's observation (1949) of the correlation was based on a sample of all words of a given corpus including function words. For conceptual accessibility, which is a nominal variable, a correlation coefficient cannot be calculated. However, we can have a look to see whether its predictions are the same as the ones of the frequency contrast, which we would expect if the two were epiphenomenal. Table 8.4 illustrates both relevant constraints (length difference and conceptual accessibility)

Table 8.4 *Predictions of FREQ cross-tabulated with CONACC and LENGTHSYL (The first number refers to irreversible, the second to reversible binomials with* and)

	LENGTHSYL correctly predicts order	LENGTHSYL wrongly predicts order	CONACC correctly predicts order	CONACC wrongly predicts order
FREQ correctly predicts order	98 / 348	15 / 104	35 / 54	3 / 14
FREQ wrongly predicts order	24 / 138	7 / 195	4 / 22	4 / 29

[11] This rather modest correlation poses no problems for the statistical modelling process, which may be problematic if strong collinearity were to arise.

pitted against frequency in the sample of irreversible and reversible binomials with *and*.

The results in Table 8.4 show that frequency and the other two variables make conflicting predictions in a considerable number of cases (see numbers in bold print). What is particularly interesting about the results is that there are more cases where CONACC and LENGTHSYL correctly predict order and FREQ does not than the opposite. This result tallies with the comparative results from above (see Section 8.1), as FREQ turned out to be a weaker constraint than the other two variables. Based upon these numbers, it can be concluded that relying solely on FREQ as a substitute for CONACC and LENGTHSYL would bring about a considerable loss in predictive accuracy, as, contrary to Fenk-Oczlon's claim, the variables do not make the same predictions.[12] In conclusion, the results obtained do not support the reductive view that frequency is the only variable necessary for an adequate explanation.

Let us turn to another reductive attempt put forward by Hawkins (1994; 2000). In propagating his Early Immediate Constituents principle, Hawkins assumes that the given-before-new principle is epiphenomenal to weight/ length effects during ordering. For example, addressing the order of prepositional phrases, Hawkins (2000: 257) claims that 'pragmatic information status appears to be a by-product of the independent correlation between syntactic weight and givenness'. In a later publication, he is more cautious and concedes that there may be an independent effect of information status (Hawkins 2004: 122–3). Let us observe how this reductive claim fares in the light of our data. Since Hawkins addresses the ordering of phrases but not of smaller elements, it is the ordering of complex NPs for which this claim is most relevant. The fact that both INF as well as the short-before-long tendency are kept in the minimal model for complex phrases can be interpreted as evidence that an epiphenomenality of the discourse-functional level is unlikely. If INF could be reduced to weight, it should not improve the predictive accuracy of our model, once a length/weight factor is considered, because in all cases where a contrast with regard to information status would be found, this would coincide with a short-before-long sequence. However, leaving INF out of the respective models results in a 2–3% loss in predictive accuracy.[13] Therefore, both information status and length are independently at work in influencing order in the coordinated constructions investigated. These results tie in well with similar observations that have been made for Heavy NP shift and particle placement (Arnold et al. 2000; Gries

---

[12] The results obtained here converge somewhat with findings by Gries (2003: 30, note 26), who shows that *concreteness*, which I used as one contributor to CONACC here, yields an effect independent from the variable frequency. In his study on particle placement, the former variable yielded significant results, while frequency failed to do so.

[13] For the sample containing the coordinator *or*, it is 3%, for *and* it is 2%. Note also the gain in accuracy that we obtained for copulative compounds by considering it (see Chapter 5).

2003).[14] However, to Hawkins' credit, it must be said that the findings show that he is right in stressing the importance of length/weight, as it is a factor that predicts order in a large number of cases (see Figure 8.2, Section 8.1). Thus, it could well be termed one of the most important factors for the ordering of elements, even though differences in information status of the constituents cannot be reduced to it. Another relation among variables relevant for the present investigation has been researched by Rosenbach (2005). Rosenbach (2005: 613), focusing on the English genitive variation, addresses the question as to whether 'animacy effects are an artifact of syntactic weight', an assumption that is based on the finding that the two variables are correlated. Similar to the aforementioned findings on the relation between syntactic weight and information status, she finds an independent effect of both factors. Note that animacy was not considered in this work as an independent variable, but as a contributor to conceptual accessibility. Nevertheless, my findings tie in with Rosenbach's results as both CONACC as well as length differences were found to independently influence ordering across all investigated samples.

In conclusion, no evidence for any of the reductive attempts has been found. On the contrary, the results obtained suggest that all variables discussed here independently influence ordering decisions. Thus, this study, as well as the other works cited in this section, strongly suggest that multiple variables independently affect the language user when ordering elements. The greater parsimony of either reductive theory (e.g. Fenk-Oczlon 1989; Hawkins 1994) that may have motivated it would come at the cost of omitting important and significant constraints. These approaches would thus limit our ability to accurately describe the ordering process, as they leave out variables that influence the language user and should therefore be theoretically accounted for.

8.4   Interim summary

As already noted above, not all hypothesised constraints were found to significantly influence the ordering of constituents, while others are found to be effective across all samples. One particularly noticeable result is that the semantic and pragmatic constraints, thus INF, ICONSEQ, HIERARCHY and CONACC, were found to be of almost general relevance, as these yielded significant results in almost all case studies. It could even be shown that there is a tendency for these constraints to outweigh others in terms of effect size. Furthermore, we found also that frequency (FREQ) and length differences (LENGTHSYL) yielded significant results for all samples. Although

---

[14]   This issue is discussed in detail in Gries (2003: 146–56). Even though the phenomenon Gries investigates is particle placement, the explanations he gives also hold true for the present case.

not all operationalisations of length were found to be significant (see Section 8.2.3), we observed a general short-before-long tendency, congruent with other findings on ordering phenomena in English. With complex NPs, we found that both their length as well as their syntactic complexity influence the ordering process, similar to studies on other cases of variation in English (cf. Berlage 2010).

Other variables were found to be not significant in any or only in selected samples. For example, a difference in syllable weight (SYLW) was found to influence ordering if the investigated construction exhibited a clear stress pattern, in accordance with the weight-to-stress principle (see Section 8.2.2.3). The tendency to alternate stressed and unstressed syllables (RHYTHM) influences order only when time constraints do not prevent the language user from performing the necessary look-ahead (see Section 8.2.2.1). A difference in vowel quality (F1) was found to significantly influence ordering only in copulative compounds, possibly due to this constraint being only effective over a short distance. For phonetic constraints, which are motivated by a longer duration of the second constituent (VLENGTHFINAL, SONFINC, VOICFINC), no substantial evidence could be accumulated, possibly due to a weak relation between the process of phrase-final lengthening and these constraints (see Section 8.2.4). While some of the negative results can be convincingly explained, others cannot. With the variables ULTSTRESS, INIC and SONINIC, it is still unclear why they are active in some samples, but not in others.

Moreover, I evaluated reductive attempts mentioned in previous research, which claims that some ordering constraints are epiphenomenal to others. No evidence was found for any of them because the multifactorial analyses yielded the result that none of the relevant variables could be reduced to the workings of other influences (see Section 8.3).

9   A comparative discussion of the results

This chapter offers a comparative discussion of the results obtained along the dimensions of reversibility, the type of coordinator and the linguistic level on which the coordination takes place. We will first have a glance at the differences and similarities among the individual case studies by illustrating the results through multi-dimensional scaling (Section 9.1), before turning to a detailed comparative analysis. This means discussing the similarity and differences between reversibles and irreversibles (Section 9.2), comparing the influences of ordering constraints across the different levels of analysis (Section 9.3) and contrasting the results of the two coordinators *and* and *or* (Section 9.4).

9.1   At a glance: multi-dimensional scaling

I will begin the comparative analysis of the results with an overview of the results of the individual case studies, which provides us with a first impression of differences and similarities. The multifactorial models built for the respective data samples allow for a fine-grained analysis of influential factors, yet interpreting their outcomes is complicated as they yield results for a multitude of factors. It is thus useful to describe the (dis-)similarity between the respective samples in a simpler way, revealing what we may call the 'big picture' in the data. One technique that makes this possible by means of visualisation is *Multi-Dimensional Scaling* (MDS). The essential feature of MDS is that it takes as input values from an unlimited number of dimensions and scales them down to a lower number, in most cases two dimensions, which can be easily plotted in a coordinate system (see Baayen 2008: 146–8). Here we take as input the different coefficients of the variables in the minimal adequate models for the respective samples and scale them down to two dimensions. If certain variables were found non-significant, the value 0 was entered. The output of MDS is values in a two-dimensional coordinate system, which can be interpreted straightforwardly. If two points are close to each other, then the ordering in the corresponding data samples is influenced by similar and similarly strong effects. Conversely, two points that are a great distance from each other denote different coefficients of the variables in the respective models, thus differing forces underlying the order of elements. Note that the resultant axes do not have significance beyond displaying the mentioned (dis-)similarity.[1] Furthermore, two things should be borne in mind before interpreting the resulting figure. First, MDS is not a hypothesis-testing method, and thus great distances in the coordinate system do not license judgements as to a possible statistically significant difference between certain samples. The technique merely visualises the structure in the data we entered and thus must be viewed as an illustrative rather than an inferential method, similar to cluster analysis. Secondly, remember that we did not test exactly the same constraints in all samples for various reasons; for example, contextual factors could only be tested with token samples and syntactic complexity is naturally confined to more complex phrases, etc. I entered o values for those constraints that were not tested with a particular sample. This fact of course limits the comparability of the samples, which should be kept in mind when interpreting the results. The result of the MDS analysis can be seen in Figure 9.1.

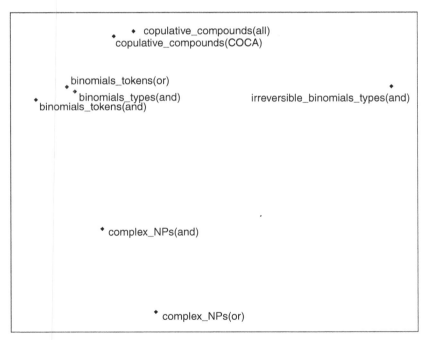

Figure 9.1 Results of multi-dimensional scaling

<hr />

[1] MDS was carried out using the R statistics software package, more specifically the *cmdscale* command. A distance matrix that served as an input for that command was created employing the *dist* function, using the Euclidean distance measure.

Despite these reservations, a number of interesting differences are brought to light by MDS. Most conspicuous is the great distance between the group of irreversibles and all other samples. The characteristic of irreversibility thus leads to the greatest distinction among the samples we investigated. We can furthermore observe that the different levels of analysis form relatively homogeneous groups. The two samples of copulative compounds are not very distant, which is hardly a surprise since the samples of the two groups strongly overlap. In addition, the binomial constructions are closely grouped together, and this group is relatively similar to the samples of copulative compounds. The coordination of complex NPs is placed at a greater distance from the other groups. However, when interpreting these results we should remember that we did not test exactly the same factors across the three levels for reasons discussed above (see Chapter 3). Thus, the greater distance between the complex NPs and the other constructions may be a result of this; we tested fewer constraints with that group. With regard to the coordinating conjunction, no big differences can be detected in the group of binomials, while there is a certain distance between the two samples of complex NPs, which are discussed in Section 9.4.

Thus, although the results of MDS are not entirely conclusive, the most dramatic difference seems to be between irreversibles and reversibles, which we will discuss in detail in the following section. The seemingly smaller differences in the other two dimensions, viz. investigated level and type of coordinating conjunction, will be discussed subsequently (Sections 9.3 and 9.4).

9.2   Comparing reversible and irreversible binomials

Let us turn to answering one of the leading research questions of this study, which addresses whether the classes of irreversibles and reversible coordination differ with regard to ordering influences. The results of MDS in the preceding section hint at large differences between these two groups, a finding I will now discuss in detail.

First, let us explore whether the same factors are at work during ad hoc coordination that we find with irreversible, lexicalised constructions. Remember that the strong focus on irreversibles in prior research provided the starting point for this book, as I set out to investigate whether observed influences reach beyond this class (see Chapter 1). The results discussed in Chapter 8 clearly show that reversible constructions are also influenced by ordering constraints found in irreversibles, and thus they are found to be of more general validity. Hence, the 'unimpaired freedom of variation' that Malkiel (1959: 116) suspected for reversible binomials does not appear to exist. Generally speaking, there is a large overlap among factors responsible for ordering in irreversibles and cases of ad hoc coordination. However, differences between the two groups were also observed, which I shall discuss in the following. Remember that we found irreversibility to be first and foremost a lexical phenomenon. On the level of compounds and with complex noun phrases, we found only a few irreversible instances (see also below Section 9.3). Therefore, the following discussion is restricted to a comparison of irreversible and reversible binomials.

When discussing influences of the individual constraints, we already noted that some factors are active in irreversibles but not in other constructions, while others are almost universally effective. In the latter group are the length (LENGTHSYL) and frequency (FREQ) of to-be-ordered constituents and the semantic/pragmatic variables, ICONSEQ, CONACC and HIERARCHY, all of which were found to influence order in almost all investigated samples. Differences with regard to influential variables between the two groups primarily concern constraints related to the stress pattern of the coordinate construction, RHYTHM, SYLW and ULTSTRESS. It was noted above (Section 8.2.2.1) that an effect of RHYTHM may be related to a greater planning and ritualisation process during the emergence of irreversibles (cf. McDonald et al. 1993), while the effect of SYLW can be explained by a stress template that affects lexicalised, irreversible binomials (see Section 8.2.2.3). Another factor differentiating the two groups is SONFINC, as a sonorant final segment was preferred in irreversibles but not in other constructions. This variable was motivated by Wright et al. (2005) based on the typical phonological shape of monomorphemic words. This latter point brings us to a discussion of theoretical accounts that may be given for the differences between reversibles and irreversibles. One explanation would be that irreversibles share crucial phonological properties with monomorphemic words by virtue of analogy: as irreversible binomials are more strongly lexicalised, they may exhibit greater similarity with monomorphemic words than reversible coordinate constructions. Arguments corresponding to this view are found in the literature: Müller (1997) states that, with regard to their phonological properties, German irreversible binomials resemble monomorphemic words and Wright et al. (2005) motivate constraints for English binomial formation by referring to the same logic. We may term this assumption the *Lexical Unit Hypothesis* (LUH). The results for the variable SONFINC are perfectly in agreement with LUH: similar to English monomorphemic words, irreversible binomials prefer a sonorant final segment, while reversibles do not. However, other hypothesised properties were not found: no tendency for initial consonant clusters (INIC) or obstruent beginnings (SONINIC) was found with irreversibles, both of which are properties of monomorphemic words (cf. the empirical analysis based on the CELEX database in Wright et al. 2005: 536). A further similarity between irreversible binomials and monomorphemic words may be found in the stress pattern of irreversibles. Müller (1997) argues that German binomials exhibit the same stress pattern as equally long monomorphemic yet polysyllabic words. The standard of comparison in our cases would be monomorphemic words that are three to five syllables long, as the majority of irreversibles is made up of cases in which the first constituent is monosyllabic and the second is one to three syllables long. What renders a comparison problematic is the fact that polysyllabic words in English do not show a consistent stress pattern, and monomorphemic words of such lengths are infrequent. An explanation of the stress pattern of irreversibles in terms of LUH is therefore not very plausible for English, as there is no systematic pattern frequent enough to serve as a model for a process of analogy. Concluding, LUH can explain only one difference between the two groups, which concerns the sonorant ending of irreversibles. There is thus only little evidence that irreversibles are shaped according to the typical phonological shape of English words. Apart from the differences with regard to influential variables, certainly the most conspicuous difference between the two groups is the very high predictive accuracy of the model built for the sample of irreversible binomials, which allows us to correctly predict 84.2% of the data. For reversible binomials featuring *and*, formally similar to irreversibles, we obtain only a value of 60.6% (see Chapter 6). Interestingly, Benor and

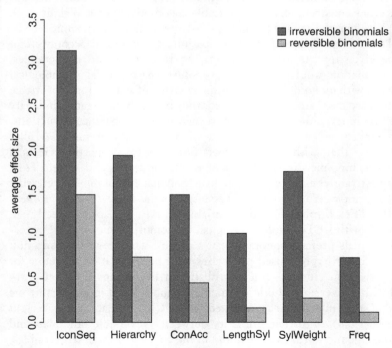

Figure 9.2 Average effect sizes of ordering constraints in irreversible and reversible binomials

Levy's (2006) model, which jointly considered reversible and irreversible binomials, made around 77% correct predictions, which is a value falling in between these two numbers. The higher accuracy of the model for irreversibles means that ordering constraints predict their internal order much more precisely than in reversible constructions. Two effects may be responsible for that result: first, it could be the case that ordering constraints are less often violated in that group; secondly, the ordering constraints may influence a greater share of data points in the sample of irreversibles. Since the variables investigated are based on differences between the to-be-ordered constituents, one may ask whether the to-be-ordered constituents in the group of irreversibles generally exhibit more pronounced contrasts. I will discuss these assumptions individually, starting with the question of violation of/adherence to ordering constraints.

We can explore this issue by comparing the effect sizes of constraints across irreversible and reversible binomials. One expression of effect sizes in the model output are the coefficient values, which correspond to the violation of/adherence to ordering constraints – the greater the coefficient value, the fewer violations of the respective ordering constraint. The mean coefficients of predictors shared between the two groups are displayed in Figure 9.2 (see Section 8.1 on standardising the coefficients).

The uniformly higher bars for irreversible binomials in Figure 9.2 denote greater effect sizes for all constraints in that group, which indicates that constraints are much less often violated. This means that irreversible binomials adhere to ordering constraints more strictly than their reversible counterparts. Let us have a more detailed look at the effects of the two most important scalar variables length (in number of syllables) and frequency. Figure 9.3 shows the two constituents' average values regarding these constraints in irreversible and reversible binomials sensitive to their position.

Figure 9.3 shows that there are clear tendencies for the more frequent and shorter constituent to be in first position in both samples. Yet the slopes in the figure differ between the two groups. The greater slopes for irreversibles reveal that, regarding length and frequency, the contrasts between constituent 1 and constituent 2 are much more pronounced in that sample. Furthermore, the constituents in first position are conspicuously shorter and more frequent than their counterparts in the sample of reversibles. This greater pronouncedness brings us to the second possible difference between irreversibles and reversibles, which poses the question as to whether the constituents in the first group generally exhibit more contrasting properties and thus are more dissimilar to each other than those in the latter class. This can be easily tested: starting with semantic contrasts, if the two constituents differ more strongly along semantic/conceptual dimensions, then a greater percentage of them should be influenced by semantic ordering constraints than in the reversible class, regardless of whether these

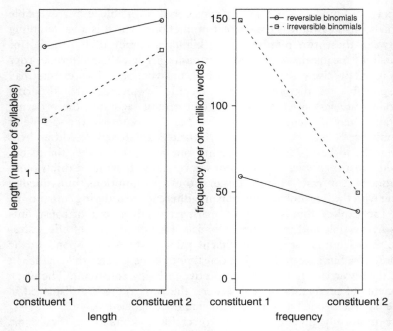

Figure 9.3 Frequency/length of constituents by position in irreversible and reversible binomials

constraints are adhered to or not. Figure 9.4 displays the percentages of data points that are influenced by the semantic ordering constraints we investigated in irreversible and reversible binomials.

The result of greater contrasts between constituents is clearly borne out for the class of irreversible binomials: the higher bars for this class show that all semantic factors are more frequently active in irreversibles than in reversibles.[2] The two rightmost bars indicate that at least one semantic constraint is active in 37.1% of all irreversible binomials, while this is true for only 20.1% of reversibles. A second area worth scrutinising is if the hypothesis of a greater contrast is also true for the two aforementioned scalar variables length and frequency. The bar chart in Figure 9.5 displays the average differences between the two constituents along these dimensions for irreversible and reversible binomials, disregarding the issue of a possible adherence to/violation of corresponding ordering constraints.

---

[2] Chi-square tests yield significant results for all pair-wise comparisons: IconSeq: $\chi^2 = 4.94$, df = 1, p = 0.027, $\varphi = 0.07$; Hierarchy: $\chi^2 = 20.67$, df = 1, p < 0.01, $\varphi = 0.12$; ConAcc, $\chi^2 = 9.67$, df = 1, p < 0.01, $\varphi = 0.08$; Total: $\chi^2 = 29.50$, df = 1, p < 0.01, $\varphi = 0.15$.

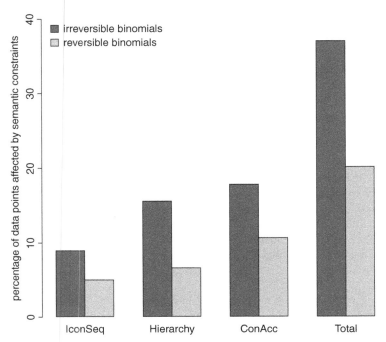

Figure 9.4 Semantic constraints in irreversible and reversible binomials

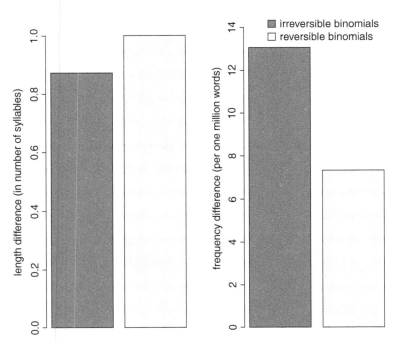

Figure 9.5 Length and frequency differences in irreversible and reversible binomials

Regarding length, the average difference between constituents in irreversibles is 0.87 syllables, while it is 1.0 syllables in reversibles, hence the
contrast between the constituents is actually greater with reversibles.
However, a t-test reveals that this difference is only marginally significant
($t = -1.77$, df = 372, p = 0.08). With regard to frequency, the assumption of
greater contrasts in irreversibles is borne out, as the frequency difference is
more pronounced in that group (13.06 per 1 million words), than in the group
of reversibles (7.32 per 1 million words) which constitutes a statistically
significant difference ($t = 2.38$, df = 308, p < 0.05). In summary, the
empirical investigation of contrasts yields the result that there are in fact
conspicuous differences between irreversible and reversible binomials: the
to-be-coordinated constituents in the former group exhibit greater contrasts
or dissimilarities on all semantic dimensions, as well as with regard to their
lexical frequency. This means that corresponding ordering constraints
influence a larger share of the data, or yield more pronounced effects in
that group.

With regard to contrasts and similarities of to-be-ordered constituents, a
further possible difference between reversible and irreversible binomials is
worth investigating. Gries (2011) shows that idioms of the structure V-NP,
such as *bite the bullet* are characterised by alliteration much more often
than non–idiomatic expressions of the same structure. Since irreversible
binomials may very well be argued to also belong in the class of idioms (see
Chapter 2), the question arises as to whether this holds true for them as well.
A cursory look at the data already reveals a number of alliterating examples in
that class: e.g. *bread and butter*, *house and home*, *life and limb*. A quantitative
analysis of the samples of irreversibles and reversibles confirms that impression. In irreversible binomials, 15.8% of all instances feature the same initial
phoneme, while this is true of only 7.9% of the data in reversible binomials
(see Figure 9.6).

The result for alliteration shows that, while the coordinated constituents
in irreversible binomials show more pronounced contrasts on a number of
dimensions, there is also a property revealing a greater similarity between the
constituents in that class.

In conclusion, the main findings are the following. All investigated
ordering constraints are more strictly adhered to in irreversible binomials, which is reflected in the greater effect sizes in the model.
Irrespective of adherence rate, the to-be-ordered constituents show more
pronounced contrasts to each other, as a greater share is affected by relevant
semantic ordering constraints, and differences in frequency are more
pronounced.

The question arises how these differences between the two groups can be
accounted for. The explanation I propose is what I term the 'selection
pressures hypothesis'. Most ordering constraints are more often active and
more strictly adhered to in the sample of irreversibles, as compared to

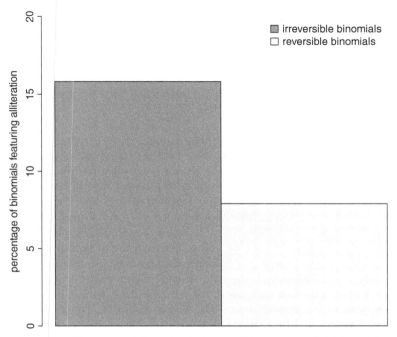

Figure 9.6 Alliteration in irreversible and reversible binomials

reversibles. If we adopt a somewhat Darwinian perspective and view these constraints as 'selection pressures' that weed out some and facilitate other orderings (see Pinker and Birdsong's 1979: 506), we observe that irreversibles do in fact better satisfy these pressures. Hence, it is possible that adhering to these constraints may lead to the emergence or selection of irreversible binomials in a diachronic process such as the following: certain orderings in ad hoc coordination are more preferable for the language user than others, which are those that adhere to ordering constraints. It is likely that these preferences relate to a greater ease of processing, which is an argument that I will flesh out in Chapter 10. Some of these preferred instances become ritualised and irreversible, concomitant with a high frequency of use. It seems only logical that the linguistic community would choose those instances for this process which are easiest to produce and process, in conforming best to existing constraints. What remains to be explained is how the ordering constraints relate to ease of processing exactly, and how the alliteration tendencies observed in irreversibles break the pattern of greater contrasts in that class. A processing account of these characteristics will be given in Section 10.3, where I will also discuss the representation of irreversibles in the mental lexicon.

9.3   Comparing the different levels of analysis

Another interesting dimension of comparison is to investigate whether ordering influences vary across the different levels of analysis and thus across the different case studies. In doing so, I will address two questions: first, whether the same influences affect order, and second, whether their effects are of equal strength on the different levels.

The first question relates to the study by Cooper and Ross, who asked whether orderings on different levels 'obey a single class of freezing principles' (Cooper and Ross 1975: 99). With regard to the present case studies, this question can largely be answered in the affirmative, as it is mostly the same constraints that are active across all samples. Thus, most ordering principles seem to be general tendencies that are not bound to a specific level of coordination. Nevertheless, differences between the case studies can also be detected. These pertain mostly to contrasts between compounds and binomials, as certain constraints are only effective in the former, but not in the latter group. One variable exhibiting that contrast in affecting only compounds is syllable weight (SYLW). Already above (see Section 8.2.2) I put forth the explanation that this effect is due to the existence of a stable stress template of copulative compounds, which may influence the order of elements. The other difference pertains to an effect of stress alternation (RHYTHM), which I argued is contingent on the amount of look-ahead that can be performed during production. Since the distance between compound constituents is smaller than on the other two levels, the necessary look-ahead is also smaller, which is why effects of euphony may play out more strongly on that level.

Despite these differences, it is largely the same influences that underlie ordering across levels. This correspondence ties in with an important result of language production research. In an analysis of speech errors, Shattuck-Hufnagel (1979) shows that erroneous exchanges of elements occur on all levels of language, from phonemes to phrases. Based on the error data, she suggests a serialisation model that assumes the same serial-ordering mechanism on all levels in language. If the same mechanism is thus responsible for ordering on all investigated levels, it makes sense that ordering influences are the same across them. I will detail this mechanism in the upcoming chapter (see Chapter 10).

The second question of possible differences pertains to the strengths of influences on the different levels of analysis. This issue was also mentioned by Cooper and Ross (1975), who suggest that the strengths of ordering principles are dependent on the linguistic level that is investigated. They sketch out a scale, which rests on the assumption that the lower the to-be-ordered elements are in the linguistic hierarchy, the stronger the ordering principles should be. Let us have a look at an extract of that hierarchy (Figure 9.7; from Cooper and Ross 1975: 99).

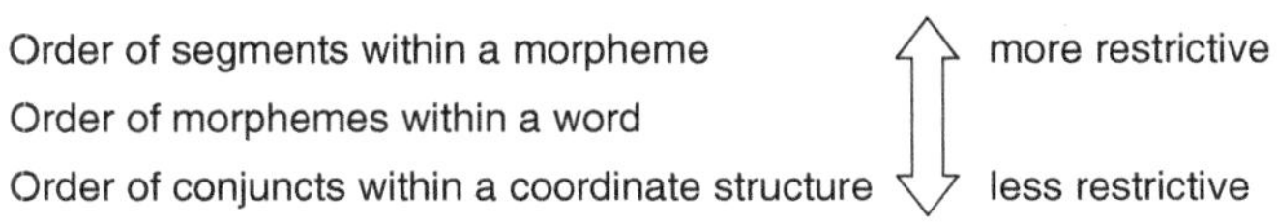

Order of segments within a morpheme	⟨	more restrictive
Order of morphemes within a word		
Order of conjuncts within a coordinate structure	⟨	less restrictive

Figure 9.7 Ordering constraints across linguistic levels

In terms of evidence for the hierarchy, Cooper and Ross provide a number of linguistic examples: for the order of segments within a morpheme, they refer to *Ablautverdoppelungen* such as *zigzag*, while for the order of morphemes within a word they mention compounds of somewhat unclear status; e.g. *Northwest*. Crucially, reversals do not occur in these examples, as **zagzig* or **Westnorth* are not possible, exemplifying the very restrictive order on lower levels. The order of constituents in irreversible binomials is, however, less restrictive, as it can be reversed in exceptional cases: for example, while *day and night* is considered an irreversible binomial by Cooper and Ross (1975), the reversal *night and day* is also possible. Based on similar observations, Ross (1982: 278) puts forward the first *Principle of Myopia*, which states that 'the shorter the elements that are coordinated, the stronger the laws that govern their order'. As lower-level elements are in general also shorter, this hypothesis corresponds to Cooper and Ross's original claim. What remains somewhat unclear about these two hypotheses is to which population of constructions the differing restrictiveness applies, as only irreversible instances are dealt with in the relevant articles. It is thus unclear whether completely reversible coordination is within the scope of their claims. If we interpret Cooper and Ross's (1975) restrictiveness scale as affecting *all* constructions that may potentially become irreversible, it becomes relevant to our findings, as the strengths of effects and the ratio of irreversibles across the different levels of analysis can be compared, as a measure of restrictiveness. Above I mentioned that irreversibles are a phenomenon affecting foremost the level of binomials. On the level of copulative compounds, 3.1% of the types were found to be irreversible,[3] while with binomials the number was 10.5%. On the level of complex NPs, almost no irreversible instances were detected. Thus, based on our data, it is not the case that more order-restricted data points are found on lower levels, as irreversibility was not found to be more pronounced with compounds. We must be cautious in interpreting these results, however, as we did not investigate a truly random sample on the level of copulative compounds but a selection based on the most typical endings of constituents (see Chapter 5).

---

[3] Since copulative compounds are considerably less frequent than binomials, the frequency threshold for reversibility was relaxed for them. Instead of 10 per 100 million, a frequency of 10 per 385 million (the size of the COCA corpus) was considered adequate.

Comparing the predictive accuracies of the statistical models on the respective levels – which we may view as an indicator of strength of the ordering constraints – yields the following pattern: with copulative compounds, the models predict about 70% of the orderings correctly, while on the lexical level, this number is only slightly lower, with values between 60% and 70%, disregarding for the moment the group of irreversibles. With complex NPs, we also achieve an accuracy of around 70%. A closer look at the effect sizes of individual constraints (see Figure 8.1 in Chapter 8) reveals the same pattern: generally speaking, effect sizes are slightly higher for compounds, then drop with reversible binomials and rise again with the sample of complex NPs. Hence no striking inter-level differences with regard to the strength of constraints can be detected. Consequently, no evidence for the *Principle of Myopia*, relating length of elements and constraint strength, has been accumulated. While the elements forming copulative compounds are not shorter than the coordinated nouns we investigated, complex NPs are clearly longer than elements on the other two levels; a difference thus could be hypothesised based on Ross's (1982) principle. In conclusion, no evidence for the two hypotheses by Cooper and Ross (1975) and Ross (1982) relating linguistic level and strengths of constraints was found. However, it is possible that their predictions would be borne out, once we have interpreted them more narrowly and considered solely irreversible constructions, including also *Reim-* and *Ablautverdoppelungen*. However, this was not what I set out to do.

Another theory whose predictions may be of relevance for the interpretation of the present results is put forward by Berg (2009). Berg develops a model that makes predictions regarding the cohesion of units on different linguistic levels. He shows that the morphological level, generally speaking, shows greater cohesion than the lexical and syntactic ones, by virtue of a greater pervasiveness and strength of hierarchical structure. He shows that coordination, which naturally lacks hierarchical organisation, is more infrequently found on lower levels. Evidence for this claim is that coordinate compounds, such as the ones I investigated, are much scarcer than binomials and coordinated NPs, as most compounds are determinative and thus feature hierarchical structure (Berg 2009: 134, see also Chapter 5). The explanation he offers for these inter-level differences comes from language processing: a lack of hierarchical structure means that the order of elements is not fixed and that two (or potentially more) constituents are activated and compete for first position (see also Chapter 10 for a detailed description of this process). This competition and selection process makes unhierarchical structures harder to process, as the order of constituents is not already determined through a structural frame. Since the number of units that are uttered in a time unit is much higher on lower levels, and since more phonemes are uttered per minute than words, these processing difficulties become much more acute there. To counter this problem, the linguistic system implements more structure on lower levels. Conversely, on higher levels, where time constraints are looser, the absence of hierarchical structure is less of a problem.

The present study complements Berg's (2009) account, as it takes a closer look at unhierarchical, viz. coordinate constructions across linguistic levels. Since, according to his model, more structure is needed on lower levels, a possible assumption would be a higher ratio of irreversibles on lower levels, corresponding to the claim by Cooper and Ross (1975). This is, however, not what we find. In contrast, the results obtained show that once we investigate solely unhierarchical constructions, differences in cohesion largely disappear and ordering constraints influence ordering similarly on all levels. Taken together, Berg's theory and the suggestion of a common serialisation mechanism by Shattuck-Hufnagel (1979) may provide a complete explanation of the occurrence of coordinate constructions and the order within them across linguistic levels. Since time constraints are more pressing on lower levels, the system becomes more hierarchical, as we move down the linguistic hierarchy. This explains why we find more coordination on higher levels. However, once hierarchical structures let serialisation 'free', the same mechanism kicks in, which explains the similar effects of ordering constraints across levels.

9.4   Different coordinators and ordering: *and* versus *or*

A further comparative perspective on the results pertains to the choice of conjunction. It is relevant for the two case studies of syndetic coordination: binomials and complex NPs. The comparison between *and* and *or* relates to an ongoing discussion as to whether a different semantics of the two conjunctions may have an influence on constituent ordering (for an overview, see Blakemore and Carston 2005b). This discussion focuses mostly on certain (exceptional) contexts, where a temporal sequence becomes part of the propositional content of the utterance. See the examples below for an illustration:

(61)   a. He started his car and drove away.
       b. He drove away and started his car.
       c. He started his car or drove away.
       d. He drove away or started his car.

The reversal of the first two verb phrases coordinated by *and* (61a, b) results in a different interpretation, while this is not the case in the examples with *or* (61c, d). It has been hypothesised that the meaning of the coordinator *and* is similar to *and then* in these cases, which means to locate temporal order within the semantics of that conjunction (see Dik 1972).[4] In contrast, the interpretation of temporal sequence could be due to pragmatic inferencing, as assuming a chronological order is the most natural interpretation (see Blakemore and Carston 2005b; see also Section 8.2.1.2 on Levelt's (1989) principle of natural order). The latter view crucially locates the effect outside the conjunction's semantics. How do the present results relate to this discussion?

Since we captured cases of temporal sequence by the ordering constraint iconic sequencing (IconSeq), we may check whether its effect differs between the two coordinators. If this temporal sequence is to be located within *and*'s but nor *or*'s semantics, the effect should be stronger for those samples featuring the former conjunction. Contrasting with that assumption, however, no such difference is observed: iconic sequencing yields largely the same, strong effect across the case studies irrespective of the coordinator. While with complex NPs the effect size in the two samples is nearly the same, with binomials the effect of IconSeq is even stronger with *or* as compared to *and*. These results thus tie in well with the interpretation that iconic sequencing is a principle best described outside the semantics of coordinators.[5] It is compatible with accounts that claim that coordinating conjunctions have only low semantic value, with *and* denoting a 'completely unspecific combinatory value' and *or* 'indicat[ing] there is an alternative or choice' (Dik 1972: 268, 275).

Let us turn to possible differences of other ordering constraints. Based on this interpretation of a light semantics of the conjunctions, we would expect to find ordering constraints to rule with equal power across the samples, irrespective of coordinating conjunction. This expectation is largely borne out, as there are no striking differences between models that differ solely with regard to coordinating conjunction. On the level of complex NP ordering, almost no differences between the respective samples were found (cf. Chapter 7), as the two models feature the same predictors and yield a similar predictive accuracy. The only noticeable dissimilarity concerns the influence of extra-linguistic hierarchies whose effect is stronger with *or*, as compared to *and*. For binomials, some marginal differences can be detected: binomials with *or* are not significantly influenced by the semantic constraint Hierarchy and also not by UltStress, in contrast to binomials featuring *and*. However, it seems hard to come up with an explanation for this contrast based on the different semantics of the coordinators. Therefore, despite these minor differences, no evidence for a consistent influence of

---

[4] Dik (1972: 271) reports typological research, which reveals that in other languages a temporal sequence is undoubtedly incorporated in the semantics of certain coordinators. This raises the question as to whether this may also hold for English.

[5] This result also tallies with observations made by Blakemore and Carston (2005b) that natural order is also obeyed in a succession of two sentences not being coordinated by a conjunction; e.g. *He started his car. He drove away.*

the respective coordinators on ordering has been found, which corresponds to an interpretation of their having a low semantic value that does not interfere with the ordering process.

9.5   Interim summary

Comparing the results for the different samples shows that, most generally, commonalities outweigh differences between the different cases studies, as it is mostly the same influences underlying order across all samples.

The biggest differences were observed between reversible constructions and the sample of irreversible binomials: the ordering constraints are much more strictly adhered to in irreversibles, which is reflected in greater effect sizes in the model for irreversibles; secondly, the to-be-ordered constituents in irreversible binomials show more pronounced contrasts to each other. Both of these properties may work as selection pressures underlying the process of their becoming irreversible, lexicalised units (see Section 9.2). I will detail this development from a processing perspective in the next chapter (Chapter 10).

With regard to possible differences between the three levels of investigation, I discussed a possible stronger influence of ordering constraints on lower levels as suggested by Cooper and Ross (1975) and Ross (1982). In contrast to this hypothesis, we found that the influences of ordering constraints are more or less stable across levels. I explained this uniform behaviour by referring to language production research, which has argued that the same serialising mechanism is responsible for the ordering of linguistic elements on different levels.

Furthermore, I compared and discussed the results for the two coordinators *and* vs. *or* in the context of possible influences of their semantics on constituent order. Since I did not find conspicuous differences between the two coordinators with regard to ordering influences, our results are congruent with the interpretation of a low semantic value of the two coordinators.

10   A processing perspective

In the preceding chapters, the results of the multifactorial case studies were reported and discussed in light of prior research. While it was possible to corroborate some assumptions and contrast others put forward in previous studies, I did not provide a theoretical discussion of the results and their implications.

In the following, a processing account of order in coordinate constructions will be given, discussing the results obtained from the perspective of language production. In particular, I will discuss the results in the context of language production models, starting with the most established model, the one by Bock and Levelt (1994), which assumes two separate stages of grammatical encoding (Section 10.1). Secondly, I will provide an account of how the results can be modelled within an interactive activation model (Section 10.2) that rests on the mechanisms of activation spreading (Section 10.2.1) and competition (Section 10.2.2) of the to-be-ordered elements. To flesh out this account, I will discuss evidence for this competition (Section 10.2.3) and relate the different ordering constraints to activation processes (Section 10.2.4). Furthermore, the strengths of the different constraints will be explained by the layered architecture of the model (Section 10.2.5). Next, in Section 10.3, the special case of producing irreversible constructions will be discussed against the backdrop of models of idiom representation. Section 10.4 concludes this chapter.

10.1   Implications for language production models

Most of the research on coordinate constructions in psycholinguistics has been conducted within the language production model by Bock, Levelt and colleagues (e.g. Levelt 1989; Bock and Levelt 1994), which is the most well-established model in the field. I will therefore begin the discussion of the results in the context of this model. In the following, I will describe its architecture and discuss what predictions it makes for the ordering process in coordinate constructions. The discussion shows that, in a strictly serial interpretation, our results are at odds with the model architecture. However,

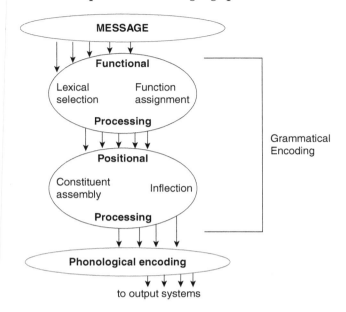

Figure 10.1 Grammatical encoding in the model by Bock and Levelt (1994)

they can be accommodated by it if incremental processing across the two crucial stages is allowed for. Let us take a more detailed look at how the model describes the ordering process.

Within the Bock and Levelt (1994) model, the crucial stage at which the ordering of syntactic constituents takes place is the so-called grammatical encoding stage. It takes as input a preverbal message from the message level and is followed by phonological encoding (see Figure 10.1 from Bock and Levelt 1994: 946).

The grammatical encoding phase involves two separate steps: the functional and the positional stage. This separation is based on the assumption that the retrieval of words during sentence production is a two-stage process of first accessing lemmas and then activating corresponding word forms (see also Levelt et al. 1999). Lemmas correspond to the meaning side of the respective words and also carry certain syntactic information, yet do not contain information about the morphological and phonological form of the word. This information becomes available once the corresponding word forms are activated (see Bock and Levelt 1994: 951). The two stages during grammatical encoding correspond to this distinction and fulfil two different functions: during functional processing, lemmas are activated based on the input from the conceptual message level; these lemmas are assigned grammatical functions in the intended utterance (e.g. Subject or Object function).

Most important for our research question, this functional structure, which is the product of this stage, 'carries no intrinsic order' (Bock and Levelt 1994: 968), thus the order of lemmas is not yet determined. This ordering takes place during the positional stage, when the corresponding word forms are activated and serialised. Within this modular architecture, both stages handle different units (lemmas vs. word forms), which encode different types of information. Furthermore, the two stages are serial and discrete, and there is thus no interaction between them. This means that the positional stage starts its serialisation process only after lemmas are selected and assigned grammatical functions during the functional stage (Bock and Levelt 1994: 960–8).

The most important consequence of this serial discrete architecture is that the two stages are subject to different influences. Since the functional stage deals with the semantics of word lemmas, it is susceptible to conceptual information, while the positional stage, which handles word forms, is sensitive to phonological, form-based influences. Levelt (1989: 276) terms this the 'informational encapsulation' of the two stages. This encapsulation allows for the formulation of concrete hypotheses as to which influences should impact the order of syntactic elements in varying contexts. During functional encoding, conceptually more accessible lemmas are assigned higher grammatical functions, such as subject role, whereby conceptual accessibility is usually understood as being influenced by a number of dimensions such as animacy, concreteness or prototypicality of the concepts denoted by the respective lemmas (cf. Bock and Warren 1985; see also Section 3.1.5). For example, all else being equal, a lemma denoting an animate referent stands a higher chance of being assigned subject role compared to a lemma denoting an inanimate referent.

During the positional stage, however, conceptual accessibility does not influence ordering, as conceptual information is no longer processed at this point. It is lexical accessibility that instead influences the activation of word forms during positional processing. Lexical accessibility corresponds to the ease of retrieval of the word form and thus is contingent on the form-properties of the word, such as its morphological and phonological make-up. Those forms that are more accessible are positioned early in sentences or generally in syntagmatic strings.

While there is much controversy surrounding the separation of these two stages, it would be beyond the scope of the present study to discuss all the available evidence for and against this model at this point.[1] Instead I will restrict myself to a discussion of its predictions for order in coordinate constructions and to the question as to how the results obtained relate to these.

---

[1] Interested readers are referred to overviews of the debate (see Levelt 1989: 275–83; Rapp and Goldrick 2000, 2004).

Let me explain first how the architecture of the model bears on the present issue of order in coordinate constructions. During the production of a coordinate construction, the two constituents' lemmas (or possibly more in the case of longer NPs) are first activated and selected during the functional stage. As mentioned above, the task of the functional stage is to assign the activated lemmas to grammatical roles of the sentence. In the case of coordinate constructions, both lemmas are assigned the same grammatical role (see Section 1.3). Consequently, based on the assumption of informational encapsulation, differences in conceptual accessibility should yield no influence on the order of constituents. Then, during the positional stage, the respective word forms are activated and serialised. It is during this stage that the order of constituents is determined. This serialisation process is contingent on the respective accessibility of these word forms, thus we would expect influences of lexical accessibility at this stage. In conclusion, the two-stage model predicts that only lexical accessibility, not conceptual accessibility, is relevant for the ordering within coordinate constructions (cf. also McDonald et al. 1993). Let us discuss how the present findings relate to this hypothesis.

Starting with possible conceptual influences, it was found that these do influence the order of elements. Across all samples, we obtained highly significant effects of constraints that obviously relate to conceptual properties of the to-be-ordered constituents: effects of temporal and logical iconicity were found, extra-linguistic hierarchies impact order and, most importantly, an effect of conceptual accessibility was found. Moreover, a comparison of effect sizes even shows that these conceptual factors yield the strongest effects (see Chapter 9 above for a detailed overview of the results). These findings are thus at odds with the predictions of the two-stages, serial model, as conceptual factors obviously impact the ordering of constituents, although this should not be the case if there was strict 'informational encapsulation'.

Turning to effects of lexical accessibility, which pertain to the phonological form of the constituents, a positive result can also be reported, in accordance with the predictions of the two-stage model. Across all case studies, effects of phonological length were observed, and constraints that relate to other phonological features, such as stress pattern or the number of consonants, were found to be significant. These effects are thus consistent with the model. In conclusion, our results corroborate the assumption that lexical accessibility effects underlie the order of constituents, yet they are at odds with the prediction of a null-result of the conceptual level.

The question that arises is whether the model can still account for this finding, or whether it needs to be modified to integrate them. Before I address this issue, note that research on languages other than English also found a conceptual effect on linearisation even without grammatical function assignment, similar to the present study. Such evidence exists for Greek (Branigan and Feleki 1999), Spanish (Prat-Sala and Branigan 2000) and German

(Kempen and Harbusch 2004). However, there is also evidence for informational encapsulation, for instance from a study on Odawa (Christianson and Ferreira 2005). Summarising, most evidence from languages other than English ties in with our findings, which underscores the need to discuss the assumptions of the serial model.

In the following I will argue that the results cannot be accounted for by a strict version of the two-stage model, but could be accommodated by the model if more incremental processing was allowed for (for a similar argument, see Kempen and Harbusch 2004). As explained above, in its traditional design the two-stage model was conceived of as a model of message production, which is strictly serial. Thus, all relevant semantic elements – at least the content words of a message – are first activated during the functional stage before an order is established during the positional stage (cf. Bock and Levelt 1994: 968). The functional stage would therefore have to be completed before the positional stage may begin the serialisation process. It is this interpretation that predicts that coordinate constructions are solely influenced by lexical accessibility effects (McDonald et al. 1993). This version of the model is adhered to by Bock and colleagues (Bock and Warren 1985; Bock 1987b; McDonald et al. 1993). Since we clearly found effects of conceptual accessibility in coordinate constructions, this version of the theory cannot account for the findings. If, however, we relax the seriality assumption by allowing for incremental processing, it becomes possible to explain the findings within the two-stage model. Incrementality in the present context means that as soon as information is available at one stage, it will be passed on to the next level. Thus, once information is available on the functional level, it may be passed down to the positional level, even though functional processing may not be complete. Such an architecture would allow for the retrieval of the word form of a lemma as soon as it is ready, regardless of any other lemmas of the message. Thus, if one of the two lemmas is more readily available due to conceptual characteristics, the retrieval of the corresponding word form may already begin. This would allow for a different speed of word-form retrieval due to conceptual characteristics, even though both lemmas are still assigned the same grammatical function during functional processing. While the ordering process would still be located in the positional stage, it may be sensitive to the speed of lemma retrieval which itself is contingent upon conceptual characteristics. An implementation of incremental processing can therefore accommodate effects of conceptual factors if, however, only indirectly via a different speed of lemma retrieval (cf. Kempen and Harbusch 2004).

It remains unclear whether proponents of the two-stage model allow for such incremental processes. While Bock and Warren (1985), and most importantly McDonald et al. (1993), are clear proponents of the strictly serial model, things are less clear with Levelt (1989). Levelt (1989: 24) explicitly states that (limited) incremental processing is possible, as a following stage may start working on the 'still-incomplete output' of the present one. Whether this applies to the grammatical encoding stage is unclear, as elsewhere he states that order in conjuncts in coordination should be driven solely by lexical factors (Levelt 1989: 281). Other versions of the theory do, however, allow for more incremental processing and can thus accommodate the results (e.g. see the discussion in Christianson and Ferreira 2005: 109–10, 129–30 for an overview of different approaches to incrementality).

In terms of a conclusion, we may state that in its traditional interpretation of a strict encapsulation of two discrete stages, the two-stage model is clearly at odds with our data. More specifically, the hypothesis that coordinate constructions are immune to conceptual ordering influences, as put forth in Bock and Warren (1985) and McDonald et al. (1993), was clearly not borne out, as both conceptual and form-related properties influence the ordering of constituents. It remains possible, however, to reconcile our results with the two-stages architecture, if we assume that the two lemmas are accessed incrementally and that lemmas that are retrieved faster may begin their phonological specification (word-form retrieval) earlier. What remains problematic, however, is that conceptual effects have even proven to yield much stronger ordering effects than form-based constraints, even though within this model they do not even pertain to the stage during which ordering takes place.

10.2   Coordination in an interactive activation model

In the following, an account of the ordering process in coordinate constructions will be given within the framework of interactive activation models. The argument that I develop is that the ordering process can best be explained in this class of models; more specifically, I argue that serialisation can be explained by the differing activation received by the to-be-ordered constituents during the production process. It should be mentioned that in other corpus-linguistic works on variation phenomena, activation-based models were found to be adequately suited for their description and explanation (Gries 2003; Schlüter 2005). The present study is therefore similar in orientation to those studies.

The account relies on two crucial concepts: the activation of constituents during production and their competition for first mention. These will be presented in turn. First, the architecture of the models and the activation process will be explained (Section 10.2.1) before I turn to an explanation how this class of models deals with the serialisation of constituents in coordinate constructions (Section 10.2.2). Then I will discuss evidence for a competition between the to-be-ordered constituents (Section 10.2.3) before explaining how the results obtained can be related to activation differences between them (Section 10.2.4).

10.2.1   Production as the flow of activation

The first step in explaining the ordering process of constituents is to flesh out the argument that their production is based on the activation they receive. This will be done by outlining the architecture of activation-based language production models, more specifically interactive activation models, relying mostly (but not exclusively) on the works by Stemberger (1985), Dell (1986) and Berg (1988).[2] Detailed accounts of their architecture can be found in the aforementioned works; thus, the description given here is confined to their most important aspects.

The most basic property of these models is that their architecture requires only two building blocks: so-called units or nodes and links between them. These units build up a complex interconnected network through which activation flows during production.[3] A certain node may receive activation from other nodes through the links. When this activation surpasses a certain threshold, the node is assumed to 'fire' and is thus selected for the current production process. Crucially, any node holds connections with many others. The activation flow in the network works in such a way that all nodes are activated ('primed' in MacKay 1987) that are connected to the target node via what are termed 'excitatory connections', which pass on activation. The network of nodes should be seen as consisting of different layers or levels, with nodes being connected both vertically across layers as well as horizontally to other nodes on the same level. The layers correspond to the levels of the linguistic hierarchy, with a level of conceptual nodes at the top and a layer of phonetic features at the bottom. To illustrate this, for example, a morpheme node has links with other morpheme nodes on the same level, as well as connections to lexical nodes on the top layer and syllable and phoneme nodes on lower layers. Apart from excitatory links, inhibitory links between nodes also exist. When two nodes are connected via these, the activation of one node results in the reduction of activation in the other. In order for the production process to work, the vertical links are generally excitatory, while horizontal links are inhibitory (Dell and O'Seaghdha 1994: 412). These inhibitory connections exist in order to prevent the intrusion of simultaneously activated nodes with the to-be-produced one. When an utterance is generated, due to this intricate network, always more than just the to-be-produced

---

[2] Interactive activation models (IAMs) have alternatively been termed 'Spreading Activation Models', or connectionist networks. While there are differences between the various theories, there is widespread consensus on their crucial properties. Since it is not the aim of this work to distinguish between intricate architectural features, as these differences are not relevant for the present investigation, 'Spreading Activation Models' is used as the cover term for models sharing the properties that will be laid out in the following.

[3] This architecture is similar to neural networks with nodes corresponding to neurons and links to the synapses between them. However, nodes are not identical with neurons, as in the model nodes correspond to linguistic units (morphemes, phonemes etc), which would be more adequately viewed as aggregations of many neurons (MacKay 1987: 9).

nodes receive activation, as 'the processing of a single utterance . . . implicates more or less the whole system' (Schlüter 2005: 269). Therefore, multiple possible targets are activated. If, for example, the node corresponding to the concept *house* is activated, it spreads down activation to the word node *house* but also to semantically similar word nodes, such as *building* or *cottage*, as these also have connections with the relevant concept node. Consequently, these word nodes compete with and inhibit each other due to inhibitory connections on the same level. The node that receives the highest amount of activation surpasses the threshold and thus fires, according to what MacKay (1987: 20) terms 'the most-primed-wins principle'. Critically, the spreading of activation and the firing of a node is a two-stage process: first, activation spreads through the network activating nodes on several layers of the network; then, if one node summates enough energy to surpass threshold, it fires and is thus selected for production (see MacKay 1987: 142; Berg 1988: 185–96).[4]

What is crucial about this network design is that it does not propose any modules or stages. In contrast to other models, activation may flow from one layer of nodes to the other, as soon as any part of a prior layer is available. There is no need to wait until a certain module has completed its production. Hence, production is rigorously parallel: not only is it possible to work on different units at the same time, but production of one and the same unit can be carried out on more than one level at the same time.

Most models assume at least five different layers of nodes (cf. Schlüter 2005: 267). For instance, Berg (1988) proposes a network that contains, from bottom to top, nodes for phonetic features, phonemes, consonant clusters, rhymes, syllables, morphemes, word stems, words and syntactic phrases. Note that there is no distinction between lemma and word form, in contrast to the model by Bock and Levelt (1994) (see Section 10.1). In the following, I will also assume merely a single level of representation for lexical units.[5]

Due to the layered design we sketched out, a certain linguistic unit – e.g. a word – does not correspond to just one particular node. As words of course consist of building blocks over several levels, it would be more appropriate to state that a linguistic unit is represented by a number of nodes on more than one level. This is due to the fact that the network does not contain symbolic form-meaning units, as we use them in linguistic description (cf. Lamb

---

[4] The assumption of two stages of activation distinguishes the cited works from Dell's (1986) model, which lacks the described distinction. As alluded to before, a two-stages approach is assumed in the present work. For a detailed discussion of this aspect, see Berg (1988: 185–96).

[5] The question of whether there is more evidence for the assumption of two separate representations of lexical units, viz. a lemma and a word-form representation, or for just a single one is beyond the scope of this book. Since in the activation model I sketch here activation may flow from one level to the next, as there are no stages or modules, the distinction is of no further relevance for the arguments to be put forth in the following.

1999: 63). A linguistic unit or utterance therefore may best be viewed as a certain activation state of the whole system, which exists across different layers of the hierarchy (Dell 1986: 287).

Furthermore, a number of things must be noted regarding the activation process and the subsequent firing of nodes. First, the activation of a node is not a two-step process from zero to full activation. In contrast, the activation level of a certain node is built up incrementally. Besides, more than one node may send activation to the target node via multiple links (Dell 1986: 287). Consequently, nodes may have varying activation levels at different points in time. Incoming activation can be summated and it may happen that only through various sources a node eventually fires. Secondly, nodes have different levels of resting activation, which is the amount of activation they have when they are not involved in processing. A node with a high resting activation level needs comparatively little activation to fire, while a node with a low resting level needs more. This resting activation is dependent mostly on the frequency with which the nodes are fired (Stemberger 1985: 150). Thirdly, the amount of activation sent from one node to another is influenced by the strength of the relevant link, which in turn is related to the frequency of contemporaneous co-activation of nodes (see, e.g., MacKay 1987: 12; for the argument's neuronal motivation, see Pulvermüller 2002: 20–2). Fourthly, activation spreads not only from top to bottom and within a certain layer, but also upwards to a limited degree, as connections between nodes are essentially bi-directional. Hence, it is possible that the activation of lower-level nodes may influence the selection of units at a higher level (see Schlüter 2005: 277–85). Fifthly, the nodes are assumed to follow a distinct activation cycle: as a node receives enough activation to surpass its threshold and fires, it receives a peak of energy; shortly afterwards, it undergoes a phase of self-inhibition, during which its activation falls below the resting level (MacKay 1987). Through this 'refractory phase', its repeated firing is avoided. Subsequently, a phase of hyperexcitability follows, during which activation rebounds, causing it to rise above resting level. Only then does activation decay until the node reaches its resting level again. The sequence of these stages is referred to as the *recovery cycle* of the node. This cycle follows different time courses dependent upon the layer on which the node is situated: the higher the level on which the node is located, the longer the individual stages take (see MacKay 1987: 144). Sixthly, another factor that can also influence the activation of nodes should be mentioned, which is so-called noise in the system (Stemberger 1985: 150–1) resulting from random variation in the activation level of nodes (Dell et al. 1997b: 805). Every node's activation level may be influenced by previous activation processes, as there is no 'blank slate' of zero-activation.

In summary, within an activation-based model, the production of linguistic units is explained by the activation of relevant nodes.

10.2.2   Serial order in an interactive activation model

Since the present study focuses on the ordering of linguistic elements, let us address the question as to how an interactive activation model solves the problem of serialisation. While the processes outlined above explain how the paradigmatic process of selection may work – namely through the spreading of activation to relevant nodes until the most highly activated ones surpass the threshold – it is not yet clear how the system puts these activated elements in the correct linear order on the syntagmatic axis (cf. Dell and O'Seaghdha 1994: 413). One level on which these decisions have to be made concerns the order of words within a phrase. For example, imagine a speaker wants to produce the sentence *The man bought the cat*. It needs to be controlled for that the correct order of elements is produced, avoiding wrong outputs such as *the bought cat man the*. More geared toward the examples that I focus on in this book would be the order of nouns within a coordinate noun phrase. In an exemplary instance such as *cats and dogs*, we assumed that the order of nouns is reversible. However, the coordinating conjunction is fixed in place, as outputs such as *and cats dogs* are not possible. In fact, such orderings hardly ever happen even in erroneous speech, as in word-exchange errors there is a strong bias to exchange two items of the same word class (cf. Fromkin 1971: 44; Shattuck-Hufnagel 1979: 336). So how does the production system come to terms with this problem? While there have been different suggestions for how to implement the serialisation process (see Dell and O'Seaghdha 1994; Dell et al. 1997a for an overview of different attempts), those models that assume a syntactic (or phonological)[6] frame seem to be most successful (e.g. Shattuck-Hufnagel 1979; MacKay 1987; Berg 1988).[7] Their crucial idea is that the positions or slots in an utterance are represented differently from the units that fill them. A frame within these models is a sequence of slots specified for syntactic category. Thus, on the syntactic level, it would contain a sequence of structural elements: e.g., for a simple noun phrase such as *the cat*, it would contain slots for determiner and noun in exactly that order. Evidence for the psychological reality of syntactic frames has been accumulated both through experimental priming studies (Bock 1986), as well as corpus-linguistic works (Szmrecsanyi 2006). The crucial feature of frame models is the separation of structure and content (see also Eikmeyer and Schade 1991), as content elements, viz. the words that are to be ordered, are separated from the structure (frame) they occur in

---

[6] Incidentally, this problem does not only arise with the ordering of words within a phrase but also with phoneme ordering within syllables (see Shattuck-Hufnagel 1979; Dell et al. 1993).

[7] Shattuck-Hufnagel (1979) was the first to detail the logic of a slot and filler model. Discussions of different serial order models can be found in Dell and O'Seaghdha (1994) and Dell et al. (1997a) and also Meyer and Belke (2007). See also Berg (2009: 4–23).

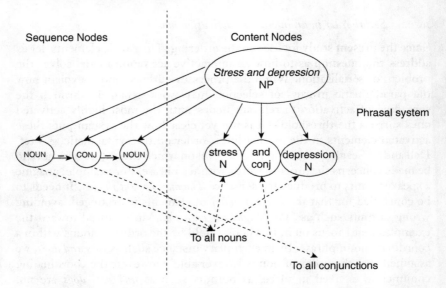

Figure 10.2 Intra-phrasal serial order in the node structure theory of sequencing (figure inspired by Dell et al. 1997a: Figure 3)

(cf. also Lashley 1951).[8] One such frame model is the node structure theory of sequencing by MacKay (1987: 47–61), which I chose to exemplify the ordering process. Figure 10.2 illustrates the production of the exemplary coordinate NP *stress and depression* in that model.

The distinction between content and structure is realised here by different types of nodes: content and sequence nodes (see dashed vertical line in Figure 10.2). Content nodes refer to particular linguistic units such as words or morphemes, e.g. *stress*, while sequence nodes correspond to a certain syntactic category, e.g. NOUN, and thus contain structural information (they are therefore also termed *structure nodes* in Dell et al. 1997a). Sequence nodes are linked to all corresponding content nodes of their category. At the top of Figure 10.2, the phrasal node of the to-be-uttered phrase has excitatory connections (solid arrows) with the word nodes *stress, and, depression* on the content side and with the sequence nodes NOUN, CONJ, NOUN. The structure node NOUN has excitatory connections to all content nodes which are nouns, while the structure node CONJ is linked to all conjunctions (see MacKay 1987: 56). The important feature of the model is that the order of elements is stored solely in

---

[8] Dell et al. (1993) show that a model that does away with the crucial distinction between content and structure is also able to explain a large share of the data on the phonological level. However, the authors caution against their applicability for ordering of words. Furthermore, it is unclear how the aforementioned syntactic priming effects would be explained by them.

the sequence nodes for which a structural frame exists, which in this case is *NOUN CONJ NOUN*. The horizontal arrows marked with a (-) symbolise inhibitory links, which ensure that when the first noun is activated, the production of the conjunction is inhibited to avoid the simultaneous firing of nodes. The activation process works like this: the phrasal node (NP) is activated and sends activation to the content nodes *stress, and, depression*, but without ordering them. It also simultaneously sends activation to the sequence nodes *NOUN, CONJ, NOUN*.[9] These then pass on activation to content nodes of the respective categories in the specified order: the noun nodes send activation to all nouns, including also *stress* and *depression*, while the sequence node *CONJ* sends activation to all conjunctions including the content node *and*. What is important for our investigation is that the order of the two nouns is *not* fixed, as both sequence noun nodes send activation to *all* content noun nodes, and thus to both *stress* and *depression* in the example. Only the conjunction is fixed in middle position by virtue of the specific frame that imposes the *NOUN CONJ NOUN* order. Crucial to the ordering process is the moment when the first structural noun node fires. As this node sends activation to all nouns, the particular content node which already has the highest activation state reaches its threshold earliest and fires. Thus, if for reasons to be explained below, the content node *stress* is activated to a higher degree than *depression* at that point in time, and both receive an equal amount of activation from the sequence nodes, it will be produced early, and thus occur in first position. As Dell (1986: 291) puts it: 'according to the theory the decision as to which noun to put first is resolved by the activation levels'.[10] After the activation of the first noun, the corresponding structural node self-inhibits and thus allows for the activation of the *CONJ* node, which then spreads activation to all conjunctions.[11] As *and* already received activation from the phrasal node, it reaches its threshold and fires. Lastly, the final sequence node (*NOUN*) fires and passes activation to all content noun nodes. At this point, the content node for *stress* can be assumed to be still inhibited, as it has already fired, yet the second content noun node (*depression*) still has a high activation level, surpasses threshold and is consequently selected for second position.

The important consequence of this model's architecture is that the ordering of to-be-coordinated constituents depends upon their respective activation levels. Moreover, the frame model explains why in the investigated constructions the conjunction cannot be moved out of place, and why, in

---

[9] In MacKay's (1987) model, sequence nodes are also activated via so-called timing nodes, which control the timing of linguistic behavior. For reasons of simplicity, they are not shown in this figure.

[10] It needs to be pointed out that Dell does not refer to coordinate constructions in this quote, yet within the logic of his model, the same process can be assumed for them.

[11] It may well be the case that activation is passed solely to coordinating conjunctions, as MacKay (1987) considered the sequence nodes to be possibly referring only to a subset of a given word class. The theory has not been specified in great detail with regard to that point, which is, however, of no great relevance for the argument elaborated upon here.

exchange errors, mostly words of the same category are involved (cf. Dell 1986; MacKay 1987: 59–61). So far I have described the ordering process solely for intra-phrasal word order. The question that still needs to be answered is whether the same argument also holds for the other two investigated levels.

It is easily conceivable that the argument can be extended to copulative compounds: as coordination is asyndetic on this level, there is no intervening conjunction for whose ordering we have to account. We may assume that the speaker activates a certain complex word node, similar to the phrase node in the example described above, which specifies the structural elements of the copulative compound. Structural templates for words are assumed in a number of models.[12] Activation is again passed to both content nodes to be produced, without specifying their order, however, as both are nominal elements and thus belong to the same syntactic class and are hence linked to the same sequence nodes. The ordering process is therefore again dependent on the differing activation of content elements – in this case, the two compound constituents.

Similar processes can also be assumed to happen with the ordering of two noun phrases, as higher-order frames for the ordering of phrases are described in Dell et al. (1993: 151) and are also assumed in MacKay's node structure theory (see MacKay 1987: 51). Syntactic priming studies provide additional evidence for their psychological reality (e.g. Bock 1986). While the mentioned works refer mostly to clause structure frames such as NP VP, there is no reason why lower-level frames for phrasal order should not exist. Thus, analogous to the ordering of words, a certain syntactic frame would send activation to phrase nodes. The order of the two subordinate NPs is not determined, as both belong to the same structural category and, consequently, the noun phrase with the higher activation level is produced early.

In conclusion, on all three levels of investigation we may assume a frame which activates structure nodes in a certain sequence, an assumption in agreement with the literature (see Shattuck-Hufnagel 1979; Berg 2009: 18). As these frames do not determine order for units of the same syntactic category, the order of coordinated elements is determined only by differences in their activation levels. Therefore, a competition between the to-be-coordinated elements for early mention can be predicted, which is an argument to be explained in the following section.[13]

---

[12] Dell (1986: 286) explicitly mentions morphological frames for the sequence of stems and affixes. For the copulative compounds we investigated, a frame on an even higher level must be assumed, as their constituents themselves may be polymorphemic, as in *actor-director*. Even if not explicitly mentioned, assuming such a frame is very much in agreement with the general characteristics of his model. For a general description of the slot-and-filler logic, including a specification of frames for words, see Berg (2009: 4–23).

[13] For a similar view of competition between phrasal constituents in free word order constructions, see Stallings et al. (1998).

10.2.3   Competing for selection

The upshot of the discussion in the preceding section is that, in a coordinate construction, during the ordering process both constituents compete to be selected for first mention. While this seems to be a plausible assumption, it would be much more convincing if there was evidence for this process. The actual competition cannot be directly observed, but indirect evidence of it should surface in the form of erroneous reversals, mirroring an unintended outcome of the process. These serialisation errors cannot be detected in the constructions under investigation, as it is one of their defining characteristics that both alternative orders are grammatically well-formed and even synonymous. One therefore cannot be certain whether a particular instance does in fact deviate from the speaker's original plan.

However, there are a number of other speech-error phenomena that provide evidence for serialisation errors through co-activation and therefore for the sort of competition I assume. One relevant phenomenon is error blends, the erroneous conflation of two words, e.g. *sotally*, which is a blend of the words *solely* and *totally* (from MacKay 1973: 785). Erroneous blends almost always involve synonyms (cf. MacKay 1973; Berg 1998: 151–7), which can be explained by the fact that the two conflated words are rivals on the paradigmatic axis. This kind of error demonstrates that the speech-production apparatus simultaneously activates more than one unit for production and shows that these compete with each other. Error blends do not, however, involve a serialisation process, as the competition for selection takes place on the paradigmatic axis, while our focus lies on competition on the syntagmatic axis.

One type of error that provides evidence for the latter form of competition is the so-called 'spoonerism', which involves the erroneous exchange of phonemes of two adjacent words:

(62)   bad goof > gad boof (from Baars and Motley 1976: 467)

Example (62) is a prototypical spoonerism, as it involves a switch of the initial phonemes (see MacKay (1970) and Motley (1973) for detailed discussions of the properties of this kind of speech error). Spoonerisms relate to the present argument of competition, as phonemes from two separate words are exchanged, which hints at the possibility that both are simultaneously active and compete for selection in a particular slot on the syntagmatic axis. In two experiments, Baars and Motley (1976) demonstrate exactly that: they show that, through creating confusion about the ordering of two lexical items – e.g. by frequently changing reading direction in an experimental condition – spoonerisms can be induced. Baars and Motley thus conclude that 'a conflict of word sequencing . . . leads to the production of spoonerisms' (1976: 472). Thus spoonerisms are indirect evidence of a word-serialisation conflict, which arises through the simultaneous activation and (partial) selection of two lexical items, thus demonstrating competition between them on the syntagmatic axis. It is worth mentioning that spoonerisms are not the only type of relevant speech error, as misorderings on the linear axis are among the most frequent errors (see Fromkin 1971), yet they most obviously demonstrate a competition of two constituents on the syntagmatic axis.

As the present study also encompasses the investigation of copulative compounds, it should be noted that ordering errors also happen with compound constituents. Misorderings within compounds occur in aphasiological speech (see Badecker 2001), as well as in the erroneous speech of healthy speakers (cf. Fromkin 1973; Stemberger 1985, as cited in Badecker 2001: 342).

Similar evidence has also been accumulated for the erroneous reversal of complete syntactic phrases (Fromkin 1971: 45), which reveals that the competition logic may also be extended to larger syntactic units, relevant for the present investigation of coordinated complex NPs.

In summary, the aforementioned discussion of speech-error phenomena demonstrates that various units can be involved in ordering errors on the syntagmatic axis, most importantly lexemes, compound constituents and whole syntactic phrases. This data thus represent indirect evidence for competition between the units whose ordering process I wish to investigate, in accordance with the serialisation account I gave above (see Section 10.2.2).

10.2.4   The variables and the activation of constituents

In the preceding sections, I explained that within an interactive activation model the order of elements in a given coordinate structure depends on their activation levels. As the language user is about to produce a certain coordinate construction, both constituents compete for selection and hence early production, as activation spreads through the network to relevant nodes for both constituents.[14]

The argument to be substantiated in the following is thus that, if one of the two constituents is more easily activated, it is produced first and consequently occurs in first position. In order to flesh out this argument, it is necessary to relate the relevant variables underlying the ordering process to activation differences of the to-be-ordered constituents. Before addressing this issue, I will briefly summarise which processes may affect the activation of nodes. According to the architecture of interactive activation models, the degree of activation of a node depends on:

- its resting activation level, in a state where it is not involved in production;
- prior production (activation) processes, which influence its degree of activation at a certain point in time (t);

---

[14] Similar views are expressed by Stallings et al. (1998) with regard to phrase ordering in alternation contexts. Corroborating evidence for that assumption also comes from experimental psycholinguistics; as Meyer (1996) shows during the production of coordinated NPs, both constituents are activated simultaneously at least to some degree.

- the activation passed to it from other nodes during an ongoing production process, which may be either excitatory or inhibitory;
- the noise in the system.

In the following, I will discuss whether and how the results obtained in the empirical studies (Chapters 5–7) can be related to these processes and consequently to an activation difference between the constituents. As shown above, any linguistic unit is produced by activating nodes on many layers of the network, and feedback among these is possible. Thus, possible activation differences on more than one level may influence the order of elements and are thus taken into account.

10.2.4.1   *Pragmatic and semantic variables*

Recall that the tendency to linearise constituents in an order of increasing information status (given before new) was found significant across all samples in which it was tested. This ordering principle can be straightforwardly related to activation differences (see also Gries 2003: 166–7). The explanatory factor here is the time course of activation of a given node in the network. Recall that nodes in the system share properties with neurons, one of which is their so-called activation contour. After firing, a node's activation level falls below its resting level, a phase we referred to as self-inhibition (see Section 10.2.1). After that phase, however, a stage of hyperexcitability follows, during which activation is higher than the resting level until it finally decays again (MacKay 1987: 143–5). Due to this rebound effect of activation, a certain time after having been fired, a node is more likely to be activated again. Thus, if a concept node corresponding to a referent denoted by one of the two constituents is activated, it goes through a stage of hyperexcitability and thus, *ceteris paribus*, has a higher activation level than its competitor and is produced earlier.

In operationalising this constraint, I coded whether the same referent was referred to in previous discourse, thus I also considered co-referential forms (see Section 4.3.1.1). This effect can therefore be explained by a repeated activation of the same concept node. However, in many cases it is the exact same form that is repeated. In those cases, activation differences should affect different layers of production at the same time, as a certain linguistic unit is distributed over nodes on several layers in the system. Not only is the concept node activated again, but nodes on lower levels (word and phoneme nodes) are also activated repeatedly. As all of these nodes undergo a phase of hyperexcitability, it may be hypothesised that these effects cumulate and render the difference in activation between the to-be-ordered forms even more pronounced in cases of referential and lexical identity. Although we did not explicitly test this claim, it is likely that it also has an influence on our results.[15]

---

[15] What must be taken into account here is that the time course of activation differs according to the level on which the node is situated (MacKay 1987: 144). Nodes lower in the network are

A further variable influencing the activation level of repeatedly activated nodes is the time span between the first and second mention, as the extra activation gained through previous activation wears off over time. Thus, a greater effect is expected at short distances.[16]An even more fine-grained investigation of the effect of information status would thus take into account the distance between the first and second mentioning of the relevant forms (cf. Gries 2003: 90).

While differences in information status can be straightforwardly related to an activation difference between the nodes of relevant linguistic constituents, other explanations have been put forward in the literature for this effect. Very similar to the present one is an explanation via accessibility differences between given and new referents made in the Levelt production models (Levelt 1989: 99–100). The explanation given here, which refers to activation, goes further, however, in relating differences in information status directly to the architecture of the production system. A complementary explanation is suggested by Bock (1977) who argues that an order of given before new is preferred as it is preferential for the hearer, since it is easier to connect new to already known content. While this argument is not incompatible with the present one, an account based on activation differences has the advantage of explaining the preference solely by recourse to the speaker, avoiding the speculative assumption that the speaker pays such close attention to the hearer's discourse model and processing needs.

The other pragmatic/semantic factors may also be related to a difference in activation levels between the two constituents. This is most obviously the case for differences in conceptual accessibility (CONACC). Recall that we motivated this constraint by arguing that certain concepts are more accessible than others (see above in Section 3.1.5) and provided independent evidence for the juxtapositions that we subsumed under this constraint. For example, several experimental studies (e.g. Bock 1982) show that concrete and animate concepts are more easily accessed than abstract and inanimate concepts. Since as a first step in the generation of an utterance concept nodes are activated, a differing conceptual accessibility can be implemented into inter-active activation models as a different resting activation of relevant nodes. Nodes of more accessible concepts can be assumed to have a higher resting activation level than those that represent concepts of lesser accessibility. This difference in resting activation levels may then lead to an early production of conceptually more accessible constituents and thus their early positioning.

---

assumed to show a much shorter activation contour, thus extra activation in the hyper-excitability stage decays faster. Thus, it is possible that this extra activation has decayed when the next ordering decision involving the same constituent is coming up. It is, however, impossible to predict the exact time course with certainty, thus we cannot be sure which layer would still add to the activation differences during the investigated ordering process.

[16] However, once the distance becomes very short we would expect the opposite effect, as the relevant node(s) may still be in the self-inhibitory phase (see Section 10.1.1).

With the variable HIERARCHY, which denotes an influence of an extra-linguistic hierarchy on order, an explanation in terms of activation is not immediately obvious. With differences in conceptual accessibility we addressed intrinsic differences between the constituents. Meanwhile, the differences denoted by HIERARCHY are not intrinsic, but arise by virtue of the two units being placed in the same hierarchy. Therefore, a difference in resting activation cannot straightforwardly be assumed. It is, however, conceivable that if a certain hierarchy exists between the two constituents, a conceptual frame is activated, which leads to higher activation of units at the top of the hierarchy. Similar suggestions have been made for proto-typicality effects on linearisation, for which a conceptual frame has been postulated (Onishi et al. 2008). Thus, even though a relation to activation is not as straightforward as with the other variables, it can be sensibly motivated. We must, however, admit that this suggestion is a post hoc explanation, as no such frame for hierarchies has yet been postulated in the relevant literature.

The variable iconic sequencing (ICONSEQ) – which denotes that an extra-linguistic order is reflected in the order of elements – yields a significant effect on the order of constituents across all samples. Levelt (1989) argues that this is an effect of the principle of natural order, which rests on the argument of the speaker taking into account the listener's needs, in accordance with the Gricean maxim of manner. However, it is also possible to explain this principle relying solely on the productive aspect of language processing: in explaining natural order, Levelt (1989: 139) refers to universal structuring principles of the memory; e.g. that events are structured in the temporal domain and are therefore remembered in a chronological order. When an utterance is prepared, this principle is obviously reflected in language, possibly due to a mechanism that influences the activation of concept nodes to different degrees, for instance by activating conceptual nodes referring to earlier events to a stronger degree than those which refer to later events. How exactly this principle affects activation is not explored, as it seems to be a higher-order mechanism that falls outside the description of language production processes since it pertains to memory organisation properties as such. It is, however, conceivable that these event structure sequences work like a frame that serialises elements by passing on activation in a certain order.

In summary, I have shown that conceptual accessibility (CONACC) and effects of information status (INF) can be straightforwardly related to activation differences. For the other two semantic constraints (HIERARCHY and ICONSEQ), an explanation in terms of activation is possible, if we assume the existence of frames which regulate activation flow. These frames can be plausibly integrated into the model; however, no independent evidence has yet been accumulated for their existence. It remains an issue for future research to address their status within language production models.

10.2.4.2   Length and complexity

Length and complexity are treated here jointly, as the basic argument in terms of activation differences between the constituents is the same for both. The factors discussed here are, using their abbreviations, LENGTHSYL, LENGTHPHO, SYNTCOMPL and MORPHCOMPL. For all these constraints, the difference in the number of subordinate units which make up the to-be-coordinated constituents is the crucial measure. This difference can be feasibly related to an activation difference: if a given constituent consists of many subordinate elements, its production involves the activation of more nodes compared to shorter constituents (cf. Gries 2003: 170–2). On the lexical level, for instance, a short word that consists of only a few phonemes may be more quickly activated than a long one. Correspondingly, Bock (1982: 31) states that 'representations with less information will finish the retrieval process faster'. Evidence for this relation between length and processing time is provided by a number of studies: MacKay (1987: 57) observes that the time to begin a pre-planned behaviour 'is shorter when the behaviour consists of a single component than when it consists of a sequence of components' (see also Sternberg 1966). Balota and Chumbley (1984) show that short words are processed faster both in production and comprehension. Additional evidence comes from a number of utterance-initiation experiments, which show that the time it takes speakers to begin articulation of longer words increases with word length (cf. Meyer et al. 2007).

We may conclude that shorter units complete the activation process faster and should thus 'win out' in the competition between the two elements. The empirical findings tie in well with these assumptions, as, across all case studies, a strong short-before-long tendency could be observed. Remember that length differences between the constituents were measured foremost in number of syllables (LENGTHSYL), a variable that yielded significant results across the board.[17] Other length measurements (MORPHCOMPL, LENGTHPHO) did not yield significant findings in all case studies. It would thus be tempting to conclude that only the number of syllables matters for the activation differences between the constituents. However, in spreading activation models, length differences on all levels should be relevant for the ordering process. The problem with an empirical investigation of the morphological and the phonological levels lies in the massive correlations between the different measurements, which we tried to disentangle by considering only

---

[17] Interestingly also Bock (1982) related the faster retrieval of shorter units to their length in syllables. Also MacKay (1987:25–6) reports that both in production as well as comprehension, words with more syllables take longer to be processed than words with fewer syllables, even when length in phonemes is controlled for. This goes to show that the length in syllables is not just a proxy for the number of phonemes, but is independently relevant for the activation process.

those data points exhibiting no difference in number of syllables.[18] This procedure resulted in a loss of relevant data, which may be the reason for the non-significant contribution of these other length measurements. A more fine-grained analysis may detect their influences.[19]

In contrast to the negative results for number of morphemes and phonemes, evidence for the simultaneous influence of several levels has been obtained for the ordering of complex NPs. Here it is both the number of syntactic nodes as well as the number of syllables or words – thus, length differences on two levels – that influence the ordering process (see the discussion in Section 8.2.3.3). The significant results obtained for length across the case studies point to a uniform effect of length, irrespective of whether the linguistic unit that is ordered is a compound constituent, a word or a phrase. In contrast to this result, Stallings et al. (1998: 410–11) argue that length is not a relevant factor with word ordering but affects solely the order of phrases. In explaining this distinction, they argue that these two ordering processes happen during different stages of the production process, referring to the production model by Bock and Levelt (1994). The present finding of an invariable effect of length across levels does, however, constitute evidence against the assumption of different stages in production and is thus another case in point for the superiority of interactive activation models in explaining the ordering processes investigated here.

In conclusion, the mechanism of activation is well suited to explaining the empirical results obtained of influences of length and complexity on ordering. With regard to which level of measurement is truly responsible for these effects, the results are not unambiguous. However, they are compatible with a view of simultaneous influences on several levels during production.

10.2.4.3   Constraints related to the stress pattern of coordinate constructions
In Section 8.2.2.1, I discussed the workings of the RHYTHM constraint and argued that its workings depend on the look-ahead the language user performs and consequently the time available. The tendency to alternate stressed and unstressed syllables can also be related to activation. In fact,

---

[18] Furthermore, it should be noted that we did not presume a prominent role of syllable nodes in the production process, which is assumed in some production models (Levelt 1989; Levelt et al. 1999). The decision for measuring length differences foremost by the number of syllables is motivated primarily by the fact that this operationalisation is compatible with much of the previous research (see Chapter 4).

[19] The issue as to which level of complexity or length is the relevant one is also very much debated in other areas of (psycho-)linguistic research. One such area pertains to possible influences on utterance initiation latencies, where it is unclear to date whether syllabic complexity or phoneme length or both are responsible (cf. Roelofs 2002; Santiago et al. 2002). With regard to errors in aphasic speech, Nickels and Howard (2004) found that length in number of phonemes increases the probability of an error and is a more robust effect than number of syllables or syllabic complexity. The present study, in contrast, is more in line with a prominent effect of number of syllables on production difficulty, yet the aforementioned methodological reservations apply.

this relation has been described in detail by Schlüter (2005: 257–306), which is why I will only briefly touch on it here. The crucial point of the argument refers to the activation curve of an activated node. Recall that, after having fired, a node undergoes a refractory phrase (also self-inhibition) during which its activation level falls below the resting state (see Section 10.2.1). After that phase, there is a rebound of energy during which activation is higher than the usual resting level. Schlüter (2005: 282) argues that, if we conceive of the property stressed/unstressed as distinct nodes that are connected to corresponding syllable nodes, this activation cycle may explain the alternation of stresses: when a stressed syllable has just been produced, the node for the property stressed is inhibited; thus, it cannot be easily reactivated and consequently sends little feedback to linked syllable nodes. However, in cases of a perfect rhythmic alternation of stressed and unstressed syllables, the property *unstressed* may be in the rebound phase at that point in time and thus send excitatory activation to connected syllable nodes, resulting in an increased activation of unstressed syllables, one of which is then selected. This way the production system may be thought of as creating the observed alternation. Schlüter (2005: 282) argues that when two (morphological or lexical) target forms compete, of which only one conforms to the principle of rhythmic alternation, then this one would receive more feedback from the stress nodes and would thus be selected, according to the most-primed-wins principle (Section 10.2.1). Based on the same rationale, the ordering alternations I investigated can also be explained. If one of the two orders means a perfect alternation of stresses, stress nodes are activated during their rebound phases, and thus, less activation is needed to produce that order in comparison to a rhythmically problematic one. While the activation contour of relevant nodes convincingly ties our findings to activation, explaining the actual ordering decisions during production is not that easy. If the processes of self-inhibition arising from the activation of the nodes for the property stress are responsible for rhythmic alternation, as Schlüter (2005) argues, this self-inhibition would have to be anticipated by the language producer and then corrected by reversing the order of constituents. Such a decision would only be possible if the language user activated both orders and then decided for the rhythmically better formed one, which is a kind of try-out mechanism that is not mentioned in activation-based models. The caveat of a missing 'mechanism for filtering out the optimal candidate' is also noticed by Schlüter (2005: 283). However, this weakness in the otherwise convincing explanation may provide the explanation for the present findings, as I found an effect of rhythmic accommodation only with instances of planned production (see the discussion in Section 8.2.2.1). When time constraints are looser, it is possible that language users try out different orders and then settle for the solution that best conforms to the activation patterns of involved nodes. This interpretation receives support from Hayes (1995: 372–3), who argues that languages' eurhythmic properties are dependent on the existence of a planning stage. The fact that the rhythm effects reported in Schlüter (2005) were observed almost exclusively in written language is compatible with this explanation, as in writing there is more time for performing the necessary planning processes. Concluding, the ordering constraint of stress alternation can be convincingly explained by the activation contour of nodes in an interactive activation model. However, this influence can only manifest itself when time constraints allow for its consideration.

Let us turn now to the variable syllable weight (SylW) that was found to influence order in irreversible binomials, as well as in copulative compounds. In Section 8.2.2.3, I argued that its effectiveness depends on the existence of a stress template. This variable can be explained in terms of activation if we assume such a template with sequence nodes to be part of an activation network (similar to phrasal nodes as described above, see Section 10.2.2). If the property of greater stress on the second element is part of a lexical frame or template of copulative compounds, the following activation flow is conceivable: the first structure/sequence node sends activation to all content nodes that correspond to constituents with light main syllables, while the second sequence node sends activation to constituents with heavy main syllables to ensure greater accent on the second constituent. When the two nominal constituents therefore compete for first position, the constituent with a light main syllable can be assumed to have a higher activation level due to activation passed on to it by the sequence node. Such a solution with stress differences being part of ordering frames is not entirely speculative, as stress information is assumed to be stored in metrical frames that are retrieved during a word's phonological encoding process in various production models (see Meyer and Belke 2007: 477–9 for an overview).

The case is slightly different with irreversible noun binomials, as no competition between the two elements can be assumed anymore. However, a lexical stress template also seems to exist for them. It is likely that this template exerted an effect on ordering during a diachronic lexicalisation process. As a binomial is becoming lexicalised, it may fall under the reign of this metrical frame and influence order accordingly. The metrical frame, however, does not affect reversible noun binomials as these are not recognised as lexical units. Since the production of irreversible binomials is a special case, as no online ordering process is involved during their production, it will be dealt with in a separate section (Section 10.3). With the constraint avoidance of ultimate stress (UltStress), a stress template is also conceivable, thus this variable's influence could be related to activation differences. However, there is very little empirical evidence for this variable, as we found it to be of marginal significance only in one sample (lexical coordination with *and*) and thus, its empirical relevance is doubtful.

10.2.4.4   Frequency

The tendency to order constituents of higher frequency before those of a lower frequency was found to significantly influence order in all investigated samples (see Chapters 5–7). It is a well-established finding that frequency influences the ease of access and processing of linguistic units. For instance, it has been shown that frequency and reading time are inversely correlated in lexical-decision tasks (e.g. Scarborough et al. 1977; Balota and Chumbley 1984).[20]

There are two possible mechanisms that could explain the frequency effect in interactive activation models. The first is a difference in resting activation levels of the nodes corresponding to the to-be-ordered constituents. It is argued that the more often a certain linguistic unit and its corresponding nodes are activated, the higher their respective resting activation levels become (see Stemberger 1985). Thus, high-frequency nodes need less activation to reach their firing threshold. It follows that corresponding constituents should be produced early, due to a 'head-start' in terms of activation, compared to lower-frequency constituents. Since complex linguistic units, such as morphemes, words and phrases, are distributed over several layers in the network, several nodes are involved in their production. Hence all involved nodes have higher resting activation levels by virtue of being frequently activated.

The second possibility for frequency to influence the activation process is via the linkage strength between nodes. In some interactive activation models, the frequent co-activation of certain nodes leads to stronger excitatory connections between these (see, e.g., Dell 1986). When nodes on several levels are activated during the production of a constituent, the connections between them are strengthened every time it is produced. Thus, the links between nodes on the relevant levels should be stronger for high-frequency units, which should speed up their production. Depending on the specific architecture of the model, we may view this second process as either a complement or an alternative to the argument of differing resting activation levels.

In conclusion, the frequency of a linguistic element may influence activation in two ways: first, the resting activation levels of involved nodes are sensitive to frequency; second, due to frequent co-activation, the links between nodes are strengthened. Most importantly, both implementations

---

[20] Notwithstanding this variable's generally acknowledged influence, it is still being discussed at which level frequency influences the access process in production models which assume a separation between lemmas and word forms (see Gahl 2008). Jescheniak and Levelt (1994) and Levelt et al. (1999) propose that frequency enhances the retrieval of word forms but not of lemmas, as low-frequency homophones seem to inherit the speed of access from their high-frequency twins. This assumption is contrasted by Gahl (2008) who, while not disputing the inheritance effect, shows that high-frequency words are shortened more strongly than low-frequency homophones. She interprets this finding as evidence for the lemma level also being influenced by frequency.

render a frequent linguistic unit more quickly activated and therefore selected.

10.2.4.5   *Other variables*

Let us turn to the remaining variables which were found to influence the ordering process in some but not all samples. With regard to the influence of further phonological constraints, it was found that the order of morphemes in copulative compounds is influenced by a difference in the number of initial consonants (INiC) between the two constituents (see Section 8.2.5.2). The element with fewer initial consonants was found to be preferred in first position beyond mere length differences between the words. This variable may also be related to activation differences between the two constituents. There are several studies reporting evidence that words beginning with an initial consonant cluster lead to longer processing and production-initiation times (e.g., MacKay 1987: 25–7; Santiago et al. 2002). This can be explained by more sequencing decisions that have to be performed before the first segment node of the word can be activated for articulation. Let us take a look at two examples from MacKay (1987: 26) to illustrate this process. The two words *crime* and *court* differ in the number of segments in the syllable onset (see Figure 10.3).[21]

In order to activate the first segment node (C) in *crime*, first a sequential decision has to be made to correctly order the two segments in the syllable onset, while no such ordering process is necessary with *court*. The mechanism underlying this ordering mechanism may be an ordering frame similar to the one I described for intra-phrasal ordering (cf. Stemberger and Treiman 1986; Dell et al. 1997a). A further difference in terms of activation is mentioned by Stemberger and Treiman (1986), who show that the second consonant of a cluster is involved in speech errors significantly more often than the first one. Stemberger and Treiman (1986) interpret this finding as indicating that the second consonant of a CC cluster in the onset has a lower activation level on the CV-tier than the first one or a singleton consonant in the onset. It follows that, during production of a CC onset, the speaker has to encode a phonological sequence that includes one lesser-activated segment. The aforementioned analyses are similar in that they predict a more

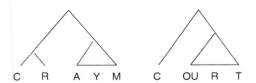

Figure 10.3 Word onsets of *crime* and *court* (after MacKay (1987: 26)

---

[21] I used the original non-phonetic transcription by MacKay (1987) for the CV-tier.

complicated activation process of the CC cluster, as compared to a singleton C onset, which may thus affect the overall activation of the to-be-ordered constituent. The ordering constraint INIC can thus be feasibly explained by activation differences.

The variable SONFINC, which states that sonorant endings are preferred in the second constituent, was found significant only in the sample of irreversible binomials. I will therefore discuss it below while addressing the special case of producing irreversible constructions (Section 10.3). It was also discovered that a sonorant beginning of the first element (SONINIC) was preferred in ordering nouns. Relating this variable to activation would mean arguing that words with a sonorant beginning are easier to activate. However, this seems difficult to motivate because it is obstruents that are more frequently found in the onset than sonorants (see Wright et al. 2005: 536). Thus, it is unclear at present if and how this ordering constraint influences the activation levels of the to-be-ordered constituents.

The findings for VLENGTHFINAL and F1, both of which were found to significantly influence order in copulative compounds, seem to defy a straightforward account based on activation processes. No convincing explanation is given for these variables in prior research (see Chapter 3). For differences in vowel height (F1), however, it is conceivable that phoneme frequency is an explanatory factor, as /i/ is the second-most frequent vowel, outnumbering all low vowels (see Fry 1947). Since frequency leads to a higher resting activation of corresponding nodes (see Section 10.2.4.4), an explanation in terms of activation differences is possible.

10.2.5   Correspondence between layer and effect size

In this section, I will propose an explanation for the varying strengths of ordering constraints by taking recourse to the layered structure of an interactive activation network. More specifically, I argue that higher layers in the production model exert stronger influences on the order of constituents than lower ones. In terms of the time course of production, this means that earlier influences yield stronger effects than later ones.

In order to develop that argument, let me first explain the influences of the different ordering constraints and their locus in an interactive activation model. Figure 10.4 illustrates the production of a coordinated sequence, X *and/or* Y. The relevant nodes are illustrated as ellipses and the links between them are displayed as lines. The influential variables (ordering constraints) are drawn as rectangles with arrows pointing at the layer/node they influence.[22] For ease of illustration, sequence nodes and also the coordinating

---

[22] Technically speaking, the rectangles are not part of the spreading activation network, they are included to visualise the effects of the different ordering constraints. As pointed out above, the activation network consists solely of nodes and links (see Section 10.2.1).

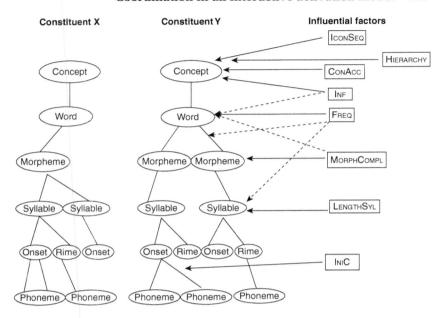

Figure 10.4 The influences of ordering constraints in a layered network

conjunction are not included in the figure.[23] The following architectural features are crucial for an understanding of the argument of competition between the two constituents. Both constituents are activated parallel to one another and their order is not fixed by sequence nodes (see Section 10.2.2). Activation happens on different levels at the same time, as there are no modules on the respective layers whose output is awaited by subsequent levels. Furthermore, feeding back of activation from lower to higher levels is explicitly possible (see Section 10.2.1). Due to these characteristics, differences in the activation of nodes on lower levels may influence ordering decisions on higher levels. Activation flows through the network until a node receives enough energy to fire. If one of the nodes on which the ordering process takes place is fired, it inhibits its competitor and hence the corresponding constituent is produced early.

Let us start at the top of the figure, which corresponds to the earliest actions during the production process. First, the language user conceives of a certain coordination 'in thought', prior to linguistic encoding. It can be assumed that, at this point, concept nodes are activated in this first step of preparing an utterance (see Dell 1986; Dell and O'Seaghdha

---

[23] The figure is inspired by Figure 1 in Dell (1986).

1994).[24] If the concepts involved in the utterance are stored in memory in a certain order, the iconic sequencing constraint (ICONSEQ) leads to their sequential activation by virtue of the principle of natural order. Thus, the variable iconic sequencing (ICONSEQ) is the earliest influence on ordering, as it involves the architecture of (pre-linguistic) memory. The next possible influences on the way from conceptualisation to articulation are the other semantic ordering constraints. Both a difference in conceptual accessibility (CONACC), as well as a differing rank in an extra-linguistic hierarchy (HIERARCHY) may influence the activation of involved concept nodes. As discussed in Section 10.2.4.1, CONACC reflects a different resting activation level of the two concept nodes, while HIERARCHY may also lead to a differing activation of the respective conceptual nodes at the time of production. The conceptual level can also be influenced by information status (INF).[25] If a constituent refers to a previously mentioned referent, the activation level of its corresponding concept node is increased through the prior activation process. If it is the same word that is repeated when the given referent is mentioned for the second time, nodes on other levels are also activated to a higher degree (these influences are displayed as dashed lines), as the word node and all other subordinate nodes have been activated during the previous production of that form.[26]

In the next step, the concept nodes spread activation to connected phrase nodes in NP ordering or to word nodes in binomials, including those that are eventually selected.[27] If, therefore, depending on the level of coordination, a phrase or word node receives more activation from a more-highly activated concept node, it may summate more energy and possibly fire earlier and inhibit its rival. Consequently, the corresponding constituent will be produced early, which explains the effects of the semantic/pragmatic constraints we obtained. From word nodes, activation is then passed on to subordinate morpheme and syllables nodes and eventually to segment nodes. Depending on the length/complexity of the constituent, a varying number of nodes is

---

[24] In most models, the conceptual level lies outside the scope of description, as most models address solely the activation of linguistic units. Still, the conceptual/semantic level is assumed here as being part of the production model along with Dell (1986: 287) and Lamb (1999). Concept nodes are situated in the topmost layer of the production network and have properties similar to other nodes in the network.

[25] As noted above, INF may influence also other nodes on lower layers if it is the same linguistic form that is repeated.

[26] Remember that we argued that the higher activation of previously mentioned referents and/ or forms is due to the hyperexcitability phase of nodes. The activation cycle described above is thought to vary according to the level on which the node is situated, with lower nodes having a considerably shorter cycle than higher ones (see MacKay 1987: 144). Due to this architectural feature, it depends on when exactly the corresponding form is produced again and which nodes may be in their hyperexcitability phase just then. It is unlikely that lower nodes such as segment nodes are relevant here due to their very short activation cycle.

[27] For reasons of simplicity, phrase nodes are not displayed in the figure. Co-activated nodes not corresponding to the two constituents have also been omitted.

activated. With morphologically complex constituents, more morpheme nodes must be activated. With syntactically complex NPs, more subordinate phrase nodes (not displayed in the figure) must be activated, and with constituents consisting of more than one syllable, more syllable nodes have to be activated. Constituents consisting of fewer units on any given level receive more activation and may thus reach their threshold earlier. Therefore, they have a tendency to occur in first position, which is reflected in the short-before-long (and less complex before more complex) preference we observed across all empirical case studies. Corresponding variables are MORPHCOMPL, SYNTCOMPL and LENGTHSYL. Below the morphological level, syllable nodes are activated, which send activation to linked onset and rime nodes which then activate phoneme nodes. The number of initial consonants (ordering constraint INIC) influences whether an onset node with more or fewer connected segment nodes is activated. The serialisation of onset consonants may take longer than the activation of a simplex onset, thus a node connected to fewer initial consonants reaches its threshold earlier, reflecting the influence of differences in initial consonants between the constituents. From the onset and rime nodes, activation is spread downwards to segment nodes. It is here that differences in the quality of the initial segment (SONINIC) become active (see Section 10.2.4). Finally, the influence of frequency must be explained. Its influence is a general one, as it is not bound to nodes on a particular layer in the network. As pointed out above, frequency (FREQ) may influence the resting activation levels of nodes on all levels, as well as the links between the nodes. For example, the resting activation level of a word node corresponding to a frequent word can be assumed to be higher than the resting activation level of a node of a word of lesser frequency. In addition, the links to other nodes may also be stronger if a certain node is more frequently activated (see exemplary arrows pointing at the word node and at a link between activated nodes).

Having dealt with the question as to how the different constraints influence the activation on different levels, let us now address the issue as to how this architecture may explain the different strengths of the variables. Remember that, in the previous chapter, we found that generally conceptual and semantic factors yield stronger influences on order (larger effect sizes) than other constraints across all case studies (cf. Section 8.1). This finding invites the explanation that the variables' strength is contingent on the layer of nodes they affect in the production network, as it can be observed that the average effect size of ordering constraints corresponds roughly to the hierarchy of layers in the network, with higher layers yielding stronger effects.

This can be explained by the architecture of the production model, as activation flows predominantly from top to bottom. If two constituents are to be produced and compete for selection, their activation levels should be more strongly affected by upper layers. For example, if there is an activation difference between the two corresponding concept nodes, as reflected in the conceptual ordering constraints I investigated, one of the two concept nodes sends greater activation down to connected nodes of its corresponding constituent. Hence, the word or phrase node of that constituent receives more activation compared to its competitor and, *ceteris paribus*, is selected early. In this way, semantic/conceptual ordering constraints exert an immediate effect on the selection of constituents during serialisation.

In contrast, influences on lower layers, which are reflected in, e.g., phonological ordering constraints, can influence the selection process only indirectly. Since these influences translate into activation differences on levels below the crucial word, morpheme or phrase node, they may influence the activation of these nodes only through feedback. While the feeding back of activation is explicitly possible in interactive activation models, it is assumed to be a somewhat weak effect, hence the influence of lower levels on higher ones is limited (cf. Rapp and Goldrick 2000). It is furthermore assumed that feedback decays over the distance that activation spreads up and is limited due to time constraints during production (Berg and Schade 1992: 409), as selection on a higher level may happen before lower levels have fed back activation (see Schlüter 2005: 289–91). Therefore, activation differences between nodes on lower layers in the network can only yield a smaller effect on the selection of the constituent to be produced first. In summary, the aforementioned architectural features explain why higher layers exert stronger effects and furthermore predict that the lower the activation differences are located – which may influence order via feedback – the weaker their influence. This is congruent with our empirical findings.

Let me illustrate the above-mentioned effects by exemplifying the production process of a reversible binomial. The first step is that two concept nodes are activated, which spread down activation through the network, thereby activating corresponding word nodes and other subordinate nodes. Through the activation flow from top layers and the feeding back of activation from lower levels, a word node has at some point summated enough activation to fire. Due to predominant feeding forward of activation, word nodes gather more activation from concept nodes as they gain in feedback from morpheme or syllable nodes, or even lower layers. Thus, if differences in conceptual accessibility or one of the other semantic constraints lead to differing activation levels of concept nodes, this discrepancy should have a strong effect on the activation of the different word nodes, resulting in one of them being closer to threshold than its competitor. At this point in time, it is still possible that feedback from lower levels influences the firing of one or the other word node. Thus, if one of the two nodes receives more activation via feedback, this process may influence the selection process. However, as feedback is weaker than the feeding forward of activation, the activation differences between the two nodes generated by this process should on average have a weaker effect on ordering. Hence, the finding that phonological and phonetic variables, such as INIC, SONFINC or SONINIC, or FI, yield the weakest effects can be explained by the corresponding nodes being situated on the lowest tiers of the activation network: as the corresponding nodes are furthest away from the word level and since the strength of feedback diminishes with greater distance, their influence can only be small.

In summary, the difference in effect size of the variables corresponds to the layer in the network on which the corresponding nodes are located. While the architecture of the model limits the influence of lower levels, it does not completely preclude it, which is congruent with our findings. This is due to the fact that a strong activation discrepancy between nodes on a lower level may overrule smaller activation differences on higher levels. Congruent with the assumptions of interactive activation models, the correspondence between effect size and layer of influence should thus be understood as a probabilistic tendency, not as a deterministic hierarchy.

10.2.6   Activation differences and empirical results

Above I discussed how the constraints that were found to significantly influence the ordering process relate to activation processes in a spreading activation model. For most but not all factors such a relation could be shown, supporting the view that activation differences underlie the ordering of constituents in coordinate constructions.

A further question must be addressed: If the factors can be neatly related to activation differences between the constituents, why can we not predict 100% of all orderings correctly, if we know about the constraints and their effects? There are (at least) three possible reasons for predictive accuracies well below that value. Firstly, it could be that we did not take into account all factors influencing the activation of the two constituents. Even though we tested quite a large number of different constraints, it is not unlikely that other unknown influences impact activation levels. A second reason is that there may be 'noise' in the system and thus activation of nodes and activation due to prior production processes that we did not consider (cf. Dell 1986). As the system is almost constantly active, since certain representations are probably entertained also during thought, there is no blank slate from which we can begin a linguistic observation. Therefore, noise may influence activation differences between the two constituents in unpredictable and, crucially, empirically unobservable ways. The ordering process should be particularly susceptible to noise effects if the two constituents' activation levels are not much different, if, for instance, there are no semantic contrasts, and differences in length, complexity and frequency are small, which is not uncommon. This lack of contrasts is in itself the third reason for a less than ideal predictive accuracy. It may happen that none of the variables we related to activation applies, as very similar constituents are coordinated that simply do not exhibit the relevant contrasts (see the next section for a discussion of this point, comparing reversibles and irreversibles).

10.3   The processing and representation of irreversible binomials

10.3.1   Irreversible binomials and models of idiom representation

Above I discussed the ordering process in coordinate constructions in an interactive activation model of language production. The description was geared towards the ordering process in cases of reversible ad hoc coordination. I showed that the results we obtained through corpus-linguistic analysis can be explained by an activation difference between the constituents. However, in Chapter 1, I mentioned that such an ordering process may not happen with irreversible, lexicalised constructions. I will therefore discuss how production of these units proceeds and thereby refer to models of idiom representation.

In Chapter 2, I mentioned that irreversible binomials share certain characteristics with idioms: their form cannot be altered and their semantics may be non-compositional. Irreversible binomials may thus be assumed to be represented in the mental lexicon similar to idioms (cf. Kuiper et al. 2007). I will review storage models of idiomatic constructions in the following to examine whether and how these apply to irreversible binomials. While there is extensive literature on the properties of idioms and fixed expressions, their storage and production is a field that is much less explored (see Sprenger et al. 2006: 162). Those studies that address the issue generally agree that fixed expressions are stored as units in the mental lexicon. For example, Levelt (1989: 187) states that 'idiomatic collocations are entries in the mental lexicon'. Let us more closely examine the claim of unit status. Early accounts held that 'idioms are stored and retrieved from the lexicon in the same manner as any other word' (Swinney and Cutler 1979: 525), which is also termed the *Lexical Representation Hypothesis*. In a strong version of this hypothesis, these quasi-lexical units store no information about syntactic or grammatical properties, and their internal components have no representation as individual items, as the expression is only stored as one unit. In such an interpretation, an idiom such as *kick the bucket* would have no connections to the lexical entries it consists of, such as *kick* and *bucket*. There is empirical evidence, however, which is at odds with this assumption, as speech errors involving lexical items that are part of idioms do occur (see Stemberger 1985: 173). It has been concluded that idioms cannot only be stored as units, but their components must also be stored separately. This insight led to the emergence of hybrid models. These models argue that, although idioms are stored as units on some level, the speaker still analyses them into their component words (e.g. Stemberger 1985: 172–3). This means that a separate entry exists on one level, but this is still connected to the individual components of the expression in the production network. In the following, I discuss two such models. Both of them share the assumption that lexical retrieval involves the activation of first lemmas and then word forms (see also

Section 10.1). The first is the hybrid account put forward by Cutting and Bock (1997), who assume that an idiom has its own lexical-conceptual (lemma) node and thus is stored as a unit on this level, but that this node is still connected to the corresponding word form nodes on lower levels. Such an architecture can explain why an idiom can be primed by one of its component words (cf. Sprenger et al. 2006). The production of an idiom may work like this: when a speaker wants to convey a meaning such as *John died* that can be encoded by an idiom, the concept for *die* will be activated. It then spreads activation to relevant lemma nodes such as the lemma node for *die*, but also to the lemma node for *kick the bucket*. If the latter is selected due to its activation surpassing threshold, it passes on activation to the word form nodes of its components, which then spread activation to segment nodes, etc. One important property of the Cutting and Bock (1997) model is that they assume that idioms make use of regular phrasal frames for serialisation similar to those illustrated above (see Section 10.2.2). Sprenger et al. (2006) take issue with such an assumption; they claim that it leaves the syntactic properties or idiosyncrasies of certain idioms underspecified. The example they discuss is the idiom *be a wolf in sheep's clothing*. As an assumed phrasal frame for the NP *a wolf in sheep's clothing* contains two noun slots, both the activated lemmas for *wolf* as well as for *sheep* may be inserted, thus the speaker may erroneously produce the utterance *be a sheep in wolf's clothing*, which would corrupt the meaning of the idiom. Therefore, Sprenger et al. (2006: 177–8) argue that the syntactic relations and thus the positions of the individual elements of the idiom need to be specified. As a mechanism for this task, they propose a so-called 'superlemma' of the idiom (Sprenger et al. 2006: 176), which contains syntactic information, and passes on activation to connected simple lemmas in a specified order. Hence, 'when the simple lemmas get activated they will already be provided with their exact position' (Sprenger et al. 2006: 178). In summary, both Cutting and Bock's (1997) and Sprenger et al.'s (2006) models are similar in propagating a hybrid account; however, they differ with regard to a feature that is crucially relevant for the binomials we investigated, viz. the positioning of lexical elements.

In the following, I will discuss how these models cope with the production of irreversible binomials. In contrast to idioms, only some of them are semantically non-compositional, e.g. *odds and ends*. However, in most accounts it is assumed that both compositional, as well as non-compositional fixed expressions have the same status in the mental lexicon (cf. Sprenger et al. 2006; Kuiper et al. 2007). Therefore, I assume that they fall within the scope of the mentioned representation models (see also Kuiper et al. 2007). In any hybrid model, an irreversible binomial such as *odds and ends* would have its own lexical entry which would still be connected to its component words *odds*, *and* and *ends*. In Cutting and Bock's (1997) model, the unit node of the irreversible does not specify the order of elements, but uses the regular phrasal frame for coordinate NPs (see Figure 10.2 above), hence the order

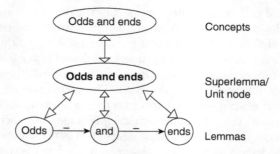

Figure 10.5 Activation of an irreversible binomial in the superlemma model[28]

of the two nouns would not be specified. Similar to reversible constructions, their positions would only be determined by differences in activation levels. Sprenger et al.'s (2006) proposal is crucially different in this respect, as the superlemma they propose contains syntactic and positional information and thus specifies the order of nouns. The process of activation in their model is illustrated in Figure 10.5.

The concept node would activate the superlemma node of the respective binomial (in this case *odds and ends*), which then activates corresponding lemmas in the specified order. The activation of a separate phrasal frame with structural nodes is not necessary, as the positional information is inherent in the superlemma, which thus predetermines order.

Now, which of the two models accounts better for the production of irreversibles? At first glance, the superlemma theory seems to be better suited, as it explicitly specifies the fixed order. This assessment is also argued for by Kuiper et al. (2007), who also discuss the status of irreversible binomials in the two models. They judge Cutting and Bock's model (1997) to be less than perfectly suited because, in speech-error data of fixed expressions, they do not find reversals of irreversible binomials, which they interpret as evidence for the superiority of the superlemma theory. However, we should not discard Cutting and Bock's (1997) model prematurely. Recall that the ordering constraints exert a stronger influence on irreversible binomials than on reversible cases (see Section 9.2). From the point of view of activation, this means that activation differences between the two constituents are much more pronounced with irreversibles than with reversibles. If, as in Cutting and Bock's (1997) model, the order of constituents is not specified and depends on their activation, these much greater differences may explain the apparent irreversibility without having to postulate an additional mechanism, as these lead to strong ordering preferences. However, their model

---

[28] The figure is modelled after Figure 5 in Sprenger et al. (2006: 176).

would predict that occasionally a reversal should happen if, for instance, due to noise in the system, the activation differences are equalised, which should not happen in the superlemma model. It is thus an empirical question as to whether these reversals occur or not. As mentioned above, Kuiper et al. (2007) aim to answer this question through the analysis of speech-error data. Since they find no reversals of irreversible binomials in their dataset, they interpret this as evidence for the superlemma theory, which predicts that such misorderings should not occur. Unfortunately, they do not reveal the number of relevant data points in their sample, which makes it impossible to determine whether this finding may be solely due to chance.[29] What underlies Kuiper et al.'s (2007) expectation to not find such reversals is the assumption of strict irreversibility. However, as noted in Section 4.1.2, it is hard to draw a line between strictly irreversible binomials and reversible constructions, which is why I described reversibility as a gradable phenomenon and operationalised irreversibles in a way so as to allow for occasional reversals. Thus, it may be too strong a claim to assume equal irreversibility for all instances within this class and an equal unit or superlemma representation for all cases. Incidentally, the observation of gradability is not specific to irreversible binomials, but is relevant for other idiomatic expressions, as it has been argued that idiomaticity should generally be viewed as a gradable phenomenon (cf. Wulff 2008). The resulting question is: For which cases should we assume unit representation? The relevant models remain mute on this subject. Some cases seem to be clear, as certain binomials never occur in reverse order, which are also intuitively felt to be strictly irreversible, e.g. *law and order* and *odds and ends*. Therefore, a superlemma node with positional information should be postulated for these instances. A common characteristic of these examples is that they have a high token frequency, which may provide the answer to the problem as to which representation we should assume for the heterogeneous class of formulaic irreversibles. A possible suggestion would be that unit storage itself is gradable and dependent on frequency: if a certain fixed expression is used frequently, a unit representation is gradually built up. This suggestion is very much in line with assumptions about entrenchment processes (Langacker 1987: 59–60) and emergentist views on the lexicon such as exemplar-based models (see Bybee 2010: 14–32), which propose that representations are sensitive to

---

[29] Other findings reported in the same article give rise to scepticism regarding their evaluation of Cutting and Bock's (1997) model. Kuiper et al. (2007) report order reversals involving words of identical word class, which are part of Dutch idioms, for instance the reversal of two nouns (Kuiper et al. 2007: 341). Crucially, according to the superlemma model and thus also according to the assessment of the authors, these errors should likewise not occur. However, these findings are not discussed with regard to the comparison between the two theories. Incidentally, a relevant speech error is also reported in Stemberger (1985: 174), involving the exchange of two nouns within an idiom: *He doesn't have any closets in his skeleton.* These examples may thus be viewed as evidence in favour of Cutting and Bock's (1997) approach, which assumes regular phrasal frames also for idioms.

frequency. It would mean that a superlemma with positional preferences gradually emerges through frequent use of the binomial. The process may work like this: a certain coordinate construction contains two elements with strong activation differences; therefore, it is preferably produced in one particular order, with only occasional reversals due to noise in the system. If this construction is produced frequently, we may assume that a super-lemma node is gradually built up, containing positional information. This node may first be a relatively weak schema, but it becomes gradually stronger due to frequent production. Through its emergence, the positional specification becomes more and more pronounced, with the result that eventually, reversals do not occur anymore. Such a strengthening of representation through repetition is the key concept of exemplar-based models (Bybee 2010: 14–32) which can be implemented in interactive activation models, as suggested by Snider (2008).[30] Incorporating a storage mechanism that is sensitive to frequency provides the missing link in our description of the representation of irreversibles, as it may implement the varying degrees of (ir-)reversibility of binomials.[31] Further corroboration for this assumption comes from a study by Siyanova-Chanturia et al. (2011), who provide experimental evidence for the existence of frequency-sensitive storage of irreversible binomials.

In conclusion, I have shown that the representation and processing of irreversible binomials can be explained within current hybrid models of idiom representation. While on the basis of our data it is not possible to conclusively decide between the model by Cutting and Bock (1997) and the superlemma account (Sprenger et al. 2006), the suggestion of a gradually emerging superlemma node with positional preferences seems best suited to capture the gradual nature of irreversible binomials.

---

[30] See also Arnon and Snider (2010: 77).

[31] The assumption of a gradually emerging schema/superlemma predicts that the probability for a reversal should drop with rising frequency of the binomial type. If in our sample of irreversibles we correlate the probability for the observed number of reversals with the token frequency of the coordinate construction as a whole, this prediction is borne out, as a significant negative correlation is found ($r_{pearson}= -0.79$, $p < 0.01$). (To obtain the probability of the observed number of reversals, binomial tests were calculated, assuming a baseline probability for a reversal of 0.5. The tests calculated the cumulated probability of obtaining the observed number of reversals or any lower number. This probability was transformed logarithmically and correlated with the logarithmic frequency count of the coordinate construction as a whole, calculating the Pearson-correlation-coefficient.) While this finding lends some credence to our hypothesis of gradual emergence, it is not without problems. This is due to the fact that the frequency of a binomial influences the calculated probability, even if irreversibility stays the same. Using another operationalisation by merely comparing the ratios of reversals for data points of varying frequency is equally problematic, as with low-frequency binomials there is a high chance of finding zero reversals merely due to chance. These findings would thus not correspond to a *true* irreversibility that can be assumed to correspond to its storage in the mental lexicon. It is thus unclear how this hypothesis should be tested with corpus data – experimental evidence is probably needed for its validation.

10.3.2   A processing explanation for the characteristics of irreversibles

Let us turn to another issue regarding the processing of irreversible bino-mials that pertains to the differences between reversibles and irreversibles that were found. In Section 9.2, I found that in irreversibles ordering constraints were much more often adhered to. Furthermore, irreversibles show a higher probability of being affected by ordering constraints, and their constituents therefore exhibit more pronounced differences to each other. In Section 9.2, I discussed the possibility that these characteristics may work as selection pressures, which can be explained through preferences of the processing system. I will now flesh out this argument and explain the differ-ences between the two groups by taking recourse to the interactive activation model.

The first characteristic of irreversibles is that most ordering influences are seldom violated in that class as compared to reversible cases. This finding can be straightforwardly related to processing, now that the serialisation of constituents in an interactive activation model has been explained. Since I have shown in Section 10.2.4 that the ordering constraints can be related to activation differences between the to-be-ordered constituents, this difference means that the constituent that is assumed to be more highly activated is more often found in first position in the class of irreversible binomials, as compared to reversible instances. This can be explained by situational influences on activation levels that are not captured by the ordering constraints and which influence the two classes differently: during ad hoc serialisation in sponta-neous speech, there may be confounding influences such as noise in the system, which may impact the activation levels of the constituents and therefore result in an order of constituents different from expected. Such influences on the activation levels of the constituents may, for example, result from previous production processes. Irreversibles, however, can be assumed not to be influenced by these situational influences to the same degree, as they have undergone a lexicalisation process. We may view this process as a collaborative production/processing effort of many production instances, which ultimately result in a formulaic, irreversible unit (see also Section 10.3.1). Although every individual instance of production during this process is similarly affected by situational influences, on the whole it is the order that best conforms to the high-low activation pattern, as evidenced by the ordering constraints, that is more frequently produced. Therefore, this ordering stands a greater chance of 'fossilising', i.e. developing into an irreversible, formulaic unit. In conclusion, a mitigation of confounding situa-tional factors in the course of the emergence of an irreversible binomial may explain the higher adherence rate to ordering constraints in that class.

A further difference between the two groups to be accounted for is that irreversibles are more often influenced by ordering constraints irrespective of their adherence. I argue that this characteristic can also be explained by the architecture of the processing system: since ordering constraints can be related to activation differences between constituents, and as these constraints affect irreversibles more often, I conclude that this class exhibits more pronounced activation differences between constituents. These greater differences mean less competition between the constituents for first position, which contributes to a smoother production process.

Central to this argument is the notion of 'inhibition' (e.g. Dell and O'Seaghdha 1994). Recall that interactive activation models assume inhibitory links between elements on the same level (see Section 10.2.1). If a word (or other form) is activated for production, it inhibits the activation of its competitors via these links, which ensures that only one form is eventually selected for production. Thus, during the production of a binomial, its two constituents inhibit each other as they are activated for production. As one of them gains excitatory activation, it sends inhibitory activation to the other.

Significantly, the extent and direction of inhibition is dependent on the activation differences between the two constituents. In a situation of large activation differences, which is the case if many ordering constraints apply, one constituent has a much higher activation level than its competitor and thus strongly inhibits the lesser activated constituent, while this constituent hardly inhibits the highly activated one. In contrast, if both constituents have similarly high activation levels, because few or no ordering constraints apply, the inhibition of both constituents is nearly equal: i.e., there is stronger mutual inhibition between the two competitors. In the latter situation, where there is strong mutual inhibition due to roughly equal activation levels, serialisation and thereby production of the whole construction is slowed down, as it takes longer until one of the two constituents' nodes reaches the firing threshold and thus is selected. Conversely, if there are large activation differences, there is little inhibition, and the selection of the constituent to be produced first may proceed largely unimpeded, resulting in a smoother production process. Consequently, as activation differences are much more pronounced in irreversibles, it follows that these are easier to produce and process.

A second argument for an easier processing of irreversibles is that the first constituent in irreversibles is characterised by many activation-boosting characteristics. Since ordering constraints apply to irreversibles more frequently and as these are adhered to more often, it follows that the first constituent in irreversibles is generally very frequent, short, conceptually accessible, occupies a higher position in an extra-linguistic hierarchy, etc. Consequently, it can be considered to be much more highly activated than first-position constituents in reversibles (see also Figure 9.3 in Chapter 9). Viewed as a whole, irreversible binomials are constructions whose first element is much more highly activated and therefore more easily selected and produced, which can be assumed to render the binomial easier to process.

In summary, both findings, the greater adherence rate in irreversibles and the greater differences between the constituents in that class, can be related to mechanisms of the processing system, with irreversible binomials conforming better to its preferences. What remains to be accounted for is the finding that irreversibles exhibit alliteration effects more often. I argue that this finding can also be explained through processing preferences by relating it to the activation contour of nodes during production. Recall that in Section 10.2.1 I explained that, after firing, nodes undergo a short phase of self-inhibition followed by a phase of hyperexcitability and increased activation. This means that during that phase, the same node is more easily activated, which invites its re-use. Another widely used term for this process is 'priming', or more specifically, 'self-priming', as we are dealing with the re-use of the exact same node. The consequence of this activation contour is that the use of the same nodes is advantageous to the processing system if there is a certain temporal distance between the two uses. This processing mechanism may be reflected in a repetition of similar forms. Since the alliteration effect means a re-use of the same phoneme after a certain distance, it can be argued to be a reflection of this preference. Corroborating evidence for this argument comes from similar results of self-priming in other areas of phonology (e.g. Berg 2004; Schlüter 2005). These repetition effects affect such instances more strongly, which allow for more paradigmatic planning because a unit that instantiates a repetition – e.g. by beginning with the same phoneme – can then be selected. Irreversible binomials can be understood as being the result of a collaborative planning process, which would explain their greater susceptibility to these effects.[32] In conclusion, the differences between irreversibles and reversibles can be explained via processing preferences, which can thus be assumed to be the 'true' selection pressure for the class of irreversibles. It seems logical that the speech community would produce those instances more frequently that are easier to process and thereby facilitate their development into formulaic constructions. While no online ordering decision is necessary anymore once a binomial is lexicalised and has unit representation (see Section 10.3.1), many characteristics of this process can still be observed in them, which is why we may view irreversible binomials as representing fossilised processing preferences.

10.4   Interim summary

In this chapter I have offered a processing account of the ordering process by discussing the results obtained in the framework of language production models. It was shown that serial models that assume two stages of grammatical

---

[32] Gries's (2011) finding of alliteration effects in other idiomatic constructions ties in well with the present finding, as also for these a certain planning process can be assumed.

encoding can accommodate the results only when adapted to allow more incremental processing. Interactive activation models can account for the data more naturally. I offered an explanation of the serialisation process within this class of models by drawing on the concepts of activation and competition. The most important argument is that the order of constituents depends on their respective activation levels. The constituents compete for selection and the more highly activated element is chosen for early production and thus first position. To corroborate that claim, I showed that most ordering constraints that were found to affect serialisation can be related to activation differences between the competing constituents. Furthermore, I suggested an explanation of the different effect sizes of the ordering constraints by showing that there is a correspondence between the strength of ordering influences and the layer in the production network which is influenced by them: those constraints which influence the production process during an early stage (conceptual/semantic factors) yield stronger effects than those which impact later stages (phonological factors).

Moreover, I discussed the representation and processing of irreversible binomials within current models of idiom representation. I suggested a gradually emerging unit representation – which can be implemented in the *superlemma* model by Sprenger et al. (2006) – which contains information about the position of its components and which is dependent on the frequency of use of the binomial. Furthermore, I discussed the differences between irreversibles and reversibles and fleshed out the argument that the properties of irreversible binomials are the result of processing preferences that influence their development into fixed, lexicalised expressions.

11   Implications and outlook

This chapter addresses the implications of the present study for other areas of linguistic study and suggests avenues for future research. The first section discusses the possible ramifications of the results obtained for other alternation phenomena in English. In particular, I explore whether the factors that influence the ordering of elements in coordination also impact other contexts of variation, and whether the finding that conceptual/semantic variables yield stronger effects than morphological and phonological factors also holds for these contexts.

The second section discusses possible correspondences between the ordering of constituents during online processing and word order in English grammar. It furthermore offers a typological perspective on performance–grammar correspondences as reflected in the distribution of word orders in the grammars of the world's languages.

11.1   Implications for the study of other alternations in English

In recent years, there has been an increased interest in the study of variation phenomena in English with a number of studies focusing on the alternation of formally divergent yet semantically equivalent constructions (e.g. the contributions in Rohdenburg and Mondorf 2003). Most results contribute to the finding that a large number of variables from different levels of the linguistic hierarchy influence each case of variation, defying simple mono-causal explanations. This insight has been facilitated by the availability of large-scale corpora and the rise of more sophisticated methods of quantitative analysis, most importantly, multifactorial models, as applied in the present study. While this development is of course to be welcomed, since it means a step towards greater descriptive accuracy (see the discussions in Gries 2003 and Bresnan et al. 2007), the large number of influential factors in every individual case can easily become overwhelming. For instance, regarding the phenomena of dative alternation and preposition stranding in English, Gries (2003: 189) states that these 'are . . . highly complex phenomena with numerous determinants from many different levels of linguistic analysis'. The focus

183

of most studies on individual variation phenomena invites the conclusion that every case of variation is a highly complex and idiosyncratic alternation, susceptible to its own multifarious influences. In contrast to this interpretation, some variables such as length/weight have been shown to influence speakers' choices in more than one case of variation (see, for example, Arnold et al. 2000). It is therefore conceivable that a common set of variables can be identified that influences a large number of variation phenomena. Such a result would of course be very welcome, as it may indicate that many alternation contexts are guided by the same processing principles.

With regard to this possibility, the present study may have something to offer to the study of other alternation phenomena, as the explanations I have given for order in coordination may be generalised to other contexts. In particular I will explore the possibility that the same difference in strength of effects that I obtained with ordering in coordinate constructions can also be found with other alternations in English. More specifically, I first address the question as to whether the same factors that influence order in coordination also underlie other alternations. I then discuss whether the dominance of conceptual/semantic variables also holds for these other contexts (see Section 10.2.5).

In order to address these issues, I will choose two variation phenomena that are well researched: the so-called dative alternation and the choice between the two genitives in English. Both lend themselves well to a comparison, because – similar to coordinate constructions – the order of constituents in these contexts is variable (examples from Bresnan et al. 2007: 3, and Rosenbach 2005: 614, respectively).

Dative alternation:

(63)   a. Susan gave the children toys.
        b. Susan gave toys to the children.

Genitive alternation:

(64)   a. the king's palace
        b. the palace of the king

With the dative alternation, the language user may choose the double object construction, in which the two crucial NPs are assigned the grammatical roles of indirect and direct object, occurring in exactly that order. In terms of argument structure, this means a succession of recipient before theme. In the alternative variant, the prepositional *to*-dative, the order of the two phrases is reversed, with the theme in first position and the recipient featuring in a prepositional phrase following it. In the case of the choice between the two English genitive constructions, two noun phrases may take on two different (semantic) roles, commonly termed the *possessor* (~owner) and the *possessum* (~that which is owned). Most importantly, their order may also differ. With the *s*-genitive, the *possessor* precedes the *possessum*, while with the *of*-genitive it is the other way round (see example (64) above). While these two contexts are similar to coordinate constructions in that the order of constituents may vary,[1] there are also obvious differences. With the dative alternation grammatical role assignment differs across the two alternatives, while this is the case with neither coordination nor with the genitive. These differences and their implications are discussed further below. Since it would not be feasible to carry out additional empirical analyses for these alternations, I will review available literature and provide a survey of empirical research results.

An analysis of recent research on the two phenomena reveals that important variables that relate to activation and underlie ordering during coordination are active also in these two contexts. Turning first to the dative alternation, it has been shown that the animacy of recipient and theme influence the choice of construction. Animate themes 'prefer' the prepositional dative, while animate recipients tend towards the double object construction. Inanimate constituents exhibit the reverse tendency (e.g. Arnold et al. 2000; Szmrecsanyi 2006). This means that an order of animate before inanimate is preferred, which is congruent with the effects of conceptual accessibility we found to be at work in coordinate constructions.[2] In addition, the information status of recipient and theme influences the choice between the two structural alternatives, with given constituents being preferred before new ones (e.g. Arnold et al. 2000; Bresnan et al. 2007). The length of the two constituents also yields a significant effect: if the recipient is shorter than the theme, the double object construction is preferred; if in turn the theme is shorter than the recipient, the prepositional *to*-dative is chosen more often (Bresnan et al. 2007). Thus, with the three variables, information status, animacy and length, three influences that are highly relevant for order in coordination also underlie the dative alternation.

Turning to the genitive alternation, we find that it is again animacy, length and givenness that also impact this alternation (e.g. Rosenbach 2005; Hinrichs and Szmrecsanyi 2007; Wolk et al. 2013): animate possessors prefer the *s*-genitive, in keeping with a preference of animate before inanimate; similarly, definite, given constituents and shorter phrases also prefer that variant, tying in with a given-before-new and short-before-long succession respectively. There is a further phonological variable that influences this alternation, viz. a final sibilancy of the possessor, which yields more *of*-genitive choices (Szmrecsanyi 2006: 89).

---

[1] Note that with both alternations, not all instances constitute choice contexts. For example, with the dative alternation certain verbs make one of the two alternatives obligatory (e.g. *donate*, which requires the prepositional *to*-dative), and there are semantic restrictions on the use of one or the other genitive (see Szmrecsanyi 2006: 87–9 for an overview). Nevertheless, there are many contexts in which the language user truly has a choice, as in the examples above, which renders the two phenomena suited for the present analysis.

[2] Animacy is an important contributor to conceptual accessibility (see Chapter 3 above).

There are a number of other variables that are relevant for serialisation in coordinate constructions but do not seem to influence the choice between the dative and the genitive. Most importantly, these are the other semantic constraints, iconic sequencing and the influence of extra-linguistic hierarchies, both of which do not seem to apply to the contexts discussed here. The iconicity variable pertains mostly to temporal sequences that do not feature in the two alternation contexts considered here. There is also no influence of the variable extra-linguistic hierarchy, since the two crucial constituents of the genitive and the dative constructions typically denote a human referent (the recipient in the dative and the possessor in the genitive) and an object (the theme in the dative and the possesssum in the genitive), which are not ranked on a common extra-linguistic hierarchy.

With regard to a possible influence of frequency, the analysis of the literature yields the result that the variable has not been tested with either the genitive or the dative alternation, although an influence is certainly likely in keeping with the activation logic outlined in the previous chapter. In summary, the meta-analysis shows that there is considerable common ground between the choice of dative and genitive constructions and also between these alternations and the coordination contexts I empirically investigated. Conceptually more accessible (animate), short constituents and constituents that denote given information are preferred before elements that are of lesser conceptual accessibility (inanimate), long and new to the discourse.

Let us now turn to the second question, viz., whether the strength relations between variables in coordinate constructions can also be observed with the other alternation contexts. The question as to which variables yield an effect on the different alternations is of great importance in the serial production model by Bock and Levelt (1994), and therefore I will review its predictions for the dative and the genitive alternation briefly here. Remember that their model assumes two subsequent stages: the functional and the positional stage, which are subject to different influences (see also Section 10.1). For the dative alternation, it is the functional stage that is most relevant, as during its production, theme and recipient are assigned different grammatical roles. In the double object variant, these are direct and indirect object, and direct object and oblique with the prepositional dative (see Bock and Levelt 1994: 951). Since the choice of construction thus hinges on grammatical function assignment, it should be solely conceptual influences, e.g. contrasts in animacy, that steer the choice between the two variants (see also Bock and Warren 1985). This prediction is clearly not borne out by the empirical studies on the phenomenon, as it is shown that also the length of the two phrases influences this alternation. For genitive choice, the predictions of the serial model are different, as possessor and possessum do not differ with regard to their grammatical function. Hence, the choice between the two genitives happens during the positional stage and should thus be immune to conceptual influences (but cf. Rosenbach 2005: 637–8). Since it has been shown that animacy is a very important variable in choosing between the two genitives, this hypothesis is also at odds with the empirical data. In conclusion, the serial model that assumes an 'informational encapsulation' (Levelt 1989: 276) of the functional and the positional stages cannot account for these findings, as both conceptual and form-related variables influence both alternations. Interactive activation models can account for the findings in a more natural way, as they do not postulate self-contained stages or modules and therefore allow for multifarious influences of different linguistic levels on the alternation phenomena.

Let me now address the question as to whether the finding that conceptual/semantic constraints yield a stronger influence than others can be generalised to these other contexts. For coordinate constructions, it was found that conceptual constraints yielded larger effect sizes than phonological and other variables. Applied to the genitive and the dative alternation, one may test whether animacy as a conceptual factor affects the choice of construction more strongly than form-related, phonological factors, e.g. length. Both length and animacy are important predictors for both alternations, as they appear in all empirical studies on the phenomena (see Altenberg 1982, Rosenbach 2003, 2005, Szmrecsanyi 2006, Hinrichs and Szmrecsanyi 2007, Szmrecsanyi and Hinrichs 2008 on the genitive, and Bresnan et al. 2007 and Wolk et al. 2013 on the dative alternation). Rather than simply determining their influence, it is a comparison of their strengths that we are most interested in. Beginning with the genitive, one may have a look at the output of the multifactorial models calculated for the phenomenon, which allow for a comparison of the effect sizes of the respective variables. Comparing the odds ratios for all categorical variables in Hinrichs and Szmrecsanyi (2007: 462) reveals that animacy is by far the strongest predictor among them. It is stronger than an influence of final sibilancy of the possessor and factors relating to persistent use of one or the other variant, or an avoidance of nested genitives. This assessment is thus in line with the prediction that semantic variables should yield stronger effects. What remains to be shown is that the effect size of the variable animacy is also stronger than the effect of the variable length on the choice of genitive construction. Such a comparison is difficult, as variables of different levels need to be compared, because length is a scalar variable, while animacy is a categorical one (see also Hinrichs and Szmrecsayni 2007: 463–4). Effect-size values for the influence of length are considerably lower than the ones for animacy, but they denote only the influence of a one-word increase in length of the possessor, in contrast to the categorical difference between an animate and an inanimate possessor. In order for the two influences to be compared, the effect-size measures need to be standardised. For regression models, Gelman and Hill (2007: 56–7) suggest the standardising of all predictor variables by subtracting the mean and dividing them by two standard deviations, which results in effect-size measures on a common scale (number of standard deviations). Unfortunately, this has not been done in any of the modelling attempts of the genitive thus far. Fortunately, the study by Rosenbach (2005) provides information on how her data is distributed across all values of length and animacy. We may thus calculate standardised effect sizes based on her data. Calculating regression models for both of these variables and performing the necessary standardisation yields coefficients of 2.15 for animacy and 2.03 for length. This means that the standardised influence of animacy is slightly higher than the influence of length, which is in line with the hypothesis of stronger effects of conceptual influences. However, it must be noted that this is no more than a preliminary analysis, and the numerical difference in effect size is certainly not a large one.

Turning to the dative alternation, we obtain similar results. Both in Bresnan et al. (2007) and in Wolk et al. (2013) animacy is the predictor with the greatest effect size, followed by definiteness and length. Since both animacy and definiteness are categorical, we may conclude that the conceptual influence of an animacy contrast is stronger than a pragmatic difference in information status, similar to the results obtained for coordination (see Section 8.1). However, to compare the results to the variable length of theme and recipient, standardisation is again necessary, and this has not been carried out in any of the empirical studies on the dative alternation. Thus we cannot be sure how an effect of length compares to either animacy or definiteness.

The results for both alternations are encouraging in that there seems to be initial evidence for a stronger influence of the conceptual factor animacy compared to other influences, e.g. phonological factors. However, more empirical research is needed to further evaluate this difference in strength. Ideally, a variety of different alternations would be tested which involve the ordering of syntactic constituents, using empirical data from either the same or at least very similarly designed corpora. Moreover, one would then need to apply a consistent operationalisation of variables across phenomena. Thus, contrasts in animacy, length and other variables need to be measured in exactly the same way across all case studies. If the coefficients in the regression models were then standardised as described above, it would be possible to compare the effects of different variables and consequently test whether conceptual influences are truly superior in strength to other influences.

In summary, I found that many of the factors underlying ordering in coordination are also relevant for the dative and the genitive alternation in English. Furthermore, I obtained initial evidence that the hypothesis put forward for coordinate constructions – viz. that the effect size of influential variables is contingent upon when they influence the ordering process – may also hold for other alternations, as reflected in a stronger influence of conceptual/semantic influences over phonological ones.

11.2   Performance–grammar correspondence and typological perspectives

This section discusses possible implications of the results for the study of word order in grammar. More specifically, I explore whether the processing preferences empirically investigated – i.e., that constituents with certain characteristics are preferred in early positions – correspond to word-order relations in the grammar of English. Furthermore, I discuss whether a correspondence between performance and grammar is relevant to typological research in being reflected in preferred word orders in the world's languages.

Recently there have been a number of suggestions arguing that properties of the grammar and structure of language ultimately stem from processing preferences (e.g. Hopper 1987; Berg 1998; Hawkins 2004; Bybee 2010).[3] This view rests on the assumption that there is a close link between usage and grammar. One influential proposal in that regard is the Performance–Grammar Correspondence Hypothesis by Hawkins (2004: 3) which states:

Grammars have conventionalized syntactic structures in proportion to their degree of preference in performance, as evidenced by patterns of selection in corpora and by ease of processing in psycholinguistic experiments.

The general argument by Hawkins is that certain variants that are preferred in performance, thus in actual language use when speakers are given a choice, should be reflected in the grammar of a given language. Applying this hypothesis in the present context means, first of all, asking whether the ordering tendencies in performance, which were revealed through empirical study, are also found in the ordering of constituents in the grammar of English. Since English exhibits a quite fixed SVO order, the question arises as to whether the ordering constraints underlying coordination may offer an explanation for this sequence of grammatical roles. As I have focused on the ordering of nominal constituents in this book, I restrict myself at this point to a discussion of the order subject before object, as both roles typically take the form of noun phrases. More specifically, I ask whether the grammatical role of subject incorporates features that lead to the early mention of constituents in coordination, since the subject is usually the leftmost NP in a sentence. In contrast, objects may be characterised by features of constituents which occur in second position in coordination. In order to explore this issue, it is necessary to clarify what the properties of subjects and objects are.

Research on the characteristics of grammatical roles has focused on the features of the subject (see the discussion in Keenan 1976 for an overview). Determining its features has been shown to be a notoriously difficult

---

[3] The following section on performance–grammar correspondences is inspired by a workshop conducted by Holger Diessel and Karsten Schmidtke-Bode at the Leipzig Spring School on Linguistic Diversity in 2008. See also Diessel and Schmidtke (2008).

enterprise, as there seems to be no finite set of defining characteristics. Frequently the notion of subject is viewed as a merely syntactic category; therefore, criteria such as verb agreement are used for its identification. Since both constituents in coordinate constructions occupy the same grammatical role (see Chapter 1), the syntactic perspective would, however, not be revealing in the present context. There are, however, a number of characteristics of subject (and object) beyond its syntactic behaviour that are relevant in the present context. Most frequently mentioned in the literature is the close relation between subject and topic, as subjects usually 'identify what the speaker is talking about' (Keenan 1976: 318), and thus encode the topic of a sentence (see also the other contributions in Li 1976). Subjects have therefore traditionally been viewed as 'grammaticalized topics' (Givón 1983a: 5), while objects were considered 'secondary grammaticalized topic[s]' (Givón 1983a: 6). While there are exceptions in which subject and topic are encoded by separate NPs, there is a strong probabilistic relation between the two notions in English (see, e.g., Taboada and Wiesemann 2009 for recent empirical evidence). Although I did not directly test for topic status in the empirical studies conducted, the variable information status is closely related to it because the topic constitutes in most cases given information (see Arnold et al. 2000: 30). Therefore, a certain correspondence can be observed, as the preference to mention given information first in a coordinate construction corresponds to the tendency of subjects being the topic of a sentence.

Further correspondences may be detected on the conceptual plane. The established view in language production research is that there is a close relation between conceptual accessibility and grammatical functions (e.g. Bock and Warren 1985; Bock and Levelt 1994). Bock and Warren (1985) suggest a hierarchy of grammatical functions of SUBJECT > DIRECT OBJECT > INDIRECT OBJECT based on Keenan and Comrie (1977). As has been shown in numerous experiments (e.g. Ertel 1977; Bock and Warren 1985; Christianson and Ferreira 2005), higher grammatical roles, most importantly the subject role, are characterised by a higher conceptual accessibility, whereas conceptual accessibility is influenced by animacy, concreteness, imageability, etc (see Bock and Warren 1985: 48; also Levelt 1989: 265–71). Since we found that differences in conceptual accessibility are a significant and important factor in ordering constituents in coordination, the correspondence is obvious: conceptual characteristics that lead to first mention also characterise the subject and, more generally, higher grammatical functions. When turning to features pertaining to the formal realisation of grammatical roles, further similarities can be detected. Temperley (2007: 310–11) shows that subject NPs tend to be shorter than object NPs in English, which is congruent with the short-before-long constraint we found to be at work in constituent order in coordination.

In summary, many factors that underlie serialisation in coordinate constructions characterise the differences between English subjects and objects.

Subjects tend to encode the topic, are highly conceptually accessible, and are short; i.e., properties that correspond to those of the first constituent in coordinate constructions. It bears mentioning that these properties of subjects are not deterministic, but probabilistic in nature. Particularly with the notion of topic, it has been shown that disjunctions of subject role and topic status do occur in English (see Givón 1983a; Taboada and Wiesemann 2009). Furthermore, in passive constructions, atypical constituents are promoted to subject status due to their contextual prominence. The notion of subject can therefore be understood as a prototypical category, with the prototype exhibiting all of the features mentioned above. Since these properties are related to a high activation of constituents, one may view subjects as a 'grammaticalized category of high activation'. The processing preference of putting highly activated constituents in first position in choice contexts is thus reflected in conventional word order in English because, given its rigid word order, subjects occur almost always in initial position. This correspondence is very much in line with the Performance–Grammar Correspondence Hypothesis by Hawkins (2004) and thus more generally with approaches that postulate a processing motivation of grammar.

Thus far I have discussed the link between processing and structure only for English. There may, however, be a correspondence between the results obtained and preferred word orders in the grammars of other languages. Thus, there may be implications for typological research. In discussing these implications, I make the simplifying assumption that the notion of subject in other languages is roughly similar to that in English. This notoriously difficult issue cannot be discussed at this point, but note that most properties of subjects seem to be shared across languages (see the contributions in Li 1976; also Christianson and Ferreira 2005). The question arises whether the same link between processing and structure found in English can be found in other languages. Pertaining to that question, Diessel and Schmidtke (2008: 3) mention an interesting correspondence between processing preferences in one language, Japanese, and the distribution of word orders in the world's languages. In Japanese, a language with a far less rigid word order than English, both the orders subject-object (SO) and object-subject (OS) are possible. Yamashita (2002) shows in a corpus study that speakers strongly prefer an order of subject before object in those contexts where also the reverse would be possible; i.e., evidence for a processing preference to place subjects first, which again emphasizes the link between first mention and subjecthood. Diessel and Schmidtke (2008) argue that this preference is a universal one reflected in the grammars of the world's languages, as a large majority of the languages studied so far prefer the subject in initial position (cf., e.g., Hawkins 1983; Tomlin 1986; Dryer 2005). Of over 1,000 languages listed in Dryer (2005), 88% exhibit either SOV or SVO order. The ratio of languages in which the subject precedes the object is even higher with 96%, while only *c.* 3% have the subject in last position. Based on this data, the predictions of a correspondence between processing and grammar are also borne out from a typological perspective: the tendency to place highly activated constituents early in syntagmatic strings during processing is grammaticalised in the sense that many languages prefer subject-initial word order.

While the link between processing in the choice contexts I investigated and preferred word orders in the grammars of a large number of languages is intriguing, further research is necessary to validate it. Many issues call for further exploration from a cross-linguistic and typological perspective. One question is whether the serialisation of constituents in coordination works similarly across languages. Thus far, I have based a possible link between grammar and performance solely on the performance in English, yet it is far from clear that processing coordinate constructions is the same in other languages. Little is known about this issue, as there are only few studies that investigate ordering in coordination in languages other than English, or even cross-linguistically. The few studies that are available indicate similarities of the ordering process to that in English. To be mentioned here are Szpyra (1983), Pórdany (1986) and Müller (1997), who study Polish, Hungarian and German binomials respectively. One study that is explicitly cross-linguistic in perspective is Pinker and Birdsong (1979), whose results indicate that most constraints work the same in French and English, yet some phonological constraints may be language-specific.

Another interesting topic from a typological perspective would be the investigation of how the difference between irreversible binomials and reversible, ad hoc coordination relates to the typological categories natural versus accidental coordination (Wälchli 2005). Earlier (see Section 1.2.2) I mentioned that the category of irreversible binomials in English is roughly similar to the typological category of natural coordination, which is often characterised by coordinator omission in a number of languages (Wälchli 2005: 67–89). For English irreversible binomials, I found that ordering constraints yield much more pronounced effects compared to ad hoc coordination, resulting in irreversibility. It would be interesting to explore whether this is also the case with languages that formally distinguish the category of natural coordination through asyndetic coordination (without coordinator). It could be that these asyndetic constructions in those languages exhibit even stronger irreversibility. Since this coordinator-less variant is argued to be more lexicalised (Wälchli 2005), it seems likely that this greater degree of lexicalisation is correlated with a lower degree of reversibility (Wälchli 2005: 218 alludes to that). If that is true, then one could explore which degree of (ir-)reversibility is needed for a coordinate expression to be tightly coordinated and thus for it to occur without coordinator. Other possible interactions pertain to the influence of specific ordering constraints and asyndetic coordination such that certain ordering constraints may be more important than the influence of others. These questions are certainly worth an empirical investigation, as they would shed more light on the properties of natural and asyndetic coordination and how these categories compare to languages such as English, which does not feature such a clear formal contrast but only differentiates between reversible and irreversible coordination.

If we turn from the specific case of coordinate constructions to the more general level of serialisation in language production as a whole, there are even more unresolved questions. The exploration of cross-linguistic differences has only just begun, as psycholinguistic research has been focused on the study of English until very recently (see, e.g., Christianson and Ferreira 2005). It is therefore unclear whether processing factors underlying serialisation are universal, or if they interact with other linguistic properties. One factor for which such an interaction has been shown is the length of to-be-ordered constituents. It was found that the short-before-long preference, which in language production research had been assumed to be a universal constraint, is reversed in head-final languages. For example, Yamashita and Chang (2001) show that Japanese speakers prefer a sequence of long-before-short in certain constructions, a finding that calls for a drastic adjustment of theories of language production, or at least reduces their applicability to only languages of a certain structural type. To further complicate the matter, Lohmann and Takada (2012) show that the influence of the factor length interacts with syntactic context, as both the long-before-short and short-before-long preference can be found in Japanese. The example of just this one factor and its effects in only two languages shows that findings from one language cannot simply be generalised to others, even if a universal validity is well motivated on theoretical grounds. Empirical studies on processing and serialisation in a large sample of languages are thus called for to further elucidate these issues – certainly a task of gigantic proportions. Even if we just focus on order in coordinate constructions, the task ahead is enormous. Testing the ordering constraints discussed in this book in a large sample of languages would only be the first step, as it is entirely possible that additional factors can be motivated for other languages, which would then have to be added to the list of potential ordering constraints. However laborious, such an empirical analysis would be of great value, as it would much advance our understanding of constituent ordering in shedding light on the question as to what extent the process is language-independent or language-specific.

12   Summary and conclusion

This study set out to investigate the order of elements in English coordinate constructions on three levels: the order of compound constituents in copulative compounds, word order in noun binomials and the order of complex noun phrases within a superordinate NP. This book's point of departure has been the observation that research in linguistics has strongly focused on fossilised irreversible binomials, which raises the question as to whether postulated factors for these quasi-idiomatic constructions are of a wider generalisability and thus represent processing factors relevant also for cases of reversible ad hoc coordination. This question could be largely answered in the affirmative. The results obtained show that a number of factors are truly relevant across the board and may therefore be viewed as empirical pillars guiding ordering choices: these are the length and frequency of constituents, and whether these denote referents given in the discourse. Furthermore, the semantic/pragmatic factors conceptual accessibility and iconicity of sequence have been found to be uniformly relevant ordering constraints. Thus, these influences are not construction-specific in applying only to a certain class of coordinate constructions, e.g. irreversible binomials, but represent generally relevant variables for coordination as a whole. Other variables, most of which are located on the phonological plane, have been found to be significant in selected samples, but could not be shown to be of general relevance. Most of these factors were motivated by observations of selected minimal pairs in irreversible binomials, in which constituents differed only with regard to this one factor. It is quite possible that these contrasts do not occur in real language data with sufficient frequency to reach significance. Thus the negative result obtained does not rule out an influence, yet indicates only a marginal relevance of these factors in natural language data.

Overall, the results obtained point to a large convergence across the three investigated levels, as mostly the same factors influence ordering across the case studies. Some factors were shown to solely influence copulative compounds, which could be explained by their greater degree of lexicalisation. Noticeable differences were detected between reversible and irreversible binomials, of which the most important one is that ordering influences affect the latter group much more strongly than the first one. This notion of a greater strength can be broken down into two separate concepts. The first is a much higher adherence rate with irreversible binomials; i.e., less violation of ordering constraints than with reversible binomials. Secondly, it was shown that the to-be-ordered constituents in irreversibles are more often influenced by ordering constraints and tend to exhibit more pronounced differences to each other on conceptual as well as formal dimensions. I interpreted both of these differences as supporting what I termed the 'selection pressures hypothesis', with those pairings being more likely to become irreversible binomials whose constituents exhibit more pronounced contrasts on relevant dimensions.

In order to explain the findings theoretically, I offered a psycholinguistic account of the ordering process, which included a discussion of different language production models. Those models that postulate two stages in grammatical encoding and distinguish between different forms of accessibility predict that solely lexical accessibility affects ordering in coordinate constructions. However, this prediction is clearly not borne out by the data, as semantic/conceptual factors also affect ordering in the data. Therefore, models that allow for effects across different levels and do not postulate self-contained modules are better suited to explain the obtained results. One such family of models is interactive activation models whose predictions for ordering in coordinate constructions were discussed in detail (see Chapter 10). While different versions of these production models vary with regard to their implementation of serialisation tasks, most of them handle serialisation via frames or sequence nodes, which determine the position of linguistic elements. However, these frames do not specify the order of individual lexical items, as slots in the frames are merely sensitive to syntactic category. For the present case studies, this means that the order of constituents in coordinate constructions is not specified, as these belong to the same syntactic class. The prediction of these models is thus that their order solely depends on the respective activation levels of to-be-ordered constituents. Discussing the results within the framework of these models yielded a number of important insights. Congruent with the predictions of these models, the relevant variables identified could be shown to relate to activation differences between constituents straightforwardly. For example, since high frequency leads to a high resting activation level of nodes in the production network, the tendency to produce more frequent constituents before less frequent ones can be described by a difference in activation levels. Similar explanations were given for the other relevant ordering constraints, in linking them to the process of activation. Furthermore, regarding the factors' varying strengths of effect, it could be shown that the average effect sizes of ordering factors roughly correspond to the layer on which respective nodes are located. For example, as conceptual nodes are located on a higher layer in the network, their activation should have a greater effect than that of lower-level nodes, which corresponds to the result of semantic/conceptual constraints yielding stronger effects on ordering. The architecture of the production network may thus explain the ordering constraints' varying degrees of strength.

The psycholinguistic perspective was found to also hold explanatory value for the characteristics of irreversible binomials, which I argued are reflections of processing preferences. The first characteristic of irreversibles – a greater adherence to ordering constraints – could be explained by a mitigation of situational influences during the emergence of irreversibles through many instances of repeated production. For the second characteristic, the more pronounced contrasts between the constituents in irreversibles mean less competition between them, which facilitates the serialisation process. Since both of these characteristics pertain to properties of the processing system, I argued that ease of processing is an important factor underlying the emergence of formulaic, irreversible binomials.

With regard to the mental representation of irreversible binomials, models of idiom representation that assume hybrid storage for fixed multi-word phrases were discussed. Hybrid storage means that, while there is a holistic representation of the expression as a whole, it is still linked to the representations of its parts, e.g. individual words of which the expression consists. Discussing two different versions of hybrid models resulted in a (slight) superiority of the superlemma model in accounting for the status of irreversible binomials (see also Kuiper et al. 2007). I proposed that the mental representation of this class of expressions may best be explained by superlemma nodes, whose emergence is sensitive to the frequency of their processing. Such an explanation is congruent with current exemplar-based theories, which assume redundant representation on several levels and furthermore claim that unit storage is a function of frequency (see the overview given in Arnon and Snider 2010).

With regard to implications of the current study, ramifications for two possible fields were discussed. Since the current investigation is located at the heart of a very active area of research – viz., the study of factors underlying variation phenomena – I first sought to compare the obtained results to those of two other English variation phenomena: the dative and the genitive alternation. The comparison yielded the result that important variables underlying coordination are also relevant for the ordering of constituents in these other choice contexts. Furthermore, I discussed whether the strength differences found for coordination, with conceptual variables yielding stronger effects than phonological ones, also hold for these other alternations. Initial evidence for that claim was acquired and I pointed out how this hypothesis could be further tested in future research. Secondly, I discussed possible correspondences between performance, as reflected in the ordering of constituents in coordination, and word order in the grammar of English and possibly other languages. It could be shown that there is a large correspondence between the characteristics of first-mentioned constit-uents in coordination and features of the grammatical role of subject in English, pointing to a processing-based motivation of SVO order in English. Extending the discussion to other languages revealed that this correspondence may be a universal one, as a large number of languages prefer the subject in first position. However, more research of diverse languages is necessary, as most studies on serialisation have been focused on English. In terms of an outlook, I have sketched out the issues that need to be empirically addressed in order to be able to advance research on performance-grammar correspondences from a typological perspective.

Some points should be raised regarding the methodological approach pursued and the theoretical explanation of the results. With regard to its theoretical orientation, this book combined research on irreversible binomials in linguistics with psycholinguistic studies on serialisation. This strategy proved to be rewarding, as both fields contributed to an empirically adequate description, as well as a theoretically sound explanation of the phenomenon. Regarding the former, research in linguistics provided a large number of ordering constraints from the study on irreversible binomials. Ordering factors are also discussed in psycholinguistics, but primarily as general constraints, not as specific influences on coordinate constructions. Taken together, these two fields provided the hypotheses that were tested in the modelling process and thereby enabled the empirical adequacy obtained. With regard to methodology, recall that above (see Section 1.5) I mentioned points of critique as to the compatibility of corpus data and psycholinguistic theorising and I argued that, although corpus data is not as controlled as experimentally acquired data, it may nevertheless be a resource suitable also for psycholinguistic interpretation. The results obtained and their subse-quent discussion showed that indeed corpus linguistics and psycholinguistics do not need to go separate ways, as the corpus findings can be explained by psycholinguistic theories, as I have shown above (Chapter 10). The findings even have implications for psycholinguistic theorising, as it could be shown that the corpus results are not compatible with serial models (cf. Chapter 10), and may be viewed as another piece of evidence in favour of theoretical alternatives. Similar to other studies (e.g. Gries 2003, 2005; Szmrecsanyi 2006), the present one has shown that phenomena that are thought to belong to the domain of psycholinguistics can be investigated using corpus-linguistic methods. The growing number of studies that are similar in orientation points to a mutually productive cooperation between the two fields instead of to their incompatibility. It does not seem to be a bold claim to state that more can be gained by this cooperation in the future, be it considering corpus data to test psycholinguistic theories, or by theoretically informing corpus-linguistic studies. Regarding the latter, the past years have seen a plethora of research on variation phenomena whose results, however, have been rarely discussed within psycholinguistic models. For instance, Smzrecsanyi (2006) and Hilpert (2008), who investigate syntactic priming and the comparative alternation respectively, do a fine job in empirically charting these phenomena; however, they do not attempt to explain how their results may feature within psycholinguistic models, although the results do have implications for these. In contrast, other works attempt such a psycholinguistic grounding, for example Schlüter (2005), who discussed the principle of rhythmic alternation within a spreading activation model, and Gries (2005), who integrated syntactic priming into a production model. It is my opinion that much can be gained by pursuing this path of convergence between these two fields, as it bears the chance of more adequately explaining many variation phenomena and the forces underlying them.

Appendix

Abbreviations of variables used in statistical models

CONACC	Conceptual accessibility
F1	First formant frequency
F2	Second formant frequency
FREQ	Token frequency
HIERARCHY	Extra-linguistic hierarchy
ICONSEQ	Iconic sequencing
INIC	Number of initial consonants
INF	Information status
LADE	Ladefoged's measure (F2-F1 difference)
LENGTHPHO	Length in number of phonemes
LENGTHSYL	Length in number of syllables
MORPHCOMPL	Morphological complexity
RHYTHM	Rhythmic alternation
SONFINC	Sonority of the final consonant
SONINIC	Sonority of the initial consonant
SYLW	Syllable weight
SYNTCOMPL	Syntactic complexity
ULTSTRESS	Avoidance of ultimate stress
VLENGTHFINAL	Vowel length of the final vowel
VLENGTHTOTAL	Vowel length counting all vowels
VOICFINC	Voicing of the final consonant

References

Abraham, Richard D. 1950. Fixed order of coordinates: a study in comparative lexicography. *MLA*, 276–87.

Ahlsén, Elisabeth. 2006. *Introduction to Neurolinguistics*. Amsterdam: Benjamins.

Aitchison, Jean and Todd Peyton. 1982. Slips of the mind and slips of the pen. In St Clair and von Raffler-Engel 1982: 180–94.

Allan, Keith. 1987. Hierarchies and the choice of left conjuncts (with particular attention to English). *Journal of Linguistics* 23/1, 51–77.

Altenberg, Bengt. 1982. The Genitive v. the of-Construction: A Study of Syntactic Variation in the 17th Century English. Dissertation, Lund University (Lund Studies in English 62). Lund: Gleerup.

Ariel, Mira. 2001. Accessibility theory: an overview. In Sanders, Schilperoord and Spooren 2001: 29–87.

Arnaud, Pierre J. L. 2002. *Document de travail sur les noms composés anglais*. Unpublished manuscript. Department of English, University of Lyon.

Arnold, Jenniffer E., Anthony Lesongco, Thomas Wasow and Ryan Ginstrom. 2000. Heaviness vs. newness: the effects of structural complexity and discourse status on constituent ordering. *Language* 76/1, 28–55.

Arnon, Inbal and Neil Snider. 2010. More than words: frequency effects for multi-word phrases. *Journal of Memory and Language* 62, 67–82.

Baars, Bernard J. and Michael T. Motley. 1976. Spoonerisms as sequencer conflicts: evidence from artificially elicited errors. *The American Journal of Psychology* 89/3, 476–84.

Baayen, R. H. 2008. *Analyzing Linguistic Data: A Practical Introduction to Statistics Using R*. Cambridge and New York: Cambridge University Press.

Backhaus, Klaus, Bernd Erichson, Wulff Plinke and Rolf Weiber. 2008. *Multivariate Analysemethoden: Eine anwendungsorientierte Einführung* (Springer-Lehrbuch). 12th edn. Berlin: Springer.

Badecker, William. 2001. Lexical composition and the production of compounds: evidence from errors in naming. *Language and Cognitive Processes* 16/4, 337–66.

Bailey, Charles-James N. and Roy Harris, eds. 1985. *Developmental Mechanisms of Language* (Language and Communication Library 6). Oxford, New York, Toronto, Sydney, Paris, Frankfurt: Pergamon Press.

Balota, David A. and James I. Chumbley. 1984. Are lexical decisions a good measure of lexical access? The role of word frequency in the neglected decision stage. *Journal of Experimental Psychology: Human Perception and Performance* 10/3, 340–57.

Bayer, S. 1996. The coordination of unlike categories. *Language* 72, 579–616.

Behaghel, Otto. 1928. *Deutsche Syntax: Eine geschichtliche Darstellung* (1. Sammlung germanischer Elementar- und Handbücher 1. Reihe Grammatiken Band III: Die Satzgebilde). Heidelberg: Carl Winter's Universitätsbuchhandlung.

Benor, Sarah B. and Roger Levy. 2006. The chicken or the egg? A probabilistic analysis of English binomials. *Language* 82/2, 233–78.

Berg, Thomas. 1988. *Die Abbildung des Sprachproduktionsprozesses in einem Aktivationsflussmodell: Untersuchungen an deutschen und englischen Versprechern* (Linguistische Arbeiten 206). Tübingen: M. Niemeyer.

1998. *Linguistic Structure and Change: An Explanation from Language Processing.* Oxford: Clarendon Press.

2004. Similarity and contrast in segmental phonology. *Linguistics* 42, 1049–103.

2009. *Structure in Language: A Dynamic Perspective* (Routledge Studies in Linguistics 10), 1st edn. New York: Routledge.

Berg, Thomas and U. Schade. 1992. The role of inhibition in a spreading-activation model of language production. *Journal of Psycholinguistic Research* 21/6, 405–34.

Berlage, Eva. 2010. Noun phrase complexity in English. Doctoral dissertation (revised version), University of Paderborn.

Blakemore, Diane and Robyn Carston. 2005a. Introduction to coordination: syntax, semantics and pragmatics. *Lingua* 115/4, 353–8.

2005b. The pragmatics of sentential coordination with *and*. *Lingua* 115/4, 569–89.

Blühdorn, Hardarik. 2008. Subordination and coordination in syntax, semantics and discourse: evidence from the study of connectives. In Fabricius-Hansen and Ramm 2008: 59–85.

Bock, Kathryn J. 1977. The effect of a pragmatic presupposition on syntactic structure in question answering. *Journal of Verbal Learning and Verbal Behavior* 16, 723–34.

1982. Towards a cognitive psychology of syntax: information processing contribution to sentence formulation. *Psychological Review* 89, 1–47.

1986. Syntactic persistence in language production. *Cognitive Psychology* 18, 335–87.

1987a. An effect of accessibility of word forms on sentence structure. *Journal of Memory and Language* 26, 119–37.

1987b. Coordinating words and syntax in speech plans. In Ellis 1985: 337–90.

Bock, Kathryn and David E. Irwin. 1980. Syntactic effects of information availability. *Journal of Verbal Learning and Verbal Behavior* 19, 467–84.

Bock, Kathryn J. and Willem J. M. Levelt. 1994. Language production: grammatical encoding. In Gernsbacher 1994: 945–984.

Bock, Kathryn and Richard Warren. 1985. Conceptual accessibility and syntactic structure in sentence formulation. *Cognition* 21, 47–67.

Bolinger, Dwight. 1962. Binomials and pitch accent. *Lingua* 11, 34–44.

Booij, Geert and Jaap van Marle, eds. 2001. *Yearbook of Morphology 2000.* Vienna and New York: Springer.

Börjars, Kersti, ed. 2013. *Morphosyntactic Categories and the Expression of Possession* (Linguistik aktuell 199). Amsterdam: Benjamins.

Boume, G., I. Kraemer and J. Zwarts, eds. 2007. *Cognitive Foundations of Interpretation.* Amsterdam: Royal Netherlands Academy of Arts and Sciences.

Branigan, Holly P. and E. Feleki. 1999. Conceptual accessibility and serial order in Greek speech production. In Hahn and Stoness 1999: 96–101.

Branigan, Holly P., Martin J. Pickering, Simon P. Liversedge, Andrew J. Stewart and Thomas P. Urbach. 1995. Syntactic priming: investigating the mental representation of language. *Journal of Psycholinguistic Research* 24, 489–507.

Branigan, Holly P., Martin J. Pickering and Mikihiro Tanaka. 2008. Contributions of animacy to grammatical function assignment and word order during production. *Lingua* 118/2, 172–89.

Bresnan, J., A. A. Cueni, T. Nikitina and Rolf H. Baayen. 2007. Predicting the dative alternation. In Boume, Kraemer and Zwarts 2007: 69–94.

Brinton, Laurel and Elizabeth Traugott. 2005. *Lexicalization and Language Change* (Research Surveys in Linguistics). Cambridge: Cambridge University Press.

Brown, R. and David N. McNeill. 1966. The 'tip of the tongue' phenomenon. *Journal of Verbal Learning and Verbal Behavior* 5, 325–37.

Bybee, Joan. 2010. *Language, Usage and Cognition*. Cambridge: Cambridge University Press.

Cedergren, Henrietta and David Sankoff. 1974. Variable rules: performance as a statistical reflection of competence. *Language* 50, 333–55.

Christianson, Kiel and Fernanda Ferreira. 2005. Conceptual accessibility and sentence production in a free word order language (Odawa). *Cognition* 98/2, 105–35.

Clark, Herbert H. and Eve V. Clark. 1977. *Psychology and Language: An Introduction to Psycholinguistics*. New York: Harcourt Brace Jovanovich.

Clements, George N. and Samuel J. Keyser. 1983. *CV Phonology: A Generative Theory of the Syllable* (Linguistic Inquiry Monographs 9). Cambridge, MA: MIT Press.

Cooper, William E. and Gayle V. Klouda. 1995. The psychological basis of syntactic iconicity. In Landsberg 1995: 331–42.

Cooper, William E. and Jeanne Paccia-Cooper. 1980. *Syntax and Speech* (Cognitive Science Series 3). Cambridge, MA: Harvard University Press.

Cooper, William E. and John Ross. 1975. Word order. In Grossman, San and Vance 1975: 63–111.

Cormack, Annabel and Neil Smith. 2005. What is coordination? *Lingua* 115/4, 395–418.

Crawley, Michael J. 2005. *Statistics: An Introduction Using R*. Chichester: John Wiley and Sons.

Crystal, Thomas H. and Arthur S. House. 1988. The duration of American-English vowels. *Journal of Phonetics* 16, 263–84.

Cutler, Anne and William E. Cooper. 1978. Phoneme-monitoring in the context of different phonetic sequences. *Journal of Phonetics* 6, 221–5.

Cutting, J. and Kathryn J. Bock. 1997. That's the way the cookie bounces: syntactic and semantic components of experimentally controlled idiom blends. *Memory and Cognition* 25/1, 57–71.

Dagenbach, Dale, ed. 1994. *Inhibitory Processes in Attention, Memory, and Language*. San Diego: Academic Press.

Dell, Gary S. 1986. A spreading-activation theory of retrieval in sentence production. *Psychological Review* 93/3, 283–321.

Dell, Gary S., Lisa K. Burger and William R. Svec. 1997a. Language production and serial order: a functional analysis and a model. *Psychological Review* 104/1, 123–47.

Dell, Gary S., Cornell Juliano and Anita Govindjee. 1993. Structure and content in language production: a theory of frame constraints in phonological speech errors. *Cognitive Science* 17/2, 149–95.

Dell, Gary S. and Padraig G. O'Seaghdha. 1994. Inhibition in interactive activation models of linguistic selection and sequencing. In Dagenbach 1994: 409–53.

Dell, Gary S., Myrna F. Schwartz, Nadine Martin, Eleanor M. Saffran and Deborah A. Gagnon. 1997b. Lexical access in aphasic and nonaphasic speakers. *Psychological Review* 104/4, 801–38.

Diessel, Holger and Karsten Schmidtke. 2008. The usage-based model (II): performance-grammar correspondences. Handout for a workshop held at the Leipzig Spring School on Linguistic Diversity 2008, available for download at: http://www.karsten-schmidtke.net/Handout1_ConvergingEvidence.pdf.

Dik, Simon C. 1972. *Coordination: Its Implications for the Theory of General Linguistics*. Amsterdam: North-Holland.

Dressler, Wolfgang U. 2005. Word-formation in natural morphology. In Stekauer and Lieber 2005: 267–84.

Dryer, Matthew. 2005. Order of subject, object, and verb. In Haspelmath and Bibiko 2005: 330–3.

Edmondson, Jerold A. 1985. Biological foundations of language universals. In Bailey and Harris 1985: 109–30.

Eikmeyer, H. J. and U. Schade. 1991. Sequentialization in connectionist language production models. *Cognitive Systems* 3/2, 128–38.

Ellis, Andrew W. ed. 1985. *Progress in the Psychology of Language*. London and Hillsdale, NJ: Lawrence Erlbaum Associate Publishers.

Ertel, Suitbert. 1977. *Where do the subjects of sentences come from?* In Rosenberg 1977: 259–75.

Evans, Vyvyan and Melanie Green. 2006. *Cognitive Linguistics: An Introduction*. Edinburgh: Edinburgh University Press.

Fabricius-Hansen, Cathrine and Wiebke Ramm, eds. 2008. *Subordination vs. Coordination in Sentence and Text*. Amsterdam and Philadelphia: Benjamins.

Farrell, W. S. 1979. Coding left and right. *Journal of Verbal Learning and Verbal Behavior* 8, 457–62.

Fenk-Oczlon, Gertraud. 1989. Word frequency and word order in freezes. *Linguistics* 27, 517–56.

Ferreira, Fernanda. 1991. Effects of length and syntactic complexity on initiation times for prepared utterances. *Journal of Memory and Language* 30, 210–33.

Ferreira, Victor S. and Hiromi Yoshita. 2003. Given-new ordering effects on the production of scrambled sentences in Japanese. *Journal of Psychological Review* 32/6, 669–92.

Frazier, Lyn, Alan Munn and Charles Clifton, Jr. 2000. Processing coordinate structures. *Journal of Psycholinguistic Research* 29/4, 343–70.

Fromkin, Victoria. 1973. *Speech Errors as Linguistic Evidence* (Janua linguarum 77). The Hague: Mouton.

Fromkin, Victoria A. 1971. The non-anomalous nature of anomalous utterances. *Language* 47/1, 27–52.

Fry, D. B. 1947. The frequency of occurrence of speech sounds in southern English. *Archives Néderlandaises de Phonétique Experimentales*, 20.

Gaeta, Livio. 2008. Constituent order in compounds and syntax: typology and diachrony. *Morphology* 18, 117–41.

Gahl, Susanne. 2008. Time and thyme are not homophones: the effect of lemma frequency on word durations in spontaneous speech. *Language* 84/3, 474–96.

Garrett, Merrill F., William E. Cooper and Edward Walker, eds. 1979. *Sentence Processing: Psycholinguistic Studies Presented to Merrill Garrett*. Hillsdale, NJ and New York: L. Erlbaum Associates; distributed by the Halsted Press.

Gaskell, M. G. ed. 2007. *The Oxford Handbook of Psycholinguistics*. Oxford and New York: Oxford University Press.

Gelman, Andrew and Jennifer Hill. 2007. *Data Analysis Using Regression and Multilevel/Hierarchical Models* (Analytical Methods for Social Research), 1st edn. Cambridge: Cambridge University Press.

Gernsbacher, Morton A. ed. 1994. *Handbook of Psycholinguistics*. San Diego: Academic Press.

Gibbs, Raymond W. and Gayle P. Gonzales. 1985. Syntactic frozenness in processing and remembering idioms. *Cognition* 20/3, 243–59.

Givón, Talmy. 1983a. Topic Continuity in Discourse: An Introduction. In Givón 1983b: 1–42.

1988. The pragmatics of word-order: predictability, importance and attention. In Hammond, Moravcsik and Wirth 1988: 243–84.

1991. Isomorphism in the grammatical code: cognitive and biological considerations. *Studies in Language* 15/1, 85–114.

Givón, Talmy, ed. 1983b. *Topic Continuity in Discourse: A Quantitative Cross-Language Study* (Typological Studies in Language 3). Amsterdam: Benjamins.

Gordon, Barry and Alfonso Caramazza. 1982. Lexical decision for open- and closed-class words: failure to replicate differential frequency sensitivity. *Brain and Language* 15, 143–60.

Grice, H. P. 1989. *Studies in the Way of Words*. Cambridge, MA: Harvard University Press.

Gries, Stefan T. 2003. *Multifactorial Analysis in Corpus Linguistics: A Study of Particle Placement*. New York and London: Continuum.

2005. Syntactic priming: a corpus-based approach. *Journal of Psycholinguistic Research* 34/4, 365–99.

2009. *Statistics for Linguistics with R: A Practical Introduction* (Mouton textbook 208). Berlin: De Gruyter Mouton.

2011. Phonological similarity in multi-word units. *Cognitive Linguistics* 22/3, 491–510.

Gries, Stefan T. and Martin Hilpert. 2010. From interdental to alveolar in the third person singular: a multifactorial, verb and author-specific exploratory approach. *English Language and Linguistics* 14/3, 293–320.

Grossman, Robin E., L. J. San and Timothy J. Vance, eds. 1975. *Papers from the Parasession on Functionalism of the Chicago Linguistic Society April, 17, 1975*.

Gundel, Jeanette K., Nancy Hedberg and Roger Zacharksi. 1993. Cognitive status and the form of referring expressions. *Language* 69, 274–307.

Gustafsson, Marita. 1974. The phonetic length of the members of present-day English binomials. *Neuphilologische Mitteilungen* 75, 663–77.

1975. *Binomial Expressions in Present-Day English: A Syntactic and Semantic Study*. Turku: Turku Yliopisto.

1976. The frequency and 'frozenness' of some English binomials. *Neuphilologische Mitteilungen* 77, 623–37.

Gymnich, Marion, Ansgar Nünning and Vera Nünning, eds. 2002. *Literature and Linguistics: Approaches, Models, and Applications: Studies in Honor of Jon Erickson*. Trier: Wissenschaftlicher Verlag Trier.

Hahn, M. and S. C. Stoness, eds. 1999. *Proceedings of the 21st Conference of the Cognitive Science Society*. Mahwah, NJ: Erlbaum.

Haiman, John and Sandra A. Thompson, eds. 1988. *Clause Combining in Grammar and Discourse* (Typological Studies in Language 18). Amsterdam and Philadelphia: J. Benjamins.

Hammond, Michael, Edith A. Moravcsik and Jessica R. Wirth, eds. 1988. *Studies in Syntactic Typology* (Typological Studies in Language 17). Amsterdam and Philadelphia: J. Benjamins.

Hansen, Klaus. 1964. Reim- und Ablautverdoppelungen. *Zeitschrift für Anglistik und Amerikanistik* 12, 5–31.

Haskell, Todd R. and Maryellen C. MacDonald. 2005. Constituent structure and linear order in language production: evidence from subject–verb agreement. *Journal of Experimental Psychology: Learning, Memory, and Cognition* 31/5, 891–904.

Haspelmath, Martin. 2004. *Coordinating Constructions* (Typological Studies in Language 58). Amsterdam and Philadelphia: J. Benjamins.

2007. Coordination. In Shopen 2007: 1–51.

Haspelmath, Martin, ed. 2001. *Language Typology and Language Universals: An International Handbook* (Handbooks of Linguistics and Communication Science/Handbücher zur Sprach- und Kommunikationswissenschaft 20). Berlin and New York: W. de Gruyter.

Haspelmath, Martin and Hans-Jörg Bibiko. 2005. *The World Atlas of Language Structures* (Oxford Linguistics). New York: Oxford University Press.

Hawkins, John A. 1983. *Word Order Universals* (Quantitative Analyses of Linguistic Structure). New York and London: Academic Press.

1992. Syntactic weight versus information structure in word order variation. In Jacobs 1992: 196–219.

1994. *A Performance Theory of Order and Constituency* (Cambridge Studies in Linguistics 73). Cambridge: Cambridge University Press.

2000. The relative order of prepositional phrases in English: going beyond manner–place–time. *Language Variation and Change* 11, 231–66.

2004. *Efficiency and Complexity in Grammars* (Oxford Linguistics). Oxford: Oxford University Press.

Hayes, Bruce. 1995. *Metrical Stress Theory: Principles and Case Studies*. Chicago: University of Chicago Press.

Hilpert, Martin. 2008. The English comparative – language structure and language use. *English Language and Linguistics* 12/3, 395–417.

Hinrichs, Lars and Benedikt Szmrecsanyi. 2007. Recent changes in the function and frequency of Standard English genitive constructions: a multivariate analysis of tagged corpora. *English Language and Linguistics* 11/3, 437–74.

Hopper, Paul. 1987. Emergent grammar. *Proceedings of the Berkeley Linguistics Society* 13, 139–57.

Huber, T. E. 1974. Law and order for binomials. *Ôbun Ronsô*, 61–74.

Jacobs, Joachim, ed. 1992. *Informationsstruktur und Grammatik* (Linguistische Berichte Sonderheft 4). Opladen: Westdeutscher Verlag.

Jaeger, Florian. 2010. Redundany and reduction: speakers manage syntactic information density. *Cognitive Psychology* 61, 23–62.

Jeffress, Lloyd A. 1951. *Cerebral Mechanisms in Behavior: The Hixon Symposium*. New York: Wiley.

Jescheniak, Jörg D. and Willem J. M. Levelt. 1994. Word frequency effects in speech production: retrieval of syntactic information and of phonological form. *Journal of Experimental Psychology: Learning, Memory, and Cognition* 20, 824–43.

Jespersen, Otto. 1943. *Growth and Structure of the English Language*. Oxford: Basil Blackwell.

Johnson, Neal F. 1966. On the relationship between sentence structure and the latency in generating the sentence. *Journal of Verbal Learning and Verbal Behavior* 5, 375–80.

Keenan, Edward L. 1976. Towards a universal definition of 'subject'. In Li 1976: 305–34.

Keenan, Edward L. and Bernard Comrie. 1977. Noun phrase accessibility and universal grammar. *Linguistic Inquiry* 8, 63–99.

Kelly, Michael H., Kathryn J. Bock and Frank C. Keil. 1986. Prototypicality in a linguistic context: effects on sentence structure. *Journal of Memory and Language* 25, 59–74.

Kempen, Gerhard and K. Harbusch. 2004. A corpus study into word order variation in German subordinate clauses: animacy affects linearization independently of grammatical function assignment. In Pechmann and Habel 2004: 173–81.

Kent, Ray D. and Charles Read. 2002. *Acoustic Analysis of Speech*, 2nd edn. Alabany, NY: Delmar.

Klein, Wolfgang and William J. M. Levelt, eds. 1981. *Crossing the Boundaries in Linguistics*. Dordrecht: D. Reidel Publishing Company.

Kortmann, Bernd. 2005. *English Linguistics: Essentials (System Use)*. Berlin: Cornelsen.

Krug, Manfred. 1998. String frequency: a cognitive motivating factor in coalescence, language processing, and linguistic change. *Journal of English Linguistics* 25/4, 286–320.

Kuiper, Koenraad, Marie-Elaine van Egmond, Gerhard Kempen and Simond Sprenger. 2007. Slipping on superlemmas: multi-word lexical items in speech production. *The Mental Lexicon* 2/3, 313–57.

Ladefoged, Peter. 1993. *A Course in Phonetics*. Fort Worth, Philadelphia, San Diego: Harcourt Brace Publishers.

Lamb, Sydney M. 1999. *Pathways of the Brain: The Neurocognitive Basis of Language* (Amsterdam Studies in the Theory and History of Linguistic Science 170). Amsterdam and Philadelphia: J. Benjamins.

Lambrecht, Knud. 1984. Formulaicity, frame semantics, and pragmatics in German binomial expressions. *Language* 60/4, 753–96.

1994. *Information Structure and Sentence Form: Topic, Focus, and the Mental Representations of Discourse Referents*. Cambridge: Cambridge University Press.

Landsberg, Marge E. 1995a. Semantic constraints on phonologically independent freezes. In Landsberg 1995b: 65–78.

Landsberg, Marge, ed. 1995b. *Syntactic Iconicity and Linguistic Freezes: The Human Dimension*. Berlin and New York: Mouton de Gruyter.

Lang, Ewald. 1984. *The Semantics of Coordination*. Amsterdam: Benjamins.

1991. Koordinierende Konjunktionen. In Stechow et al. 1991: 597–623.

Langacker, Ronald W. 1987. *Foundations of Cognitive Grammar*. Stanford, CA: Stanford University Press.

Lashley, Karl. 1951. The problem of serial order in behavior. In Jeffress 1951: 112–46.

Levelt, Willem J.M. 1981. The speaker's linearization problem. *Philosophical Transactions of the Royal Society of London: Series B, Biological* 295/1077, 305–15.

Levelt, Willem J. 1989. *Speaking: From Intention to Articulation* (A Bradford Book). Cambridge, MA: MIT Press.

Levelt, Willem J., Ardi Roelofs and Antje S. Meyer. 1999. A theory of lexical access in speech production. *Behavioral and Brain Sciences* 22, 1–38.

Levelt, William J. M. and Ben Maassen. 1981. Lexical search and order of mention in sentence production. In Klein and Levelt 1981: 221–252.

Levy, Roger. 2004. The statistical properties of coordinate noun phrases. Presented at the Department of Linguistics, University of Colorado-Boulder.

forthcoming. *Probabilistic Models in the Study of Language*. Cambridge, MA: MIT Press.

Li, Charles and Sandra A. Thompson. 1981. *Mandarin Chinese: A Functional Reference Grammar*. Berkeley: University of California Press.

Li, Charles N. ed. 1976. *Subject and Topic: [Papers]*. New York: Academic Press.

Lohmann, Arne and Tayo Takada. 2012. The effect of length on order in English and Japanese NP conjuncts. Talk given at the 86th Annual Meeting of the Linguistic Society of America, Portland (OR).

MacKay, Donald G. 1970. Spoonerisms: the structure of errors in the serial order of speech. *Neuropsychologia* 8/3, 323–50.

1973. Complexity in output systems: evidence from behavioral hybrids. *American Journal of Psychology* 86/4, 785–806.

1987. *The Organization of Perception and Action: A Theory for Language and Other Cognitive Skills* (Cognitive Science Series). New York: Springer-Verlag.

Malkiel, Yakov. 1959. Studies in irreversible binomials. *Lingua* 8, 113–60.

Masini, Francesca. 2006. Binomial constructions: Inheritance, Specification and Subregularities. *Lingue e Linguaggio* 5/2, 207–32.

Mayerthaler, Willi. 1981. *Morphologische Natürlichkeit* (Linguistische Forschungen 28). Wiesbaden: Verlagsgesellschaft Athenaion.

McDonald, Janet L., Kathryn Bock and Michael H. Kelly. 1993. Word and world order: semantic, phonological, and metrical determinants of serial position. *Cognitive Psychology* 25, 188–230.

Meyer, Antje S. 1996. Lexical access in phrase and sentence production: results from picture-word interference experiments. *Journal of Memory and Language* 35/4, 477–96.

Meyer, Antje S. and Eva Belke. 2007. Word form retrieval in language production. In Gaskell 2007: 471–87.

Meyer, Antje S., Eva Belke, Christiane Häcker and Linda Mortensen. 2007. Regular and reversed word length effects in picture naming. *Journal of Memory and Language* 57, 207–31.

Mitchell, Don C., Fernando Cuetos, Martin M. B. Corley and Marc Brysbaert. 1995. Exposure-based models of human parsing: evidence for the use of coarse-grained (nonlexical) statistical records. *Journal of Psycholinguistic Research* 24/6, 469–88.

Mithun, M. 1988. The grammaticization of coordination. In Haiman and Thompson 1988: 331–59.

Mollin, Sandra. 2012. Revisiting binomial order in English: ordering constraints and reversibility. *English Language and Linguistics* 16/1, 81–103.

Mondorf, Britta. 2009. *More Support for More-Support: The Role of Processing Constraints on the Choice between Synthetic and Analytic Comparative Forms* (Studies in Language Variation 4). Amsterdam and Philadelphia: John Benjamins.

Mortensen, David. 2003. Hmong elaborate expressions are coordinate compounds. Unpublished paper, UC Berkeley available for download at http://www.pitt.edu/~drm31/.

Mos, Maria. 2010. *Complex Lexical Items*. Utrecht: LOT.

Motley, Michael T. 1973. An analysis of spoonerisms as psycholinguistic phenomena. *Speech Monographs* 40, 66–71.

Müller, Gereon. 1997. Beschränkungen für Binomialbildungen im Deutschen. *Zeitschrift für Sprachwissenschaft* 16/1, 25–51.

Mullie, Jos L. M. 1947. *Korte Chinese spraakkunst van de gesproken taal (Noord-Pekinees dialect)*. The Hague: Martinus Nijhoff.

Nauclér, Kerstin. 1983. Connections between spoken and written language: evidence from three investigations on normal and pathological written performance. *Journal of Pragmatics* 7, 595–602.

Nelson, Gerald, Sean Wallis and Bas Aarts. 2002. *Exploring Natural Language: Working with the British Component of the International Corpus of English*. Amsterdam and Philadelphia: J. Benjamins.

Nickels, Lyndsey and David Howard. 2004. Dissociating effects of number of phonemes, number of syllables, and syllabic complexity of word production in aphasia: it's the number of phonemes that counts. *Cognitive Neuropsychology* 21/1, 57–78.

Norrick, Neal R. 1988. Binomial meaning in texts. *Journal of English Linguistics/*21, 71–87.

Oakeshott-Taylor, John. 1984. Phonetic factors in word order. *Phonetica* 41/4, 226–37.

Oden, Gregg C. and Lola L. Lopes. 1981. Preference for Order in Freezes. *Linguistic Inquiry* 12/4, 673–9.

Olsen, Susan. 2001a. Copulative compounds: a closer look at the interface between syntax and morphology. In Booij and van Marle 2001: 279–320.

2001b. Coordination in morphology and syntax: the case of copulative compounds. In ter Meulen and Abraham 2001: 17–38.

2002a. Coordination at different levels of grammar. In Gymnich, Nünning and Nünning 2002: 169–88.

2002b. Constraints on copulative compounds. In Scholz, Klages, Hantson and Römer 2002: 247–58.

Onishi, Kristine H., Gregory L. Murphy and Kathryn J. Bock. 2008. Prototypicality in sentence production. *Cognitive Psychology* 56, 103–41.

Pampel, Fred. 2000. *Logistic Regression: A Primer* (Quantitative Applications in the Social Sciences 132). Thousand Oaks, CA: Sage University Papers.

Pechmann, Thomas and Christopher Habel, eds. 2004. *Multidisciplinary Approaches to Language Production* (Trends in Linguistics Studies and Monographs 157). Berlin: Mouton de Gruyter.

Peterson, Gordon E. and Harold L. Barney. 1952. Control Methods Used in a Study of Vowels. *Journal of the Acoustical Society of America* 24/2, 175–84.

Peterson, Gordon E. and Ilse Lehiste. 1960. Duration of syllable nuclei in English. *Journal of the Acoustical Society of America* 32/6, 693–703.

Pinker, Steven and David Birdsong. 1979. Speakers' sensitivity to rules of frozen word order. *Journal of Verbal Learning and Verbal Behavior* 18/18, 497–508.

Plag, Ingo. 2003. *Word-Formation in English* (Cambridge Textbooks in Linguistics). Cambridge: Cambridge University Press.

Plag, Ingo, Gero Kunter, Sabine Lappe and Maria Braun. 2008. The role of semantics, argument structure, and lexicalization in compound stress assignment in English. *Language* 84/4, 760–94.

Plank, Frans, ed. 2003. *Noun Phrase Structure in the Languages of Europe* (Empirical Approaches to Language Typology 20–7). Berlin and New York: Mouton de Gruyter.

Pordány, László. 1986. A comparison of some English and Hungarian freezes. *Studies in Contrastive Linguistics* 21, 119–27.

Prat-Sala, Merce and Holly P. Branigan. 2000. Discourse constraints on syntactic processing in language production: a cross-linguistic study in English and Spanish. *Journal of Memory and Language* 42/2, 168–82.

Pulvermüller, Friedemann. 2002. *The Neuroscience of Language: On Brain Circuits of Words and Serial Order*. Cambridge: Cambridge University Press.

Purnelle, Gérard, Cédrick Fairon and Anne Dister, eds. 2004. *Le poids des mots: Proceedings of the 7th International Conference on Textual Data Statistical Analysis: March 10–12, 2004*. Louvain-la-Neuve: Presses universitaires de Louvain.

Quirk, Randolph, Sidney Greenbaum, Geoffrey Leech and Jan Svartvik. 1985. *A Comprehensive Grammar of the English Language*, 2nd edn. London: Longman.

Rapp, Brenda and Matthew Goldrick. 2000. Discreteness and interactivity in spoken word production. *Psychological Review* 107/3, 460–99.

2004. Feedback by any other name is still interactivity: a reply to Roelofs (2004). *Psychological Review* 111/2, 573–8.

Renner, Vincent. 2008. On the Semantics of English Coordinate Compounds. *English Studies* 89/5, 606–13.

Roelofs, Ardi. 2002. Syllable structure effects turn out to be the word length effects: comment on Santiago et al. (2000). *Language and Cognitive Processes* 17/1, 1–13.

Rohdenburg, Günter and Britta Mondorf, eds. 2003. *Determinants of Grammatical Variation in English*. Berlin and New York: Mouton de Gruyter.

Rosch, Eleanor, Carolyn B. Mervis, Wayne D. Gray, David M. Johnson and Penny Boyes-Braem. 1976. Basic objects in natural categories. *Cognitive Psychology* 8, 382–439.

Rosenbach, Anette. 2003. Aspects of iconicity and economy in the choice between the s-genitive and the of-genitive in English. In Rohdenburg and Mondorf 2003: 379–412.

2005. Animacy versus weight as determinants of grammatical variation in English. *Language* 81/3, 613–44.

Rosenberg, Sheldon, ed. 1977. *Sentence Production: Developments in Research and Theory*. Hillsdale, NJ and New York: Lawrence Erlbaum Associates; distributed by Halsted Press.

Ross, John R. 1967. Constraints on variables in syntax. Doctoral dissertation, Massachusetts Institute of Technology.

1980. Ikonismus in der Phraseologie: Der Ton macht die Bedeutung. *Semiotik* 2, 39–56.

1982. The sound of meaning. In The Linguistic Society of Korea 1982: 275–90.

1986. *Infinite syntax* (Language and being). Norwood, NJ: ABLEX.

Sambur, Marnie. 1999. Factors that influence word ordering of conjunctive phrases containing a male and a female name. Unpublished paper, available for download at: bespin.stwing.upenn.edu/~upsych/Perspectives/1999/sambur.htm.

Sanders, Ted, Joost Schilperoord and Wilbert Spooren, eds. 2001. *Text Representation: Linguistic and Psycholinguistic Aspects ; [Based on Papers Presented at a Conference Held July 1997, Utrecht University]* (Human Cognitive Processing 8). Amsterdam: Benjamins.

Sankoff, David and William Labov. 1979. On the use of variable rules. *Language in Society* 8, 189–222.

Santiago, Julio, Donald G. MacKay and Alfonso Palma. 2002. Length effects turn out to be syllable structure effects: response to Roelofs (2002). *Language and Cognitive Processes* 17/1, 15–29.

Scarborough, Don L., Charles Cortese and Hollis S. Scarborough. 1977. Frequency and repetition effects in lexical memory. *Journal of Experimental Psychology: Human Perception and Performance* 3/1, 1–17.

Schachter, Paul. 1977. Constraints on Coördination. *Language* 53/1, 86–103.

Schlüter, Julia. 2003. Phonological determinants of grammatical variation in English: Chomsky's worst possible case. In Rohdenburg and Mondorf 2003: 69–118.

        2005. *Rhythmic Grammar: The Influence of Rhythm on Grammatical Variation and Change in English*. Berlin and New York: Mouton de Gruyter.

        2009. All beginnings are light: a study of upbeat phenomena at the syntax-phonology interface. *Journal of English Linguistics* 37/1, 61–87.

Scholz, Sybil, Monika Klages, Evelyn Hantson and Ute Römer, eds. 2002. *Language: Context and Cognition: Papers in Honour of Wolf-Dietrich Bald's 60th Birthday*. Munich: Langenscheidt-Longman.

Schveiger, Paul. 1995. Aphasia and syntactic iconicity. In Landsberg 1995b: 373–90.

Schwanenflugel, Paula J. 1991a. Why are abstract concepts hard to understand? In Schwanenflugel 1991b: 223–50.

Schwanenflugel, Paula J. ed. 1991b. *The Psychology of Word Meanings: A Publication of the Cognitive Studies Group and the Institute for Behavioral Research at the University of Georgia*. Hillsdale, NJ: Erlbaum.

Seymour, P. H. K. 1969. Response latencies in judgements of spatial location. *British Journal of Experimental Psychology* 60, 31–9.

Shattuck-Hufnagel, Stefanie. 1979. Speech errors as evidence for a serial-ordering mechanism in sentence production. In Garrett, Cooper and Walker 1979: 295–342.

Shopen, Timothy, ed. 2007. *Language Typology and Syntactic Description*: Volume 2: *Complex Constructions*, 2nd edn. Cambridge: Cambridge University Press.

Sinclair, John. 1991. *Corpus, Concordance, Collocation* (Describing English Language). Oxford: Oxford University Press.

Siyanova-Chanturia, Anna, Kathy Conklin and Walter J. B. van Heuven. 2011. Seeing a phrase 'time and again' matters: the role of phrasal frequency in the processing of multiword sequences. *Journal of Experimental Psychology: Learning, Memory, and Cognition* 37/3, 776–84.

Snider, Neil. 2008. An exemplar model of syntactic priming. Doctoral dissertation, Stanford University.

Sobkowiak, Wlodzimierz. 1993. Unmarked-before-marked as a freezing principle. *Language and Speech* 36/4, 393–414.

Sprenger, S., Willem J. M. Levelt and Gerhard Kempen. 2006. Lexical access during the production of idiomatic phrases. *Journal of Memory and Language* 54, 161–84.

St Clair, Robert N. and Walburga von Raffler-Engel, eds. 1982. *Language and Cognitive Styles: Patterns of Neurolinguistic and Psycholinguistic Development* (Neurolinguistics 11). Lisse, Netherlands: Swets and Zeitlinger.

Stallings, Lynn M., Maryellen C. MacDonald and Padraig G. O'Seaghdha. 1998. Phrasal ordering constraints in sentence production: phrase length and verb disposition in heavy-NP shift. *Journal of Memory and Language* 39, 392–417.

Stassen, Leon. 2000. AND-languages and WITH-languages. *Linguistic Typology* 4, 1–54.

2001. Noun phrase coordination. In Haspelmath 2001: 1105–11.

2003. Noun phrase conjunction: the comitative and the coordinative strategy. In Plank 2003: 761–817.

Stechow, Arnim von, Dieter Wunderlich, Armin Burkhardt, Gerold Ungeheuer, Herbert E. Wiegand, Hugo Steger and Klaus Brinker, eds. 1991. *Semantik: Ein internationales Handbuch der zeitgenössischen Forschung = Semantics* (Handbücher zur Sprach- und Kommunikationswissenschaft/Handbooks of linguistics and communication science/Manuels de linguistique et des sciences de communication 6). Berlin: de Gruyter.

Steinlen, Anja K. 2002. A cross-linguistic comparison of the effects of consonantal contexts on vowels produced by native and non-native speakers. Dissertation, English department of the University of Århus.

Stekauer, Pavol and Rochelle Lieber, eds. 2005. *Handbook of Word-Formation*. Dordrecht: Springer.

Stemberger, Joseph P. 1985. An interactive activation model of language production. In Ellis 1985: 143–86.

1990. Wordshape errors in language production. *Cognition* 35, 123–57.

Stemberger, Joseph P. and Rebecca Treiman. 1986. The internal structure of word-initial consonant clusters. *Journal of Memory and Language* 25/2, 163–80.

Sternberg, Saul. 1966. High-speed scanning in human memory. *Science* 153, 652–4.

Swinney, David and Anne Cutler. 1979. The Access and Processing of Idiomatic Expressions. *Journal of Verbal Learning and Verbal Behavior* 18, 523–34.

Szmrecsanyi, Benedikt. 2004. On operationalizing syntactic complexity. In Purnelle, Fairon and Dister 2004: 1032–9.

2006. *Morphosyntactic Persistence in Spoken English: A Corpus Study at the Intersection of Variationist Sociolinguistics, Psycholinguistics, and Discourse Analysis* (Trends in Linguistics Studies and Monographs 177). Berlin: de Gruyter.

2013. The great regression: genitive variability in Late Modern English news texts. In Börjars 2013: 59–88.

Szmrecsanyi, Benedikt and Lars Hinrichs. 2008. Probabilistic determinants of genitive variation in spoken and written English: a multivariate comparison across time, space, and genres. In ter Meulen and Abraham 2008: 291–309.

Szpyra, Jolanta. 1983. Semantic and phonological constraints on conjunct ordering in English and Polish. *Kwartalnik Neofilologiczny* 30/1, 33–53.

Taboada, Maite and Loreley Wiesemann. 2009. Subject and topics in conversation. *Journal of Pragmatics* 42, 1816–28.

Tanaka, Mikihiro. 2003. Conceptual accessibility and word order in Japanese. http://www.ling.ed.ac.uk/~pgc/archive/2003/proc03/Mikihiro_Tanaka03.pdf.

Temperley, David. 2005. The dependency structure of coordinate phrases: a corpus approach. *Journal of Psycholinguistic Research* 34/6, 577–601.

2007. Minimization of dependency length in written English. *Cognition* 105/2, 300–33.

ter Meulen, Alice and Werner Abraham, ed. 2001. *The Composition of Meaning*. Amsterdam and Philadelphia: John Benjamins.

2008. *The Dynamics of Linguistic Variation: Corpus Evidence on English Past and Present*. Amsterdam and Philadelphia: John Benjamins.

The Linguistic Society of Korea, ed. 1982. *Linguistics in the Morning Calm*. Seoul: Hanshing Publishing Company.

Tomlin, Russel S. 1986. *Basic Word Order: Functional Principles*. London and Sydney: Croom Helm.

Turk, Alice E. and Stefanie Shattuck-Hufnagel. 2007. Multiple targets of phrase-final lengthening in American English words. *Journal of Phonetics* 35/4, 445–72.

van Langendonck, Willy. 1995. Categories of word order iconicity. In Landsberg 1995b: 79–90.

Wälchli, Bernhard. 2005. *Co-compounds and Natural Coordination*. Oxford: Oxford University Press.

Wasow, Thomas. 1997. End-weight from the speaker's perspective. *Journal of Psycholinguistic Research* 26/3, 347–61.

2002. *Postverbal Behavior*. Stanford, CA: CSLI Publications.

Wasow, Thomas and Jenniffer E. Arnold. 2003. Post-verbal constituent ordering in English. In Rohdenburg and Mondorf 2003: 119–54.

Widdows, Dominic and Beate Dorow. 2005. Automatic extraction of idioms using graph analysis and asymetric lexicosyntactic patterns. *Proceedings of the ACL-SIGLEX Workshop on Deep Lexical Acquisition*, 48–56.

Wolk, Christoph, Joan Bresnan, Anette Rosenbach and Benedikt Szmrecsányi. 2013. Dative and genitive variability in Late Modern English: exploring cross-constructional variation and change. *Diachronica* 30/3: 382–419.

Wright, Saundra K., Jennifer Hay and Tessa Bent. 2005. Ladies first? Phonology, frequency, and the naming conspiracy. *Linguistics* 43/3, 531–61.

Wulff, Stefanie. 2002. Determinants of prenominal adjective order. MA thesis, University of Hamburg.

2003. A multifactorial corpus analysis of adjective order in English. *International Journal of Corpus Linguistics* 8/2, 245–82.

2008. *Rethinking Idiomaticity: A Usage-Based Approach* (Corpus and Discourse). London and New York: Continuum.

Yamashita, Hiroko. 2002. Scrambled sentences in Japanese: linguistic properties and motivations for production. *Text* 22/4, 597–633.

Yamashita, Hiroko and Franklin Chang. 2001. 'Long before short' preference in the production of a head-final language. *Cognition* 81, B45–B55.

Zipf, George K. 1949. *Human Behavior and the Principle of Least Effort: An Introduction to Human Ecology*. Cambridge, MA: Addison-Wesley Press.

Index

CPSIA information can be obtained
at www.ICGtesting.com
Printed in the USA
BVHW060128250321
603353BV00003B/217